There Was Light

There Was Light

Autobiography of a University:
A collection of essays by *alumni*
of the University of California, Berkeley
1 8 6 8 — 1 9 9 6

Originally published in 1970;
> *edited by* **Irving Stone**

Updated in 1996 with new and selected original essays;
> *edited and with an introduction*
> *by* **Jean Stone**

Reprinted in 2002 with a new foreword
> *by* **Chancellor Robert M. Berdahl**

UNIVERSITY OF CALIFORNIA

BERKELEY

Produced by University Relations, University of California, Berkeley
Printed in the United States of America

Library of Congress Catalog Card Number 77-78738

Foreword

ROBERT M. BERDAHL
Chancellor, University of California, Berkeley

A S I READ THESE WONDERFUL ESSAYS, I think about the formative experience UC Berkeley provided for these distinguished alumni. Each of the thirty men and women in this collection write about not only the broadening of their intellectual horizons, but also their awakening to the wider world. Their experiences at Berkeley were not a linear timeline that ended upon graduation, but a trajectory for lifelong exploration and transformation.

There Was Light captures different voices. A uniform experience at Berkeley, of course, does not exist. A common theme, however, runs through the essays: It is the value of the University community—the pursuit of knowledge that binds us together. This notion of free inquiry and disciplined inquiry is the core value of a community that we call a university. And, as Hannah Arendt said so eloquently, community happens when we love the world enough to take responsibility for it by preparing the next generation to inherit it through education.

As a historian, I am drawn to these compelling portraits of Berkeley set against a wider milieu of social change and world events. Conductor Antonia Brico '23 tells of women dusting off their trombones and violins to form the novel New York Women's Symphony Orchestra during the WPA era. Nobel laureate Glenn T. Seaborg Ph.D. '37 describes the stormy night he discovered plutonium, a highly radioactive element that would help bring World War II to a close. The probing essay of UC Berkeley history professor Leon F. Litwak '51, M.A. '52, Ph.D. '58 takes the reader from the boom of postwar America to the divisive McCarthy era to the Free Speech Movement on campus.

The novelist Irving Stone '23, LL.D. '68 first proposed the idea for a book to be written by alumni to celebrate the University's centennial. He thought it essential to include contributors from a multitude of disciplines "to present a diversity of material and experience." Mr. Stone, who became an international literary figure after his graduation, worked with the alumni-writers to produce what he called a "labor of love." *There Was Light* was published in 1970.

The 1996 edition of *There Was Light* was the workchild of Mr. Stone's widow, Jean. She was his longtime editor and lifelong companion until his death in 1989. Mrs. Stone suggested marking the 125th anniversary of the University of California by revisiting the book. She thought it appropriate to seek essays from a new group of eminent alumni. So sixteen new entries joined fourteen of the original group, spanning several generations of our students.

Now we are in a new century, and on the cusp of a new millennium. What an appropriate time it is to reprint *There Was Light* as the University renews its commitment to foster a community of learners that transforms the lives of all who come in contact with it.

There Was Light is a fitting tribute to all the men and women who make UC Berkeley great.

Contents

*ESSAYS NEW TO THE 1996 UPDATED EDITION

Introduction

JEAN STONE, 1996

T HIS BOOK IS A LABOR OF LOVE. It was for Irving Stone in 1968, and it is for me in 1996. *There Was Light* celebrated the first centennial of the University of California, Berkeley.

When Irving received in his mail literature announcing the centennial year of the University of California, a momentous occasion in the history of the young state—it was only admitted to the Union in 1850, eighteen years before the University was founded—he remembered President John F. Kennedy's speech at the 1962 Charter Day in Berkeley: "When I observe the men who surround me in Washington—when I reflect that the Secretary of Defense, the Chairman of the Atomic Energy Commission, the Director of the Central Intelligence Agency, and the Ambassador to India are all graduates or former students of this University—I am forced to confront an uncomfortable truth ... that the New Frontier may well owe more to Berkeley than to Harvard!"

It seemed to Irving that the story of the University should be told by its own graduates. *There Was Light* became as well an attempt on the part of thirty-nine men and women in days of anxiety and confusion on the American campus to rediscover what was of value in their university training, what was excellent and should be retained, what was irrelevant and must be remolded to make modern education germane to a world in (violent) transition.

Now we have celebrated the 125th anniversary. Much of the world is still in violent transition. The country and state have been subjected to a long and deep recession with vast unemployment, which forced a reduction in available resources for education and a change in the charter concept of state support.

However, in its 125 years the University of California, Berkeley has become one of the world's leading universities and is determined to remain so.

Irving believed that in one sense a university is important only in terms of what it creates in its students, in his or her character as an individual, as a citizen, and as a contributor to the pattern of American life. *There Was Light* became a portrait of America about the time Rube Goldberg entered the university. The contributors would be deliberately chosen from more than thirty separate disciplines and a wide variety of race, religion, and national origins in order to present a diversity of material and experience. Autobiography, though it is admittedly the most difficult and self-serving of all literary forms, has the possibility of getting very close to the bone.

In addition to his background and the recollection of his university years, each writer was asked to describe what his objectives were when he entered and when he left the University, what he actually did with his life work, what it was he wished to establish or create in his chosen field, and the difficulties and/or obstacles he may have encountered en route. A symposium is rarely a unified oil painting. This book would emerge as a collage, an honest portrait of the changing face of the world.

Irving outlined the concept to his good friend Willard Libby, a Nobel Prize winner in chemistry, and then to Chancellor Roger W. Heyns and the Centennial Publishing Committee. He volunteered to do the editorial work; Doubleday agreed to publish. He titled the book *There Was Light* and spent the next eighteen months pursuing those contributors who had been guilty of the sublime but unfruitful virtue of modesty, and others whose over-opulent manuscripts needed cutting, Irving's included. He convinced them that the reader expected accomplishments, demanded them ... along with the failures.

He wrote: "As a professional writer all of my adult life, the experience of being an editor has been something of a revelation. ... I have acquired a quite intimate family of thirty-eight near relatives. ... I knew at all times which member of my writing family was ill, in crisis, had a house burn down with half the completed manuscript in it, ... was depressed by the state of the world, exhilarated by a new discovery or merely by having written what he considered a few good pages for this book. ... It is astonishing how close one gets to people as their editor."

He remembered many delightful moments: There was the note from John Kenneth Galbraith which said, "It's in the typewriter and writing itself. But I may have to take a hand eventually." There was the telephone call from Glenn Seaborg from his office in Washington saying, "Tell me precisely what it is that you want," and within a month receiving a manuscript in which he had covered all of my forty points brilliantly! The second manuscript to reach Irving's desk, from Rube Goldberg, was the hilarious story of how he found the prototype of his life work: an anecdote which is as much a *reductio ad absurdum* as his cartoons. There was the thrill of coming upon a natural born writer, Daniel E. Koshland Jr., whose piece on biochemistry was a joy and to have his mother, Eleanor Koshland, with whom Irving had served for two years on the California State Committee on Public Education, report hearing her son say, "Maybe I ought not to aspire to the Nobel Prize in science; maybe I ought to try for literature."

The astonishing difference of thought and feeling of the contributors sometimes caused speculation that the chapters had been written not by one species but by a dozen. Therein lies the richness of the book: Every point of view is represented not only in the arts, humanities, and sciences, but also in the startlingly polarized attitudes towards our political, economic, and educational problems. Need I point out that this is a virtue of our American university today? It produces strong individualists, not regimented men and women.

As each chapter reached his desk and later mine, I agreed with Irving that this body of work could be meaningful to the entire field of American education. So many of our high-school students still do not know what a university is, nor how importantly it can influence their lives. These cohesive chapters make abundantly clear what a university is, how it helps one to find a place in the sun and a work to do, a way of life that can sustain them and provide true excitement. The chapters glow with the love of campus, experiences of self discovery, of teachers and books and extended horizons. Many of these young men and women did not know why they were at the University—until something hit them and shaped their lives forever. The University still stands above all else on the American scene for the dissemination of knowledge, the search for wisdom and the powers of reasoning. Training under gifted scholars can provide the skills needed to play a constructive and exciting role in meeting the ever-growing world challenges. An untrained man or woman may turn out to be, even for his or her own purposes, an unresolved human being living unfocused years. The young people today are right when they say, "It is not necessary to have things, but it is urgent to be good at something, to develop one's potential."

Irving discovered the joys and vicissitudes of editing. I, on the other hand, have been an editor for more than half my life. I edited all of his work, twelve major volumes, as well as my own volume of Vincent van Gogh's letters, *Dear Theo: The Autobiography of Vincent van Gogh,* and *I, Michelangelo, Sculptor* from Michelangelo's letters. I could have told him that there is almost no stratagem or device to which an editor will not fall (rise?) to extract a completed manuscript from his contributor: flattery, cajolery, blackmail, crocodile tears, and, as the deadline approaches, sheer extortion. ... Ah, but when a manuscript finally comes in, and it is good, really good, and the editor knows that it might never have been written otherwise, what a heady feeling of accomplishment. For me, editing can be one of the weirdest combinations of fun and exasperation.

This is not the place to attempt a history of Berkeley's various protest movements, neither is it the place to ignore them. What was called the "campus revolution," which spread over the world, began quite naturally in Berkeley. Why naturally? Because San Francisco, just a few minutes across the Bay, was conceived in culture. It built an opera house and established a first-rate literary magazine while its inhabitants were demanding that it first pave its streets. A revolutionary concept.

When Irving recounted to Robert S. McNamara, Class of '37 and Secretary of Defense under Presidents Kennedy and Johnson, the details of a particularly sharp clash on the campus only a few days before, commenting that the slightest rumbling on campus brings about an eruption which causes a lava flow that covers the campus and the streets of Berkeley, McNamara listened intently then replied calmly:

"The University must learn to roll with the punches, and not take them all on the chin. That is the only way I could have survived in Washington. The University was here a hundred years ago; it will still be here a hundred years from now."

Survival value. For an individual, an institution, a nation. Perhaps the experiences, the minted, albeit variegated views of these contributors, clustered about today's critical theme of education and human fulfillment, will indicate guidelines for Berkeley's second and continuing centuries: the making of a college education not only relevant to modern society but also crucial for its continued growth. Berkeley has always been a barometer of changing times. It is not only reflective but also often the enunciator of change in the human condition; indeed, boom or bust the entrance of the drug age, high crime rate, the enormous gap between the haves and have-nots. Only the University can shed light on these problems and create solutions. It is something that the University of California, Berkeley has been doing for many years and charter rules or no charter rules, support or no support from government, it will continue to do so. It is a great university.

I cannot supplant an introduction by Irving Stone but I can "frame it," add to it to introduce this volume and new contributors more than twenty-five years later to celebrate the University's 125th anniversary.

For Irving it was a labor of love, as it is for me now.

There Was Light

"I loved, most of all, the very aspect of the Berkeley experience that came into such strenuous question a decade later, in the early 1960s: I loved the anonymity of the place."

JOAN DIDION

Joan Didion

ERKELEY IS SO MUCH A PART of who I am that I find it almost impossible to reflect rationally on what it "meant" to me, what I "got out of it," what it "did" for me. All I know is that I arrived there at eighteen with two new Samsonite suitcases, a portable Olivetti typewriter, an inchoate yearning to become someone better than I was, and not the slightest business being there. I wasn't prepared, I was ignorant, I knew nothing at all, I was ignorant even of that. I had done nothing in high school but resist it, cutting what classes I could and daydreaming through the rest and staying up all night to read novels not on the reading list. When I got to Berkeley and noticed people writing during lectures, I could conclude only that they were writing letters home. When I finally caught onto the mechanics of taking notes, I still failed to get the point, and diligently filled notebooks with the peripheral, words caught on the fly, stray phrasings I thought felicitous. I had no idea how to organize the day, prepare for a midterm, write a paper. I had a certain spurious facility with language, but no idea how to think through what I wanted to say: the arresting first line was by default my strong point, never mind where it led. I had no real idea even of why I was there, of what was expected of me, or of what, in a more specific vein than "be better," I wanted to do.

Yet I loved it, right away. I loved walking up from the campus in the late afternoon and watching the fog blow in. I loved walking down past LSB and seeing the bay come into view. I loved passing those places on the campus where the creek could be heard but not seen. I loved spending time in bookstores, touching the smooth covers of new books, imagining that to own them would be to magically absorb them, know them, know it all. I loved sitting on the balcony in the Morrison Library and listening to recordings of poets reading their own poetry and imagining that I lived in the burnished light of this splendor, all the while knowing that I belonged downstairs in the fluorescent light of the Reserved Book Room, waiting for one or another crucial three-hour hold I had not yet even gotten around to putting on call.

I loved wasting time in coffee shops, talking and reading and knowing (once again, as always) that I was on only a temporary pass from the prison of the Reserved Book Room. I loved certain classes, loved being forced, or prodded, or shown how, to make connections I had not before known how to make. Connections between literature and language. Connections between language and politics. "When the American soldiers tore down the gates at Buchenwald, what they found was a poem by Baudelaire": I have no memory of who said this, or in what class it was said, but I remember hearing it said, and being astonished, and walking up the campus oblivious to what was being said around me, trying to grapple with the implications of what was for me an entirely new but immediately logical causal relationship between ideas and history.

I loved, most of all, the very aspect of the Berkeley experience that came into such strenuous question a decade later, in the early 1960s: I loved the anonymity of the place. I loved being left alone, loved the absolute absence of the kind of enforced community that I so disliked, found false and sentimental and at base authoritarian, in other institutions (notably high school) I knew about. I loved the freedom, which of course included the freedom to fail, to slip under, to go down and out—in what was still, after all, a relatively benign situation. There were a lot of ways you could fail at Berkeley, and also a lot of ways you could make a recovery, and in either case nobody would much care. Failing academically was the least of it. You could stop getting up in the morning, you could let your shoes run down at the heel, you could have a failure of the will, or of the imagination. We all saw it happen to people we knew. This constant possibility of failure, of dropping below the line unnoticed and unremarked upon, introduced an element of dread to daily life at Berkeley, a chill in the late afternoon even more pronounced than the chill endemic to all campuses at that time of day. I remember dirty coffee cups, scraps of muddied paper overflowing trash baskets. I remember the dispiriting prospect of the evening ahead, promising nothing but the inevitable six o'clock dinner.

Yet this dread was its own challenge, and could provide its own risky exhilaration: the freedom to fail was also the freedom to be, to make one's own way, to choose the road not just less traveled by but less traveled by for good reason, because it was mined, say, or led nowhere. There was, of course, a down side to this free-market aspect of the Berkeley experience: it was entirely possible to graduate with an eccentric or incomplete education. Everything I know about European history was learned indirectly, and in a real sense accidentally, picked up from novels or poetry. On a campus where there were, at this time, seven or eight Nobel laureates in the sciences, I learned no science at all, managing to fulfill my science requirement with a geology lecture class favored by football players.

At twenty-one, still unprepared, still ignorant, even more aware of my own limitations than I had been at eighteen, I left Berkeley to go to work in New York. I did not graduate with honors. I barely graduated at all: I had somehow managed to overlook a required course in Milton, and only through the vast tolerance and generosity of the English department was one provided, an intensive seminar, on the cosmology of *Paradise Lost,* for one student, me. (I think of this seminar whenever I hear complaints about how "big" Berkeley is, how "impersonal.") My diploma was mailed to me, and when it arrived in New York, I put it in a box and had no occasion to look at it again until some years later, when I was living in Los Angeles and needed to show a diploma to get a stack permit at UCLA. Berkeley seemed to me then an experience I had left incomplete, an open question and in some sense an accusation.

I had, nineteen years later, an extraordinary opportunity. I had a second chance at Berkeley. In the spring of 1975, I was asked to come back to the English department as a Regent's lecturer, a reversal of positions that moved me profoundly, an opportunity, or so I thought, to close the circle, answer the open question. In some ways, nothing had changed: I still avoided Milton, still disliked Spenser, still could not read *The Faerie Queen*. I still procrastinated, still spent more time in bookstores than at my desk, still dreaded the fall of four o'clock. I had a room at the Faculty Club, and I still felt myself an undergraduate, a secret agent, an impostor who had somehow managed to infiltrate this citadel of grown-up life. The single class I was teaching met in Wheeler Hall, and my stride still adjusted automatically to the familiar way the steps flatten out on the uphill side. I was still unsettled by the familiar questions: what was I doing with what I had been given? What was I making of what I had learned? Aside from maybe a thousand fragments of poetry, what in fact had I learned? Why had I not learned more? Why had I not learned Russian, Chinese, physics, the colonial history of Africa, the kings of France? What Berkeley had offered me was for all practical purposes infinite: why had my ability to accept it been so finite? Why did I still have so many questions? Why did I have so few answers? Would I not be a more finished person had I been provided a chart, a map, a design for living?

I believe so.

I also believe that the world I know, given such a chart, would have been narrowed, constricted, diminished: a more ordered and less risky world but not the world I wanted, not free, not Berkeley, not me.

"In the 1960s Dean Rusk, Lyndon Johnson, General Westmoreland, Lewis Hershey, and Ronald Reagan accomplished what not even the most talented of our teachers had ever hoped to achieve. The undergraduates became politically concerned. . . . Now, I would suppose, Berkeley is the most intense intellectual and political community in the world; perhaps, indeed, it is the nearest thing to a total university community in modern times. As such it would be silly to suppose it could be altogether tranquil."

JOHN KENNETH GALBRAITH

John Kenneth Galbraith

ONE DAY IN THE AUTUMN OF 1930 I was gazing at the notice board in the post office of the main men's residence at the Ontario Agricultural College at Guelph, Canada. It was usually an unrewarding vision but on this day it advertised a number of research assistantships at the Giannini Foundation of Agricultural Economics at the University of California. The annual stipend was $720 for unmarried scholars. I copied down the details and applied. Some time later I received a letter from George Peterson, associate professor of Agricultural Economics, saying that I had been selected. I was surprised and so were my professors, who detested me and thought the people at Berkeley were crazy. I quickly accepted; in that second year of the Great Depression the monthly salary of sixty dollars, if not princely, was by far the best offer of any kind I had. In fact it was the only offer of any kind I had. From that day on the University of California has engaged my affection as no other institution—educational, public, or pecuniary—with which I have ever been associated. One Sunday afternoon in the summer of 1968, with my wife and oldest son (who followed me to be an assistant at the University of California Law School) I strolled across the California campus—over Strawberry Creek, by the Campanile, down by the Library, out Sather Gate. I was taught, as were most of my generation, that no one should allow himself the weak luxury of sentiment or even emotion. To this day when I write "Love" at the end of a letter I always remind myself that it is only modern affectation, in all respects a matter of form. I was suddenly overwhelmed by the thought that I loved this place—the paths, trees, flowers, buildings, even the new ones. I was deeply embarrassed.

In the thirties, for some reason related either to the eccentricities of the California crop year or climate, the University of California opened in August. Accordingly in July of 1931 I borrowed $500 from an aunt, one of the few members of our rural family still to command such capital, and, almost literally, set sail for California. I boarded the steamer which plied between Port Stanley on the north shore of Lake Erie and Cleveland, where, by prearrangement of our local jeweler and oculist, I met his nephew who had a graduate fellowship at California in astronomy. At five o'clock the following morning we set out in the 1926 Oakland automobile my companion had acquired for this trip. The car was in terrible condition and almost immediately got worse. To save money he had bought a five-gallon gasoline tin and a one-gallon container for oil so that we could stock up on these products whenever, as happened in those days, our path led us through a region being ravaged by a price war. Such at least was the theory. About thirty miles out of Cleveland my friend stopped to check the gas (the gauge was broken) and look at the oil. The car absorbed the whole five gallons of gasoline and the whole gallon of oil. For the rest of the trip we averaged around a quarter gallon of gas and a half pint of oil to the mile. To this day I shudder at the cost.

The journey took ten days not counting twenty-four hours at Casey, Iowa, where we laid up with a broken connecting rod. That, too, had a lasting effect. It was raining hard, and as we waited for the repairs, we listened to the local farmers, who used the garage as a club, discuss Hoover. I became a life-long Democrat. It was about six o'clock on a bright summer evening when we got to Berkeley and drove up Bancroft Way to the International House. The hills behind were very bleached and sere but the low sun glistened on the live oaks and the green lawns and the masses of pink geraniums, which elsewhere are only geraniums but in Berkeley are the glory of the whole city. The sun also lit up a vast yellow-buff facade of the International House with the large Spanish arches of the portico below. We passed into the great hall, then gleaming new, and combining the best mission style with the finest in Moorish revival. I thought it a place of unimaginable splendor.

Eventually the International House was to prove a bit too expensive even for one who earned sixty dollars a month and was, as a result, one of the more affluent members of the community. My capital had been depleted by that terrible car. But for the first few months at Berkeley this nice Rockefeller benefaction—it had counterparts in New York, Chicago, Paris, and Tokyo—housing several hundred students of both sexes from the United States and many foreign lands, was to be my window on the Berkeley world. Never before had I been so happy.

The world on which I looked down could not be recognized in important respects by Mario Savio. I must stress that I had just emerged from the Ontario Agricultural College and this could have distorted my vision. Once not long ago I was asked by *Time* magazine about this academy; I replied, thoughtlessly, that in my day it was certainly the cheapest and possibly the worst in the English-speaking world. This was tactless and wrong and caused dissatisfaction even after all these years. (No one questioned my statement that the college was inexpensive.) But at OAC students were expected to keep and also to know and cherish their place. Leadership in the student body was solidly in the hands of those who combined an outgoing anti-intellectualism with a sound interest in livestock. This the faculty thought right. Anyone who questioned the established agricultural truths, many of which were wildly wrong, was sharply rebuked, and if he offended too often he was marked down as a troublemaker. A fair number of faculty members had effectively substituted the affable and well-clipped manner and mustache of the professional countryman for the admitted tedium of science. Unquestionably the place did build health. At Berkeley I suddenly encountered professors who knew their subject and, paradoxically, invited debate on what they knew. They also had time to talk at length with graduate students and even to come up to International House to continue the conversation. I first discovered at Berkeley from Henry Erdman, who had until recently been the head of the Agricultural Economics Department, and Howard Tolley, who had just succeeded him as the director of the Giannini Foundation, that a professor might like to be informed on some subject by a graduate student—not just polite but pleased. So profound was that impression that I never stopped informing people thereafter. The pleasure I have thus given has been very great. (Howard Tolley, after a year or two, went on to Washington to become head of the Agricultural Adjustment Administration under FDR. I shall mention him again in a moment. In 1968, after the elapse of a third of a century, I was back in Berkeley one Sunday to urge the case and, more important, since everyone was persuaded, to raise money for Eugene McCarthy. I was not at all surprised to see Henry Erdman in the front row. He believed strongly in keeping informed.)

Although we had stipends, we agricultural economists were second-class citizens. Our concern was with the prices of cling peaches, which were then appalling, and the financial condition of the Merced irrigation district, which was equally bad, and the prune industry, which was chronically indigent, and other such useful subjects. I earned my research stipend by tramping the streets of Los Angeles and also Oakland and San Jose to ascertain the differing preferences as to package and flavor—sage, orange blossom, clover—of Mexican, Jewish, Negro, and (as we then thought of them) ordinary white Americans, for honey. No differences emerged. This kind of work was not well regarded by the non-agricultural, or pure, economists. Thorstein Veblen was still being read with attention in Berkeley in the thirties. He distinguished between esoteric and exoteric knowledge, the first having the commanding advantage of being without "economic or industrial effect." It is this advantage, he argues, which distinguishes the higher learning from the lower. Ours, obviously, was the lower.

We suffered from another handicap. Agriculturists, in

an indistinct way, were considered to be subject to the influence of the California Farm Bureau Federation and, much worse, of the opulent and perpetually choleric baronage which comprised the Associated Farmers of California. Actually our subordination was not all that indistinct. Both organizations told the dean of the College of Agriculture and the director of Extension what they needed in the way of research and also conclusions. They were heard with attention, even respect. No one was ever told to shape his scholarly work accordingly; men were available who did it as a matter of course.

The nonagricultural economists, whatever their differences in other matters of doctrine, were united in regarding the farmers, even more than the bankers or oil men, as an all-purpose class enemy. In time I acquired a certain reputation in economic theory and other branches of impractical knowledge and also as a rather circumspect critic of the agricultural establishment. So I was accorded an honorary status as a scholar, my agricultural handicaps notwithstanding. I was then even more happy.

The Department of Economics at Berkeley has never been considered quite as eminent as that at Harvard. The reason is that the best Californians have always been at Harvard. As this is written in the autumn of 1968, of the twenty-three full professors of economics at Harvard no fewer than seven, nearly one third, were recruited at one stage or another in their careers from the University of California at Berkeley. And economics at Berkeley has long had a marked personality. In the early thirties, years before the Keynesian revolution, Leo Rogin was discussing Keynes with a sense of urgency that made his seminars seem to graduate students the most important things then happening in the world. I learned Alfred Marshall from Ewald Grether, who taught with a drillmaster's precision for which I have ever since been grateful. Marshall is the quintessence of classical economics and much of what he says is wrong. But no one can know what is wrong if he does not understand it first. My memory also goes back to M. M. Knight's seminar in economic history, a gifted exercise in irrelevancy. Once Robert Gordon Sproul, then the president of the University, said in one of his booming speeches that, after all, a university was run for the students. Knight, a brother of the noted Frank H. Knight of the University of Chicago, attacked this doctrine for two full sessions. A university, he argued with indignation, was run for the faculty and, to affirm the point, he announced his intention of introducing a resolution at some early faculty meeting to exclude the students from the library. They got in the way.

We graduate students were also fond of Paul Taylor, who spoke out unfailingly for the small farmer in California; Charles Gulick, who spoke out for the farm workers, who then as now aroused great animosity and a measure of righteous anger for wanting a union and a living wage; and Robert Brady, who was the friend of the consumer and other lost causes. Brady taught courses in the business cycle and set great store by exhaustive bibliographic research. One of my friends met this requirement by going to the card catalogue in the library and copying into the appendix of his thesis everything that appeared there under the headings Cycle, Business, and Cycle, Trade. Brady sent over for some of the later items which were new to him and they turned out to be works on bicycles, tricycles, and motorcycles published by the Cycle Traders of America. We always heard there was quite a scene.

A few years after I left Berkeley I became deputy head of the Office of Price Administration in charge of the World War II price controls. This was a post with unlimited patronage—eventually, as I recall, I had some 17,000 assistants. In addition to Richard Nixon and Mrs. Nixon and many other promising people, numerous of my former professors, including Howard Tolley, Harry Wellman (later the acting president of the University), and Robert Brady turned up on our staff. Brady had scarcely arrived before he was assaulted hip and thigh by the Dies Committee—now better known as HUAC—for saying in a book on German fascism that American capitalism was only technically better. To complicate matters further, Dies had got hold of the edition published by the Left Book Club in England. It had something on the cover about not being for public sale. I handled the defense on the Hill with the handicap of knowing that everything I said in favor of Bob would immediately be used against me. Brady later attributed his troubles to the oil companies and said I was their tool. He had proposed that people conserve oil by not draining the crankcase for the duration or ten thousand miles, whichever was less. I did not endorse the idea. This was mostly because with everything else it never got to my attention. But if it had, I might have remembered that Oakland and the way it changed itself and wondered if it would have made much difference.

The graduate students with whom I associated in the thirties were uniformly radical and the most distinguished were Communists. I listened to them eagerly and would have liked to have joined both the conversation and the Party but here my agricultural background was a real handicap. It meant that, as a matter of formal Marxian doctrine, I was politically immature. Among the merits of capitalism to Marx was the fact that it rescued men from the idiocy of rural life. I had only very recently been retrieved. I sensed this bar and I knew also that my pride would be deeply hurt by rejection. So I kept outside. There was possibly one other factor. Although I recognized that the system could not and should not survive, I was enjoying it so much that, secretly, I was a little sorry.

In the ensuing twenty years many of those I most envied were accorded an *auto-da-fé* by HUAC, James Eastland, or the late Joseph R. McCarthy. Their lives were ruined. Phrases about the unpredictable graces of God kept constantly crossing my mind.

One man who did not get called by Joe McCarthy was Robert Merriman, a vital and popular graduate student and teaching assistant who came down to Berkeley from Nevada in the early thirties. As an undergraduate he had been wholesome and satisfactory and even took an interest in ROTC. But Berkeley had its effect and so (as he told friends) did the great waterfront strike of 1934, where he saw soldiers deployed against the strikers. Hugh Thomas' brilliant book, *The Spanish Civil War*, tells the rest of his story. Interrupting a traveling fellowship in Europe in 1936, Merriman went to Spain, where (one assumes as an uncalculated consequence of ROTC) he commanded the Abraham Lincoln Battalion on the Jarama and then went on through many battles to be chief of staff of the XV International Brigade. A major and by not long a veteran, he was killed (possible executed after capture by the Nationalists) on the Aragon front in 1938. He must have been the bravest of our contemporaries; he so impressed Ernest Hemingway that he became in part the model for Robert Jordan (a professor from Montana) in *For Whom the Bell Tolls*. The California campus has ornaments for lesser heroes who died nearer home for more fashionable beliefs. There are some naïve, haunting lines written by John Depper, a British volunteer, of the Battle of Jarama that might serve:

> Death stalked in the olive trees
> Picking his men
> His leaden finger beckoned
> Again and again.

A year ago in Chicago I was on a television discussion program with Robert Merriam, a White House aide to President Eisenhower and once Republican candidate for mayor of Chicago against Richard Daley. He said that for many years he had been investigated assiduously by the FBI because of his name. Merriman was not completely forgotten.

I would not wish it thought that our life in the thirties was limited to politics and great matters of the mind. One roamed through San Francisco, climbed Mt. Diablo, went up to the Sierra, where someone was always imagining that the Depression might make panning gold profitable again, and consumed (I most diffidently) alcohol stolen from the chemistry laboratories and mixed with grapefruit juice and, after repeal, a blended whiskey of negligible cost called, to the best of my memory, Crab Orchard. I have difficulty in believing that the latter-day intoxicants and suffocants do more. In any case we were all greatly impressed one night when a girl who had been over stimulated by these products ceremoniously removed her clothes in the patio of the International House and spent the late hours of the evening doing orgiastic obeisance to the heavens above and, more than incidentally, to the windows of the men's rooms around.

In those days people came to Berkeley from all over the world and, naturally enough, no one ever left. The reasons were social and economic as well as cultural. As a student, teaching fellow, or even a non-student one could be a respected member of the community and it counted against a person not at all to have no income. But the moment one left Berkeley he became a member of the great army of the unemployed. As such he was an object of sympathy and lost his self-respect. In general, graduate students avoided taking their final degrees lest they be under temptation, however slight, to depart. When, in 1933 and 1934, jobs suddenly and unexpectedly became available in Washington— NRA, PWA, AAA—almost everyone got busy and finished up his thesis. Even my Communist friends reacted favorably to the exorbitant salaries which economists commanded in the New Deal.

Among the people who appeared in Berkeley, my mind returns to a slim, boyish-looking girl who, improbably in light of her build, claimed to have been in Texas Guinan's chorus before turning to the higher learning. More recently she had been in Tahiti and then in Bora Bora, where she had gone native and had as proof a comprehensive suntan. Now she was doing graduate work in anthropology on the basis of credentials, partly forged and partly imaginary, from a nonexistent undergraduate institution in the city of New York. I fell deeply in love with her; on our second or third date, as we were walking up Strawberry Canyon back of the stadium, she asked me if I thought it right, as an economist, to be wasting both her time and mine. Nothing in my Canadian and Calvinist background had prepared me for such a personal concept of efficiency. A little later, after an all-night party in San Francisco, she insisted on being taken to the Santa Fe Station. She had just remembered that, on the day following, she was scheduled to marry a banker in New Mexico. Much later I met her in New York. She was just back from Haiti (not Tahiti) and preparing to marry a Pan Am pilot. She told me she was working on her memoirs and was being encouraged to the task by Westbrook Pegler. I was by then a promising young member of the Harvard faculty. I first worried that she would publish her recollections and then, after a time, that she would not.

Though we graduate students expected the revolution very soon and planned to encourage it, we did not expect any help from the Berkeley undergraduates. Not that they would oppose—they would simply, as usual, be unaware that anything was happening. A singular accomplishment of American higher education, as one reflects on it, was the creation of a vast network of universities, public and private, which for a century, until the sixties, caused no one any political embarrassment of any kind. In other countries they created trouble from time to time, but not here. A control system which subtly suggested that whatever the students most wanted to do—i.e., devote themselves to football, basketball, fraternities, college tradition, rallies, hell-raising, a sentimental concern for the old alma mater, and imaginative inebriation—was what they should do, was basic to this peace. The alumni rightly applauded this control system and so, to an alarming extent, did the faculty. An occasional non-political riot was condoned and even admired; some deeper adult instinct suggested that it was a surrogate for something worse. At Berkeley in the thirties this system was still working perfectly. Coming up Bancroft Way to the International House of an evening one saw the fraternity men policing up the lawns of their houses or sitting contentedly in front. Walking along Piedmont at night one heard the shouts of laughter from within, or occasional bits of song or what Evelyn Waugh correctly described as the most evocative and nostalgic of all the sounds of an aristocracy at play, the crash of breaking glass. Here were men with a secure position in society and who knew it and who were content. On a Friday night they would do their duty at the pep rally shaming the apathetic; on Saturday they would be at the stadium and on Saturday night,

win or lose, they joined with the kindred souls of earlier generations, men they did not hesitate to call brother, to whoop it up as
a college man was meant to do. The *Daily Californian* was the
approving chronicle of this world—of the Big Game, the Axe, the
cards turned in unison in the cheering section to depict an Indian
or a bear, the campaign to send the band to Oregon to support the
team. In 1932 Norman Thomas came to the campus and spoke to
a small assembly in a classroom. Neither Hoover nor Roosevelt
dreamed of favoring us. Hoover did speak to a vast audience
of indigent citizens from the local Hooverville down on the
Oakland flats and was cheered uproariously when he told them
that, at long last, the Depression was over. They had not heard.
Only once was there a suggestion of student involvement. The
financial condition of the state of California in those days was
appalling. State workers were being paid with tax-anticipation
certificates. Even the governor, James (Sunny Jim) Rolph, sensed
that something was wrong. In 1932 and 1933 there were threats
to cut the University budget. When it seemed that these were serious, the students were encouraged to assemble and ask their relatives and friends to petition their legislators to relent. Perhaps
that was the camel's nose, the seed of the Frankenstein. As to persuading the legislature, however, it was considered less important than a promise by the University to retrench voluntarily and
to begin with the Agricultural Extension (Farm Adviser) Service.
No one said so but we agriculturists certainly felt that our prag-
matic approach to scholarship had paid off for everyone.

In the 1960s Dean Rusk, Lyndon Johnson, General
Westmoreland, Lewis Hershey, and Ronald Reagan accomplished what not even the most talented of our teachers had ever
hoped to achieve. The undergraduates became politically concerned. When the time comes to award honors to those who
made our universities the center of our political life, it will be a
great injustice if the men of affirmative, as distinct from the negative, influence are featured. Now, I would suppose, Berkeley is
the most intense intellectual and political community in the
world; perhaps, indeed, it is the nearest thing to a total university

19

community in modern times. As such it would be silly to suppose that it could be altogether tranquil. Often in these past years, following some exceptionally imaginative outbreak on Telegraph Avenue I've heard a colleague say: "You know that sort of thing could never happen here." I've always been too polite to say why I agreed. And the statement could be wrong. As other university communities succumb to the concerns so long a commonplace at Berkeley, they, too, cease to be tranquil.

Not everyone is as restrained as I am about Berkeley. A few weeks ago I shared a seat on an airplane with a young colleague newly recruited, like so many before him, from the University of California. I asked him if he missed it. He replied, "Christ, yes! At Berkeley you worked all morning in the library and then at noon you went out into the sun and there was always a demonstration going on or something. Man, that was living!"

The days passed. During my second year my stipend was raised to seventy dollars a month, allowing me to save a little money and also to have a larger social life. Then in my third year I was sent to Davis, which, for the benefit of non-Californians, is in the Sacramento Valley not far from Sacramento. It is now a full-fledged university but in those days it was the center of agricultural research and instruction too closely associated with orchards, insects, and the soil to be carried on at Berkeley. It cultivated, in other words, the lowest of the lower learning. At Davis I was the head of the Departments of Economics, of Agricultural Economics, of Accounting, and of Farm Management. I also gave instruction in all of these subjects and, with the exception of one elderly dean, who gave lectures to non-degree students, I was also the total teaching staff in these disciplines. During the year I also had time to write my Ph.D. thesis and I do not recall that I was especially rushed. Certainly such was my love for Berkeley that I went there every weekend. At Davis my pay was $1,800 and I was able (by way of repayment of my own college debts to my family) to send my younger sister to college.

The Davis students were also highly stable. My course in beginning economics was required for some majors. The scholars so compelled tramped in at the beginning of the hour, squeezed their yellow-corduroy-clad bottoms into the class-room chairs, listened with indifference for an hour and then, by now conveying an impression of manfully suppressed indignation, tramped out. Only once in the entire year did I arouse their interest. I gave some support to the textbook case for lower tariffs. Coming as they did from the sugar beet fields, olive orchards, cattle ranches, and other monuments to the protective tariff, they knew that was wrong and told me so. My best-remembered student that year was a boy who had an old Ford runabout and spent his weekends putting up signs on the highways which warned motorists to repent and prepare at a fairly early date to meet their God. In response on an examination to a question about the nature of money, he stuck resolutely to the proposition that it (not the love of money but money itself) was the root of all evil. I tried to reason with him, but in vain. So I flunked him, for his contention seemed to me palpably untrue. That was my only personal encounter in those years with any form of student dissent.

One day in the spring of 1934 I was in Berkeley putting the finishing touches on my thesis. A Western Union boy came into the room with a telegram offering me an instructorship at Harvard for the following year at $2,400. I had not the slightest idea of accepting, for I was totally happy at California. But my rapid advance in economic well-being, plus no doubt the defense of my faith against that student, had made me avaricious, and I had heard that one won advances in academic life by flashing offers from other universities. I let it be known over the weekend that "Harvard was after me," and, on the following Monday, went by appointment to see the dean of the College of Agriculture to bargain. I carried the telegram in my hand. The dean, a large, handsome, and highly self-confident man named Claude B. Hutchison, who later became the mayor of Berkeley, was excellently informed on all matters in the college and his intelligence system had not failed him on this occasion. He congratulated me warmly on my offer, gave me the impression that he thought Harvard was being reckless with its money, and said that, of

21

course, I should go. In a moment I realized to my horror I had no choice. I couldn't now plead to stay at two thirds the price. The great love of my life was over. I remember wondering, as I went out, if I had been right to flunk that nut.

"If you are bored with Berkeley,
you are bored with life."

CLARK KERR

Clark Kerr

MY FIRST VISUAL CONTACT with Berkeley was the sight of the Campanile looming up at the end of Telegraph Avenue. The Campanile remains my favorite view off and on the campus, and I was so fortunate that the window of my office, when many years later I became President of the University, looked straight out at it with the Berkeley hills and the Big C behind.

It was the fall of 1932. I had driven up from Palo Alto across the Dumbarton Bridge and past the tomato fields and canneries of southern Alameda County, then almost entirely rural. I was driving my 1928 Model A Ford—a convertible coupe—on my way to International House to visit a friend. There I made my first contact with life at Berkeley.

My friend and I were having a snack in the coffee shop when there burst in a small mob of people shaking their fists and screaming slogans. We were asked to join the mob. We refused. It was led by a red-haired young man of great dynamism. I asked his name. It was Lou Goldblatt. I later came to know Lou well when I was Impartial Chairman on the West Coast Waterfront appointed by the United States Secretary of Labor. I was the arbitrator between the International Longshoremen's and Warehousemen's Union of Harry Bridges and the Waterfront Employers' Association of Frank Foisie. I last saw Lou at a reception in San Francisco in the late 1970s. I met Harry Bridges at the door and asked him (forgetting for a moment that they had parted company) whether Lou was there. He pointed across the room and said, "There he is—that Maoist." When the Bancroft Library needed an introduction to Lou's oral history (others being hesitant of the association), I wrote one noting our profound political disagreements but acknowledging him as a historical figure in the history of the West Coast and Hawaii—one of many Berkeley graduates who became historical figures in many ways in many parts of the world.

So my first impressions were of the physical beauty of Berkeley centering on the Campanile and of its avant-garde ambiance—the former has been always one of the great pleasures of my life and the latter, from time to time, one of the sources of greatest challenge.

In the fall of 1932, I had enrolled as a graduate student at Stanford on the spur of the moment. I had been in California that summer as a "peace caravaner" for the American Friends Service Committee (the Quaker service organization). We were arguing before church groups and businessmen's luncheon clubs for the United States to join the League of Nations and the World Court in those fiercely isolationist days. I was planning to enter Columbia Law School that fall but had a few free days before I needed to start back East. So I took a fling at entering Stanford for one year before Columbia. I went to registration with my college transcript from Swarthmore College in my hand. When I reached the head of the line, I was referred to the Registrar. He looked at my transcript, and I was accepted.

I stayed the year at Stanford but shortly planned to go on to Berkeley. First, because when I had written to my major professor at Swarthmore to tell him where I had ended up, I got back an immediate reply to the effect that I had made a terrible mistake, that, if I were foolish enough to be in California at all, I should transfer as quickly as possible to Berkeley, which was much the better university. Secondly, I had become interested in the self-help cooperatives of the unemployed and wanted to write a thesis about them. My faculty friends at Stanford were politely supportive but were not really interested. They had read about unemployment but none of them had ever met an unemployed person and, according to the economic textbooks of that day, unemployment was in any event bound to cure itself. I heard that there was a professor at Berkeley who was interested in my topic and was out in the field on his own investigations. I went to see him and he offered me a research assistantship at $400 per year. This led to my third great impression of Berkeley.

I quickly discovered that Berkeley was much more a part of the real world than "the farm." Paul Taylor, my professor at Berkeley, was a great expert on farm labor. I had barely registered for my seminars when the great cotton pickers' strike in the San Joaquin Valley broke out. It was the biggest and bloodiest rural strike in American history. He sent me out into the field to talk with farmers, sheriffs, strikers. This was life in the raw as I had never seen it. There had been vigilante massacres in Pixley and Arvin at the southern end of the great valley. Strikers were living on the banks of irrigation ditches, which were both sources of water and receptacles of sewage. There was hunger. There was violence as strikers entered the fields with sticks and stones to drive out non-strikers. There was hatred. Not only between strikers and farmers, but, among the strikers, between the "Okies" led by their politically conservative lay preachers and the "Mexicans" led by Communist Party officials. It was a long way from the peaceful Oley Valley in eastern Pennsylvania where I had been raised on a family farm. A long way also from the Quaker atmosphere of Swarthmore. And a long way from the isolation of the Stanford campus. A great big dose of reality.

Taylor told me to talk to people, to write down what they said exactly as they said it, and to send my notes to him immediately. He came down to see me on occasional weekends. One time I drove him back to Berkeley on a Sunday night in my Model A Ford. Taylor was a taciturn man as the following will illustrate. We stopped at a gas station. I was asleep on the passenger side. I woke up when the door was yanked open and a man grabbed me by the throat yelling, "What have you done with my wife?" It turned out that he had an identical Model A that he had parked on the other side of the single gas pump. Paul had come out of the restroom, gotten into this second Model A, and driven off with the sleeping wife. Just as the Highway Patrol car arrived to investigate the alleged abduction, Paul came back, quietly got into my car, and drove off, never saying a word.

It was through Paul that I met Dorothea Lange, his second wife, the great photographer. I have written a chapter on Paul and Dorothea for a book published by The Smithsonian Press, *Dorothea Lange: A Visual Life*. Paul wrote about, and Dorothea took pictures of, America during the Great Depression that will stand forever as records of that tragic time. It was a great experience for a young graduate student at Berkeley to be in the field with them.

It was through Paul Taylor that I first got to know the formidable Ira B. "Doc" Cross. Doc was one of the great lecturers in Berkeley history. Every undergraduate knew him or knew about him. He fell in rank just below Henry Morse Stephens (1900 to 1919) in modern European history and Charles Mills Gayley (1889 to 1923), who lectured on Shakespeare in the Hearst Greek Theatre. Doc held forth in Wheeler Auditorium, and with total discipline—"What is it that the male student in the twelfth row, three seats in from the aisle, finds so much more interesting in the *Daily Cal* than my lecture? Please stand up and tell us." He was an iconoclast and had many prejudices—all held with absolute assurance. One was that married graduate students were not serious, a waste of time. He would never have one as a teaching assistant—never! But once he did. My wife, Kay, and I had a small apartment in an old house on College Avenue. One afternoon just as the term was underway, I heard someone pounding up the steps and then a heavy pounding on the door. I opened it. There was the legendary Doc. He said, "If I am willing to forget my principles, I expect you to forget that I did not ask you earlier. My course is oversubscribed. I need another T.A. I expect you to be there tomorrow morning." And so I was. Shortly he gave me about my only and certainly my best advice about teaching. The Economics Department then had a "bullpen" on the first floor of South Hall. All the professors were there for an hour or two after lunch each day seeing students and each other. Doc saw me come in the door and yelled at me, attracting the attention of all in the room: "Speak up Kerr, speak up—the girls in your class tell me that they have to hug you to hear you!"

Cross had been known as the Stormy Petrel of the Berkeley City Council and the Academic Senate. He had calmed down somewhat and now gave seminars for San Francisco bankers. One day, Paul Taylor and I were working over a manuscript at the table in Paul's kitchen. In came Doc. He had in his hand a copy of a populist weekly (*The Guardian* from someplace in Oklahoma). He read a column about a farmyard and how twice a year, when the wild geese flew overhead on their migrations, the fat tame geese on the farm below would try their wings unsuccessfully a few times and return a few feeble cries, as the wild geese above flew freely by, proud and undaunted. Then Doc walked out. He had become a tame goose and he knew it; Paul and I were still flying freely in the air. I could have wept.

Doc later took very good care of me. He gave me the Newton Booth Fellowship, which he conferred each year on a chosen student. Later he gave me his precious card file of set "jokes" for use in my classes, but his style and mine were too different. Later still, after I became Chancellor, he passed on to me his academic gown, just as President Sproul some years later gave me his presidential gown to wear. I felt greatly honored on each occasion.

Doc was not a great scholar but he was a great character. Berkeley now has many more great scholars than then but many fewer characters.

ia. ia.

As World War II was coming to an end, Governor Earl Warren in California was worried about disruptions in labor relations resuming from the turbulent thirties. He proposed, and the University accepted, the idea of an Institute of Industrial Relations to work with both industry and labor and to make studies in the area. Dean Ewald T. Grether, on behalf of both Business Administration and Economics (for I was given a joint appointment), asked me to be the first director. I was then at the University of Washington. The University of California at Berkeley in those days preferred Ph.D.'s from other universities (no "inbreeding"). As graduate students we had all come to know that policy, and to respect it. Kay and I would drive around the Berkeley hills looking at the houses and the views—our favorite views came when the morning fogs were rising through and above the eucalyptus trees—but knowing how unlikely it was that we would ever be back. I even thought that perhaps I could get a job in the "City" and perhaps teach an occasional course in the University's Extension—we might possibly get that close to our Shangri-La. Then came Greth's unexpected letter. It was an impossible dream come true.

It was then that I got a fourth impression of Berkeley—as a great door to opportunity. The GIs came flooding in and enrollment jumped by more than fifty percent—25,000 instead of the pre-war 15,000. They sat in the aisles and stood along the walls. They were the best students we ever had, and that made us better teachers. My big lecture course was in labor economics and held in 101 California Hall—then an amphitheater holding (nominally) 400 students. My topic was a hot one in the daily headlines, and Letters and Science had made my course one of the select ones to fulfill its breadth requirements. So I had a full house. Among other things, I brought in guest lecturers from industry and labor to present their views directly. The students were tough in their questions, and industry leaders would tell me how anti-industry they were and labor leaders how anti-labor. I would tell them both that the students had sharp, inquiring minds and were fearless in asking questions even in such a large class. And they were.

One of those outside lecturers was Boris Shiskin, the research director for the AFL-CIO nationwide. In addition to all those students, I left the back doors into the amphitheater open, and a whole pack of the many campus dogs shared the platform with me. They were all very well behaved. Except once. The AFL-CIO speaker was attacking the National Association of Manufacturers. After one very critical comment, one of the dogs let out a loud yelp and tore up the stairs to the main entrance and the others also yelping followed him. The speaker turned to me and said, "Professor, you did not tell me your class had so many representatives of the NAM!" The students applauded wildly.

The GIs came back from the military far more mature than earlier students, more determined to get their degrees and to start making their way in the world. Some had already taken more life-and-death responsibility than the average professor would in a whole career. They were a joy to teach. Even to grade. One student, on a one-question exam which asked what he would do if faced with a very difficult problem, simply wrote, "Hire Professor Kerr as my consultant and do exactly as he told me." He turned in his blue book and, smiling smugly, left the room.

The GIs were also the wave of the future. The Land Grant universities created after the War Between the States (UC being one) had welcomed the children of farmers. The GI Bill of Rights welcomed everyone regardless of family income or race. And many came. We were moving toward universal access. When I was later involved in developing the Master Plan for Higher Education in California (1959–60), I thought back to the arrival of the GIs in 1945 and that there should be such opportunity always; and California became the first state in the nation and the first political entity in the world to guarantee access to higher education to all qualified persons.

The GIs had another great impact specifically at Berkeley. Many had attended private and public universities, before their military service, where they were accustomed to much more in the way of student facilities. Berkeley was, in this respect, the last of the German-type universities with the university providing classrooms, laboratories, and professors, and leaving the students to take care of themselves. No residence halls (except for those financed by gifts), no modern student union, few intramural sports fields, and so on. They complained a lot, and I listened to those complaints with great sympathy for I had seen Stanford and Swarthmore and Washington. The grievances came to a head with a losing football season and, after a defeat in Memorial Stadium, to a great bonfire in the stands fueled by debris. This brought the attention of the alumni. The Alumni Association set up a committee to look into the grievances.

The resultant report was called "Students at Berkeley" (1948). It asked for residence halls, a modern student union, better cultural facilities, more sports fields, better advising agencies for students, and much else. When I became Chancellor in 1952, I dusted off that report and with the help of the Alumni Association and the officers and executive committees of the ASUC (1952–53 to 1957–58), started to turn it into accomplishments—the new Student Union, Zellerbach Hall, residence halls for one-quarter of the student body, the Haas Recreation Center in Strawberry Canyon, more sports fields, and many other projects. In the end, every recommendation in "Students at Berkeley" came true. And this set a pattern for every other campus, beginning with UCLA and including the three new campuses. Few bonfires have ever had such advantageous results. Consequently, when the Regents named the Clark Kerr Campus with its residence halls, its sports facilities, its conference center, it recalled for me the expectations of the GIs in my classes at the end of World War II. I always kept them in mind—the Clark Kerr Campus was in substantial part their dream campus, the campus of the GIs.

≈ ≈

The other great postwar development, beyond the avalanche of GIs, was the oath controversy. This demonstrated another outstanding aspect of Berkeley—a proud faculty protective of its rights. Here was my fifth great experience in getting to know Berkeley. U.S. Senator Joe McCarthy was dominating the headlines and the airwaves. There was fear among intellectuals across the nation. Into this atmosphere was introduced the oath. It was proposed as an answer to problems in Sacramento in the 1949 session of the Legislature. It was proposed without consultation with the Academic Senate. The Regents adopted the proposal initially with some hesitation and never with full consent of all the Regents (one opponent was Governor Warren of the Class of 1912). The faculty slowly rose in what became increasing opposition.

The issue was never Communism, much as it may have appeared that way to some in the public. What was really at issue was that the Regents seemed to identify the members of the university faculty as particularly suspect among all citizens in the state. Faculty members had already signed, without objection, an oath of allegiance to the Constitution, why should they also have to sign a special political oath? Why was the Academic Senate not consulted? Berkeley had then, and still has, the most powerful Senate among all American universities largely as the result of the "revolution of 1919" led, among others, by the then young Joel Hildebrand of great subsequent scholarly fame, a great, and relatively conservative, leader of the faculty.

I saw this battle at first hand. As a young faculty member, I served as a member of the Committee of Five selected to lead the opposition to the oath (I was myself a signer, as were over ninety-five percent of the faculty). I subsequently served as a member of the Committee on Privilege and Tenure, later as chair, in trying to carry out a compromise accepted by the Regents that those who refused to sign could go before the Committee on Privilege and Tenure as an alternative. All those who appeared before the committee and who were willing to discuss their reasons of conscience for not signing were "cleared"; and this was all but six. With my Quaker background, I was particularly sympathetic to reasons of conscience for not signing an oath, and particularly a political oath. Also, my father was a stubborn independent who thought nothing should ever be unanimous and he would vote "no" on principle. But a majority of Regents, after having agreed to this alternative, then rejected our report and fired *all* the non-signers, thirty-one in total! I thought this was a terrible breach of faith, and said before the Regents that I did not think that "any-one in good faith" could possibly vote for such an action. But they did. In the end, however, the State Supreme Court declared the special oath to be unconstitutional, and the non-signers were subsequently invited back and a few accepted. Later a Berkeley faculty committee nominated me to become the first Chancellor of the campus, mostly because of my role in the oath controversy, which was the only way they then knew me. The wounds were healing—the Regents accepted the nomination.

34

These are some of the ways that I got to know and develop a great affection for and devotion to the Berkeley campus: as a place of great beauty, of an avant-garde ambiance, of active participation in the life of society—not an ivory tower—of opportunity for the GIs to advance on ability and motivation into positions of leadership in the American community, of a faculty marked by pride and high spirit.

If you are bored with Berkeley, you are bored with life. Let there always be light at Berkeley, and a Campanile!

Maxine Hong Kingston addressed the English Department's graduates at the commencement ceremony in the Greek Theatre in 1992. The following are her notes from that speech.

Maxine Hong Kingston

IN 1962, I GRADUATED FROM UC BERKELEY with a degree in English. Some of those teachers who taught me are teaching now. I did not attend the ceremony. Some thirty years later, I can perhaps recover that period. The students I hung out with—and they included my husband-to-be, also an English major, whom I met during my senior year—turned out to be lifelong friends, all poets and painters, English majors and history majors. My community, a bohemia of friends, believed it was not cool to participate in ceremonies staged by the military-industrial-educational establishment. Not cool, and wrong, and evil to be, however small, a part of the wars that government is always planning. A graduation ceremony ought to be a celebration, and I didn't feel like celebrating. I also felt like a failure; there were quite a few C's in my major, a low GPA. In those days, according to rumor, there was a grade in the English department called a Chinese C, or according to other rumors, a Chinese D. It meant, out of pity, go ahead and pass the Chinese Americans; they're going to be engineers anyway, and their English didn't need to, and couldn't, get any better. At graduation time, I was afraid that I didn't know anything. I hadn't been trained to *do* anything; I wasn't prepared to make a living. I had no business getting a degree in English. I'd gotten the liberal arts education of an aristocrat when I was a peasant and the daughter of peasants. My parents wouldn't be at graduation. I hadn't dared ask them to shut the laundry to come see me graduate. They had never closed the laundry during daylight hours; they had to make the money to send six of us to college. They had sent me to Cal as an engineering major. I had entered Cal in the engineering program, and I don't remember ever telling them that in my sophomore year I'd switched to English. I was one of three girls in the engineering department—we weren't called women in those days—actually, we weren't called anything. The engineering professors started each lecture, "Good morning, gentlemen," or "Good afternoon, gentlemen," until I disappeared. I transferred out when we had to declare ourselves Civil, Mechanical, Mining, or Electrical engineering students. I hated applied science, a closed, claustrophobic system. I didn't like being able to see the end product, a bridge, a mine shaft, a set career. Shouldn't a university education be the time and a way to think freely? I wanted to learn how to push my mind and my life past any known limits to the universe. I switched to English: for the fun of it, for the joy and ease of reading, for the talking with like minds about books, and poetry and truth and beauty. But the decision to be an English major was also frivolous. I was getting an education that was of no practical use whatsoever.

In June, with my only marketable skill, typing, I got a job as a clerk-typist at an insurance company in San Francisco. I was fired. I got another job as a clerk-typist at a property owners' association at the Claremont Hotel. I got fired from that too. I got another job as a clerk-typist at the Cal Engineering Department. I got fired from that. I was fired from the first three jobs after graduation. I give every one of you permission to get fired from at least three jobs. I also stole time from my employers. I could type ninety words a minute, but pretended I typed sixty. I finished my assignments and worked on my novel, which I pulled out of the typewriter and hid—like Jane Austen—whenever I heard anyone coming.

The world is not friendly to writers. It is not friendly to English majors. There is no job out there that will let one earn a living with the academic skills we'd been taught; there is no job where you get paid for reading wonderful books and discussing them.

Today, some thirty years later, I want to suggest an idea

that has taken me, in my slowness, all this time to understand: *that I had received the perfect education.*

The teachers at Berkeley had given me the best they had, all they knew. It was a miracle of an education. In all its hodge-podge and vagaries, here's what I learned: to doubt, to ask questions, to appreciate ambiguity, multi-quity, to hold multi-quity like rainbows in one's hands and clear eyes. I came away from Berkeley knowing how to doubt everything, how to deconstruct *any*thing. The Cal liberal arts education blows away old answers, and leaves questions.

The most interesting and scary of the questions was this one: "With this degree in English, what will I do to make a living?" Isn't that a beautiful phrase? "Make a living." A gerund, a verb form, an idiom made of two verb forms. Not a definitive once-and-for-all deadend noun like "money" or "job." To "make a living," one needs to discover and invent work that makes one feel alive, that doesn't deaden the spirit, that enlivens the family and friends and community, that gives the world life. "To make a living": an action verb—your work will keep changing as you change, and you make the world change. You create and make up new jobs that are good for a human being. You alter a cramping job so that it supports your humanity and spirit and changes the marketplace. English teachers don't give you vocational training in how to find a job and what job to try for. Virginia Woolf does not tell you specifically how you would earn £500 a year. As an English major you have to imagine that for yourself.

To give you short cuts and reassurances, and to save you from regrets, I want to say that after those three jobs where I got fired, I became better at inventing work. I helped found a sanctuary for AWOL soldiers from the Vietnam War. I started a drop-in school for drop-outs; I went up and down the road looking for boys with spray cans, and took those who'd collapsed in the grass and bushes to my drop-in school. First I fed them; then I tried to show them that reading books will get them higher than sniffing paint. Also, I helped unionize the private school where I taught after the drop-in school.

If I had felt and known then what I do now, I wouldn't have sneaked and stolen writing time. I should have asked those employers to allow me to use my desk and typewriter and free time for personal research and art. That way, I might even have given the property owners' association a chance to help feed the soul of their clerk-typist. I should also have suggested to my parents that they come to my graduation; they might have changed their work patterns to include rest, and enjoyed celebrating the results of their labor with me.

It's easier to invent new jobs than it is to write a book. After graduation, my writing, which began when I was a child, almost disappeared. I hadn't written much real writing during the years at Cal. No poems came to me. Writing criticism and essays and doing too much homework ban poetry and fiction and creative nonfiction.

What I did after graduation was paint, a nonverbal rest that got my imagination going again; I came at composition and images and perspective from a different medium. After a year of sketching and painting, I wrote my closet novel, which was shapeless and strange. I don't need to decide whether to take it out of the closet. It, and the closet, burned in last year's fire. I then wrote a scholarly essay, and got it published in a journal. It took fifteen years after graduation before I could find the language and form to write my first published book, *The Woman Warrior.* I used the map and timeline given to us by epics and myths. Notice that it took twenty years for Ulysses to get to Troy and back. It's also taken twenty years for Vietnam veterans to remember their experience, and to psychically and existentially come home.

In our culture, the education that we've gotten at Berkeley *is* the vision of the quest. This graduation is not the beginning or the end. In Native American cultures, the questing hero or heroine sees a vision, then brings it back as a story, a song, a dance, a weaving pattern, a painting, or a map to give to the tribe. This graduation is the middle of the quest. Now you take the knowledge and make sense of it, create its practical applications, invent human uses for abstractions, and bring gifts home to us, your community.

"The thrill of being paid for what I loved to do and being close to men who labored with Strathmore board and Higgins ink was somewhat dampened by having all my attempts at cartooning thrown in the wastebasket."

RUBE GOLDBERG

Rube Goldberg

MEMORY GROWS SLIGHTLY DIM after sixty-four years unless you have total recall, which I have not. But there are certain indelible imprints on the innermost recesses of the mind which are not so much a matter of memory as a part of my life at the University of California, which cannot be erased.

At the end of my junior year, as part of the vacation requirements, I worked as a mucker in the Oneida Mine in Amador County, two thousand feet under the ground. How could this have happened to me, one who is now so remote from the bowels of the earth that I shy away from digging a hole to plant a gardenia sprig?

Let's go back to my graduation from Lowell High School in San Francisco. My father, who came to this country from Germany some years before the Civil War, had not much of a formal education but was extremely well versed in Shakespeare and other classics. He had his heart set on one of his family going to college. My two brothers and sister had no taste for "higher education." He had been sympathetic towards my early inclination to become some sort of an artist, but he later harbored the idea that artists were a rather dissolute class of bohemians who ambled through life full of false hopes for the future, and whose stomachs remained empty. He decided he wanted me to pursue a vocation that would more obviously insure financial success.

My father knew a prominent man named Ignatz Steinhart, who was president of the Anglo-California Bank. The bank had large interests in the mining industry. Mr. Steinhart assured my father that my future would be secure if I became a mining engineer. Though my heart was set on drawing, preferably cartooning, I succumbed to my father's wishes because he would be paying the bills.

I was graduated from Lowell High School in the winter of 1900, six months ahead of my class, either because they had enough of me or because I wrote a scholarly thesis on the mating habits of the Mexican armadillo. I arrived in Berkeley in January 1901, at the beginning of the second semester, and registered in the College of Mining. There were no facilities for receiving students in midterm. I tried to find out in South Hall if there were any new classes beginning at that time but was sent from office to office by vague assistants who looked upon me as an intruder. It was a question of my going back to Lowell High to finish out my senior year or bluffing my way through the second half of the freshman year.

I managed to strike up an acquaintance with some of the freshmen in the mining course and followed them from class to class in chemistry, trigonometry, solid geometry, and other courses, all of which were quite strange to my unscientific mind. I put on a smock and poured multicolored liquids into retorts and test tubes and burned my fingers on Bunsen burners. I parroted equations in trigonometry but did not know the difference between a sine and a cosine. I still don't. I bought a slide rule but never learned how to use it. I saw sophomores roaming the campus wearing little blue caps with the insignia UC imprinted on the visors and I made up my mind I would be wearing one of those caps at the beginning of the fall semester.

At the end of the term I took my exams. I crammed relentlessly and memorized as much material as I could. My blue books, into which we were required to write answers to the tests, were turned in and I went home overwhelmed by a feeling of failure. But miraculously I received word that I had passed and was eligible to wear one of the little blue caps. My father was very proud, although he did not know that the principal reason for my passing was fright.

I lived at home in San Francisco during my college days, which was somewhat of a disadvantage as far as real participation in college life was concerned. I took a cable car each day to the ferry, rode over to Oakland on the boat, and then took a train up to the campus entrance, where I walked to the gym and changed into my campus regalia, all of which took up about three hours a day which might have otherwise been used absorbing the campus atmosphere. But on the ferry each day I had good company. We joked and laughed as the ferryboat plowed across the Bay and enjoyed ourselves as we might have done in a fraternity house or a social club.

Bunny Hare's father was an undersheriff of San Francisco. It was one of his responsibilities to see that people who were committed to the Napa and Stockton asylums were properly escorted to these institutions. Sometimes there were not enough deputies to escort them, and outside deputies had to be temporarily sworn in. Bunny and I were immediately notified and given the job of delivering the committed ones to their new homes. We received five dollars for each delivery. Some of our wards were manacled, some wore straitjackets, and others appeared perfectly normal, making it impossible for fellow passengers to tell which were the afflicted, our guests or ourselves.

Sometimes I envy graduates who recall their close relationship with certain professors, who talked to them privately and had a profound influence on their lives. I had no time to indulge in this luxury because of my long daily trek back and forth from home. But I did have occasional talks with Andy Lawson, a genial professor with a rare sense of humor, which seemed lacking in many of the other faculty members.

Samuel B. Christy was the dean of the College of Mining. He assumed an air of great profundity and when he wanted to make a special point he would jut his neatly trimmed Vandyke beard a little farther away from his winged collar and utter a theory that caused slight snickers in the classroom. One of his favorite pronouncements was that a wheelbarrow, to get the proper proficiency, had to be held at an angle of thirty-two degrees, going uphill. We all feigned rapt interest, which seemed to impress the dean with our great desire to push wheelbarrows uphill for the rest of our lives.

Another professor who stands out in my memory of characters is Freddy Slate, a spare little man with a red beard, a high-pitched voice, and an urgent manner of sputtering his scientific declarations. His subject was analytic mechanics, and his favorite mechanism for illustrating his epic postulates was the Barodik, which he had invented. It filled a good-sized laboratory, and its principal function was to record the weight of the earth by a series of pipes and tubes and wires and chemical containers and springs and odd pieces of weird equipment which made it look like a dumping ground for outmoded dentists' furnishings.

Each student was allowed six months of experimentation with this forerunner of modern sculpture to determine the weight of the earth. We all got fairly good marks in this course because the weight of the earth varies constantly through moisture, barometric pressure, magnetic currents, and other natural forces, so that the answer, give or take a few quadrillion tons, might be correct on any particular day or month.

At the time of my incarceration in the Barodik cell, I had no idea that this machine would furnish me with one of the principal props of my career as a cartoonist. Like the Barodik, my "Rube Goldberg" inventions are incongruous combinations of unrelated elements which cause a chain reaction that accomplishes something quite useless. It points up the human characteristic of doing things the hard way.

Later, in my cartoons, I broadened the Barodik's sequence of interlocking elements by adding midgets, kangaroos, rising cakes of yeast, hungry moths, shrinking pajamas, self-dunking doughnuts, animated anchovies, woodpeckers, man-eating trees, water wheels, and coloratura sopranos. During my long career as a cartoonist, sixty years to be exact, I have portrayed many facets of human behavior, but somehow the machine age slant on human frailties has grown to be widely accepted all out of proportion to my original conception. I am credited with any machine that looks crazy. People coming into my studio expect me to be hanging from the chandelier. It is always a disappointment to them, and me too, that I am a perfectly normal human being. I am deeply flattered and still wonder how I achieved the odd distinction of being completely cracked. Perhaps people who need a short way to describe an involved piece of machinery always pounce upon my name.

I do not remember resenting the fact that, instead of being sent to art school, I went to college. I took all the scientific courses in stride perhaps because my subconscious mind told me that I would never follow mining engineering as a profession. I always seemed to find time for myself in lampooning. I took part in the sophomore minstrels as a member of the Barodik Trio. I designed my class pin and won an award for a *Blue and Gold* cartoon. And Freddy Slate threw me out of his class for drawing his caricature.

I had great admiration for Earle Anthony, the editor of the *Pelican,* a tall, gangling young man who wore his floppy senior stovepipe at a jaunty angle and took long strides across the campus like one who had the past, present, and future all wrapped in a nice secure package. When he accepted one of my drawings it gave me a greater thrill than a good mark in calculus or geology.

When at the end of my sophomore year I went with my classmates on a geology expedition, it was more of a lark than a serious quest for knowledge. We spent the day with our hammers knocking away pieces of earth and stone and surveying the different strata so that we could determine whether the Tertiary period of the region was Pliocene or Miocene.

Another experience to which I referred earlier was frightening at the time but seems rather funny in retrospect. I put in six weeks at the end of my junior year in the Oneida gold mine. When I put on my denim shirt and loose Levis I was reminded of the costumes the insane characters wore when Bunny Hare and I took them off to the state asylum. My fears were more than realized when I got into the mine's cage along with the miners, all Polish giants who spoke little English. I carried a candlestick which consisted of an iron spike with a loop to hold the candle and a pointed end to stick in a timber while you were working.

At the 2,000-foot level I alighted in a daze with the sweating Poles and followed them along a dimly lighted tunnel, where I was given a shovel and told to pile ore into a small car. There were miners working above me in stopes, which were graded steps up from the level of the tunnel. They were drilling holes, into which they placed sticks of dynamite. I was told in sign language to hand them the sticks of dynamite, which rested in a box nearby. My day passed in shoveling ore and passing sticks of dynamite. At the end my tender hands felt like the fringe on an old sofa. I remember standing in a line of crude showers with dozens of ogres around me all splashing away and looking at the sharp bones sticking out of my skinny frame. I was never so ashamed in my life.

I stood the routine for weeks because I knew the other members of my class were doing the same thing in different mines. Each afternoon when I came up and saw the light of the sky I uttered a prayer of thanks. During the last two weeks of torture I was placed in the stamp mill, where the ore is pounded and run over sluices to be refined later for assaying. The noise nearly burst my eardrums, but I was above ground. I knew mining was not my dish! Yet inside I was rather proud for having survived the ordeal. Finally the day arrived when Benjamin Ide Wheeler handed me my diploma.

After graduation in 1904 I felt I was not ready to look for a job as a professional cartoonist. I was familiar with the techniques of every artist whose work appeared in *Puck* and *Judge* and other magazines, but knew I had not yet developed a style of my own. So, mindful of the debt I owed my father for having supported me through college, I went to work in the City Engineer's Office in San Francisco for $100 a month. My job was to design sewers and water mains, but I was dissatisfied, because each day at the City Hall, where I worked, I could spot shady characters hiding behind Doric columns, plotting, as I thought, the ruin of the innocent people of San Francisco. I quit the job after six months, resolved to find some activity related to cartooning whether I was ready for it or not.

Fate was on my side. Harry Bunker, the assistant manager of the art department of the *Chronicle,* took me on at eight dollars a week. My ambition had won over my sense of reason. My job was to sweep out the art department, wipe retouching off used photographs and file them away in the "morgue," and contribute an occasional photograph to the sports page.

The thrill of being paid for what I loved to do and being close to men who labored with Strathmore board and Higgins ink was somewhat dampened by having all my attempts at cartooning thrown in the wastebasket.

After three months I was given an assignment to draw pictures of a football game at a prep school across the Bay. Before going over I laid out my materials very neatly on my desk together with clippings of football players I had gathered from the files.

I made many sketches at the game and came back to the art department ready to do my noble best. My desk was bare. I tried to open the drawer and found it nailed tight. I asked the one person in the room, Fred Small, who nailed up my desk. He smiled and turned away. I strode into the composing room, got a hammer and some nails, came back and nailed up every desk in the room. Then I went out to dinner. When I returned I found every member of the art department trying to pry open his own drawer. Not a word was spoken. I drew my cartoon and took it to the city editor, who accepted it with a favorable comment. From that time on I was accepted as a full member of the staff and my work started to improve.

In talking with men who have achieved a modicum of success I have found that each has gone through periods of frustration and disillusioning change. The man who goes straight from college to a planned life that extends through middle age misses something. He misses the variety and the bumps that make you hold on a little tighter. He misses the contrast that helps you recognize the real thing. He misses the mystery of what tomorrow might hold. He misses the job of expectation, which has the sustaining grace of the youthful years at college.

And don't forget luck. Luck comes to you if you put yourself in its way.

"During my years at Berkeley I wasn't consciously aware of the criteria that defined first-rate science, but I was experiencing it. That early exposure to rigorous thinking and hard work helped mold my style of science today."

ROBERT TJIAN

Robert Tjian

Y RECOLLECTION OF STUDENT DAYS at UC Berkeley is remarkably vivid, not because I have a razor-sharp memory, but because I am constantly reminded of early impressions as I walk or drive around the picturesque Berkeley campus. Such positive feelings helped lure me back to Berkeley as a professor, after seven years on the East Coast as a graduate student and postdoctoral fellow.

When I was in high school, living in a small, insulated community in southern New Jersey, I desperately hoped to find a place in which I could expand my knowledge and horizons. Since I'd traveled and lived in several cities in South America, including Rio de Janeiro and Buenos Aires, I knew there was more to life than football, cheerleaders, beer, and Saturday night drives down Main Street. I wanted to meet a diverse group of educated, progressive, and creative people who would have the openness to exchange ideas and voice a passion for the new and unexpected. My instincts told me that selecting Berkeley over East Coast schools would be the right choice.

My first day in Berkeley is perhaps the most deeply etched in my memory. On the flight from Philadelphia to San Francisco, I sat next to UC law professor Noonan, (who I'm certain has no recollection of this encounter). He was very gracious and patient, answering all of my mundane questions about Berkeley. He also kindly offered to drive me to the East Bay. Riding across the bridge, I had my first glimpse of San Francicso, the Bay, and the hills of Berkeley. I strangely felt as if I were coming home, though I hardly knew anyone in the Bay Area and was visiting California for the first time. It reassured me to know that my older brother Hans and my two sisters Carol and Jane had already attended UC Berkeley with good results.

Life as a Berkeley undergraduate was less than auspicious at first. But as it turned out, my initial attempts to find an area of study were significant to my eventual career. I moved into Cloyne Court, a student co-op with a reputation for scholastic nerds. Quickly I realized that my intended major in mathematics was a naive choice. One of my housemates was such an accomplished mathematician that at the tender age of twenty, it was rumored a theorem had already been named in his honor. And after attending a few advanced math courses, I was convinced that my superficial aptitude for calculus and group theory in high school was an inaccurate indication of how talented a mathematician I could become. It seemed I was no better suited for physics. I remember getting back my first physics midterm, feeling very proud that I had scored well above the 48-point average. Then I spoke to my housemate, Ravi, a sixteen-year-old from India majoring in physics. He looked distressed after receiving his exam, so I asked him how he did. He replied, "I'm not happy at all. I got a ninety-eight and I know the T.A. made a mistake grading my exam!" At that point, I knew physics was out. I was definitely playing in the major leagues of academia at Berkeley, competing with super-bright students, the likes of whom I had never seen in high school. My early impressions of how extraordinary Berkeley students are is reinforced every time I walk into a class as a teacher rather than a student. When I teach my MCB 110 course, I look out into a class of 200 students, and I know that among them are some of the brightest young minds in the country. If I can turn them on to biology, they could develop into world-class scientists. This prospect is a great motivator for a teacher, so I am always charged up to deliver the best lectures I can muster.

Having eliminated math and physics, and knowing I certainly had no talent for music, literature, or art, I was at a loss to find a field of study I could get passionately excited about. Then I took Biology 1A, which changed everything. My professor was Gunther Stent, whose lecture style and personal accomplishments as a pioneering molecular geneticist inspired me deeply. He unfolded incredible stories of phage molecular genetics, the double helix, the lac operator, the Messelson and Stahl experiments, and the mechanisms of gene regulation. This section of the course was constantly changing textbooks and Stent managed to give us a glimpse of how the field was progressing. One-third of the way through this course, I knew that biochemistry and molecular biology would be my field of study. In contrast to other sciences, the pace at which this young field of biology moved really excited me.

In the spring of 1969, at the height of the Vietnam war protests, our classes were canceled frequently, so our Molecular Biology 110 class met off-campus. We had heated discussions about science and the war. There was a strong tradition (persisting today), where students asked tough questions, trying to test the boundaries of the teacher's knowledge. Several of my classmates were brilliant and relentless. They knew more about the subject than the teacher, which was always amusing. I learned as much from other students as I did from formal lectures and the faculty, which is a wonderful aspect of studying at Berkeley.

A unique challenge and opportunity as a student at Berkeley is the incredible choice of courses one can take. I gravitated toward classes in the sciences, although I also took several "breadth requirements" such as music, art history, and Brazilian literature, to broaden my horizons. I still wonder what made me sign up for Physical Chemistry 120, which was designed mainly for chemistry graduate students and advanced chemistry majors. As a biologist, I had to struggle to keep up, but it was exhilarating to solve tough problem sets and even grasp some fundamentals of thermodynamics and quantum mechanics. These classroom experiences only deepened my resolve to get into a laboratory and find out how science was done.

By the end of my sophomore year, I learned that at UC

Berkeley, as in the real world, one must take the initiative and create opportunities. At first, I had no luck finding a professor willing to take an inexperienced student into his laboratory. Finally, I settled for a job as glassware washer in Professor Henry Rappaport's laboratory in Latimer Hall. By summer's end I was extracting alkaloids and purifying them by chromatography to help a chemistry graduate student with his research project. My enthusiasm for organic chemistry was somewhat dampened by my encounter with alkaloid extraction from the curare root (a poison used by South American natives to tip their arrows), which left me completely without a sense of taste for a week. Although the monotony of natural product extraction was far from inspiring, I got a firsthand look at how research is done.

Despite a rich summer experience in chemistry, I still had not entered the fascinating new area of large biomolecules—the field of biochemistry and molecular biology. The following summer, I approached Professor Daniel Koshland of the Biochemistry Department. I boldly asked him whether there was any chance I could work in this lab; for free, if necessary. He sent me off to read a book on the three-dimensional structure of proteins and asked me to come back after I'd read it. Then he grilled me for thirty minutes about the structure and function of proteins. Apparently satisfied with my rudimentary and recently acquired knowledge of proteins, he offered me a position. During the next year and a half, I was consumed with the excitement and challenge of studying enzyme catalysis, testing the orbital steering theory, and getting my first glimpse of world-class science in biology. I also experienced for the first time the privilege of being paid to do something I enjoyed.

In the Koshland lab, I worked with an exceptional graduate student, Dan Storm, who was demanding and tough, but also encouraging and patient. I also met two extraordinary postdoctoral fellows in the lab, Alex Levitski and Rick Dahlquist, two of the sharpest, brightest, and most original people I've met. Their vitality, energy, and intensity greatly stimulated the ambiance of the lab. For reasons I can't fathom, they decided to take me under their tutelage. They taught me to think critically, to recognize creativity, and value originality. (They also taught me how to party and have fun.) Daily encounters with motivated young scientists who were making new discoveries strongly attracted me to the field of biochemical research. This was a unique opportunity and I knew it. The lab environment was intellectually challenging and the work demanded focus and discipline. And yet, whenever I was in the lab, I was happy. Once I had the freedom and knowledge to actually design experiments and to execute them, time became meaningless. Spending fourteen hours a day, seven days a week in the laboratory seemed normal. The experience was so intense that it superseded all activities except karate training, which I took several times a week to help discipline both my mind and body. Other areas, namely my social life, took a beating. My girlfriend Claudia (who is now my wife) somehow endured this deranged behavior and even seemed to understand and partially accept my passion for research. As a major in French literature at Cal, Claudia found my "lab persona" strange and unsettling. She still manages to put up with it.

In the spring of 1970, an event took place outside of the classroom and the lab that had a lasting effect on my life. I was invited to go fishing with Professor Horace "Nook" Barker in the northern Sierra. That weekend trip rekindled my childhood passion for fishing and also introduced me to the art of fly-fishing. I didn't actually get to fly-fish that time for lack of proper equipment, but I observed a fly-fisherman catch a rainbow trout after laying sixty feet of line out on the surface of the lake. Right then, I was captivated. I didn't get my chance to fly-fish until the first summer after graduate school when I was given an old cane rod and some ragged flies to try on Williams Creek in Southern Colorado. Hooking that first ten-inch rainbow trout with a dry fly initiated a lifelong love of fly-fishing. In 1978 when I returned to Cal as a faculty member, I reestablished my fishing partnership with Nook Barker, and we spent many summers together fishing Hot Creek, Silver Lake, Lava Creek, and Fall River. Nook taught me not only how to fly-fish, but also to appreciate good science and how to behave as a scientist. His uncompromising honesty, openness, and clarity of thought as well as unwavering self-confidence have served as the model to which I aspire.

After graduating from Berkeley in 1971, I decided to take time off before entering Harvard for graduate school. I spent two summers traveling in Europe on a Triumph 650 sportster motorcycle. In between, I attended Oxford University and learned the basics of X-ray crystallography. Dan and Bunny Koshland spent six months during that year at Oxford, and Dan kindly arranged to open doors for me, making it possible for me to work with Sir David Phillips, who had solved the first three-dimensional structure of an enzyme. This brief "sabbatical" in England also gave me the freedom to work on several "far out" projects, and I came to appreciate the elegance of biomolecular structures. It was quite an experience to learn how to use the five counter linear defractometer from David Phillips and Louise Johnson, the inventors of the machine. Phillips' quiet reserve and understated British style was in stark contrast to Dan Storm and Rick Dahlquist's hard-driven "cowboy" brand of science. That year, I also had the opportunity to spend much time with the Koshlands, which fostered a lifelong relationship with two of the most progressive, talented, and sophisticated scientists I have known. My short time in Europe was memorable because I traveled, met people, learned the power of structural analysis by using X-ray crystallographic techniques, and had time to mature as a scientist.

It's clear that my time as an undergraduate research student at Berkeley profoundly influenced my scientific career and essentially set the path I would take. I found that using just my hands and a few simple apparati, I could address fundamental questions about living cells, or how enzymes catalyze reactions 100,000 times faster than ordinary chemical reactions. I enjoyed the intoxicating pleasure of solving important problems in biology, guided by intuition and experimental savvy. I had little patience for performing complex and drawn out experiments that might take months or even years to complete, so I was instantly drawn to the clever, rapid turnover strategies of modern biology. It was a revelation that I could actually tackle even the most profound questions in biology—how DNA replicates, what makes red blood produce hemoglobin, how do oncogenes cause cancer—by doing a series of technically simple but theoretically elegant benchtop experiments, each taking no longer than forty-eight hours. I became a "results junkie." To this day, I can't resist running to the lab on Saturday or Sunday morning, to grill my students to their delight or irritation: "What's up? How did last night's transcription reaction work? Did it give you any interpretable results?"

During my years at Berkeley I wasn't consciously aware of the criteria that defined first-rate science, but I was experiencing it. That early exposure to rigorous thinking and hard work helped mold my style of science today. I learned that no matter how smart, a good scientist must also be single-minded, intensely driven, and lucky. My first piece of luck came with the decision to attend Berkeley.

"... The very thing the University has been criticized for in some quarters— massiveness—acted positively for me. Being part of the crowd afforded me an anonymity that allowed me to evolve on my own."

RALPH EDWARDS

Ralph Edwards

THE THIN HAZE THAT SOMETIMES SCREENS New York City in mid-August from incoming traffic kept the famous skyline from my view as our automobile approached from the Jersey side. It was to be my first glimpse of the "big city," and I was a very excited young man.

The year was 1936—one year after graduation from the University of California—and I had decided to make the big step and try my hand at New York radio. I had worked my way through Cal writing, acting, announcing, newscasting, and performing about every broadcasting task in radio stations in and around Oakland and San Francisco.

A postcard from New York sent by Cal alumnus Sam Taylor, now a prominent playwright, held out the possibility of a small part in a Broadway play if I could get to New York. Sam had seen me in various Little Theater roles on the improvised stage of Wheeler Hall at Cal. That postcard was all the push I needed to climax a mounting urge to gather whatever abilities I might have acquired in five years of local West Coast radio and Edwin Duerr's Little Theater, and launch an attack on the big-time headquarters of radio in its 1936 heyday—and perhaps snare a Broadway bit in the meantime.

And now here it all was—right on the other side of that haze. I was on the last lap of a trip from San Francisco, for which I contributed thirty dollars to share auto expenses to Philadelphia with another young fellow. A kind couple, Dorothy and Dayton Lummis, had offered to drive me these final few miles to New York.

Thirty dollars.

That left ninety in my pocket.

I didn't know where I was going to stay or how far the ninety dollars would carry me, but it really didn't matter; my concern of the moment was a long-awaited view of the legendary New York. Then we were on the Pulaski Highway ramp that bridges New Jersey to New York, and suddenly New York's majestic skyline loomed across the Hudson, bigger, higher than I had envisioned.

By the time we had been squeezed through the long tube of Holland Tunnel and catapulted into the canyons of Manhattan, I knew I would have no bigger assignment than this in my future. I also knew I had faced a similar challenge in my past and had emerged with a token of victory, a Bachelor of Arts degree from the University of California.

The cold fright of first seeing New York reminds me of the same feeling of apprehension and excitement I felt the first day I walked through Sather Gate on the campus at Berkeley to enroll as a freshman. I was frightened then: at the lines, the Sophomore Vigilantes, the procedures, the swirl of people all looking as if they knew exactly where they were going and why.

I have searched my memory to find something in the realm of lectures, books, professors, sections, seminars, to say "this is the most important contribution the University of California made to my life," but I can't find anything. The most important lesson I learned from my University was the ability to exist in a crowd, be fed by the crowd, taught by the crowd, understand and be understood by the crowd. Thus the very thing the University has been criticized for in some quarters—massiveness—acted positively for me. Being part of the crowd afforded me an anonymity that allowed me to evolve on my own.

Cal taught me survival; the opportunity to view the attitudes, the problems of others objectively; to recognize these problems as some of my own and to analyze them, consciously or unconsciously, from the short-range vantage point of anonymity. This helps, I believe, to develop in a student that

nature peculiar to man—humanity: consideration and understanding of other human beings; recognition of the dignity and
worth of man. If the University has taught humanity to its students, it has made a significant contribution to mankind.

I didn't know it there in August 1936, but that awareness
of my fellow man, generated at UC, was to influence a nationwide radio audience in a few years, to contribute millions of dollars for health and educational purposes, build hospital wings
and school buildings, cause one-half billion dollars in "E" bonds
to be sold, clear up a wartime paper shortage on the East Coast,
help solve other domestic problems for the Office of War
Information and bring some pleasure to hundreds of thousands
of American servicemen and their families through "Truth or
Consequences" and "This Is Your Life." These are two radio
and television shows that came out of my heart and my head. The
same unconscious schooling in human awareness found its way
into several other television and radio productions that bore
my name.

The countless, nameless students, all fighting the same
battle, make an impression on a student without his even knowing it, especially if his background is less than sophisticated. I had
come to Cal from a farm, a very small town in Colorado, and then
a high school in Oakland.

I found a haven in the vastness of the student body and
the curriculum at the University. I needed a hiding place to find
myself. Until I acquired layers of confidence and social experience, I was alone and free to study and to blend into university life
on my own terms. Having faced the challenge at Berkeley, I was
better prepared for the challenge of New York and big-time
radio.

A shouted direction to me from seemingly indestructible
Professor Charles D. von Neumayer, drama instructor, during a
rehearsal performance of *The Choephori* at the Greek Theatre
during my second year on campus, speaks for all the warm discipline and inspiration of my UC instructors: "STOP! DON'T MOVE
A MUSCLE, MY DEAR-R-R-R FELLOW!"

I can assure you, this sophomore Orestes froze in the middle of his soliloquy. Unfortunately, the position in which I was caught was not a graceful one. That was the reason for the order to freeze. The toes and sole of my right foot had been pointed straight up in the air—the heel solidly on the tomb of Agamemnon—a truly unprofessional pose. I remained in this awkward position as Professor von Neumayer, tall, thin, erect, in regal, graceful strides so much a part of Vonny, so much a part of the theater, began an interminable descent from halfway up the cement block of seats in the vast open theater and ended beside this graceless victim on the arena floor. The other twenty students sat immobile, inwardly grateful they were not the targets of attack.

"Look!" said Vonny, almost spitting out the word as he rifled an arm and aimed a bayonet of a finger at my right foot. I wanted to bring the flagrant foot down to a normal and, hopefully, more artistic position, but the good professor forbade me to do so until I—and the rest of the class—had been crash-lectured in grace, conflict of movement, and projection of naturalism.

Two and a half years later, during my senior year, after a speech I had made in a rehearsal of *A Midsummer Night's Dream*, once more under this fine professor's direction, Vonny, up in the seats of Berkeley's Greek Theatre, again stopped me. I braced myself. This time he didn't bother to walk down, but the arm uncoiled as before; the bayonet aimed directly at me.

"If I were you, my dear fellow, I would get to New York if I had to crawl, stay there if I had to starve, line up at all the theater tryouts, see all the casting directors, keep at it until some producer hired me!"

With that statement I came out of the crowd at Cal. The final layer of confidence had been wrapped around me. Even if I never walk a Broadway stage, I *could,* for Vonny thought I could.

But first I had to graduate from Cal, and that meant at least a B minus in my English Comprehensive Exam. I spent six weeks cramming for it with Don Anderson, an honor student, in a room on Oxford Street. I filled the bookshelves with every play

Shakespeare ever wrote, with the biographies and poems of Keats, Shelley, Wordsworth, Spenser, as well as with Boswell, Johnson, Restoration comedies, and Chaucer—every poet and author we had studied for the past four years. The comprehensive asked only one question: "Give evidence of the economic conditions of the world at the time of Shakespeare, as reflected in his works"—or something to that effect. I took three hours to answer, the full limit. I was afraid something more would come to me after I had left, so I bled it out.

The days until the final grades were posted were like one long, wakeful night. It was "B minus or forget it" for me. When they were posted, I climbed the marble stairs of Wheeler Hall and walked apprehensively up to the list. I looked carefully and checked the name. I could hardly believe it. I had gotten a B.

I can't remember walking down the stairs. I could only see "radio for sure now" and "graduation" flashing marquee like in my mind. I was thrilled when Dr. Sproul handed my diploma to me a few days later at graduation in my memorable Greek Theatre. It was a beginning rather than an end.

A year went by, a year of radio in San Francisco. Big names kept announcing themselves at the conclusion of New York radio shows: Ted Husing, David Ross, Andre Baruch, H. V. Kaltenborn, Paul Douglas, Westbrook Van Voorhis. They did all the work; my job was to open the mike on the cue "This is the Columbia Broadcasting System" and intone, "KFRC, San Francisco." I felt I could do what they were doing. Then came Sam Taylor's postcard from New York.

I went out to Berkeley to see Vonny two days before I left. We walked around the lovely gardens of his home near the campus and talked of mutual student friends, light moments in the past three years, bantering on one of his popular subjects, "I won't be around forever." There in the driveway of his home on the eve of my departure for New York, all Vonny said was "Give 'em hell, Ralph." We shook hands and I drove off. How do you say good-by to your University?

I remember thinking of Vonny in that automobile ride

down Third Avenue on my first day in New York. The Lummises suggested that I stay at the Pickwick Arms Hotel on East Fifty-first Street. The room was nine dollars a week, which was four dollars more than I had paid for that room on Oxford Street in Berkeley, but I figured I could always retreat to lower rent if some network executive didn't discover me the first week.

None did. Nor the next week. By the third week I had auditioned or had my name on file for an announcer's job at almost every radio station in New York. In the meantime, I had acted on two aspects of Vonny's exhortation: I had crawled (through traffic) to the tryouts at theaters and, although I wasn't exactly starving, I wasn't eating as well or as often as I would have liked.

I realized that if I were to be the 1936 Broadway success story, I was going to have to either find a very reasonably priced place to eat or get a job that would carry me until some bright producer discovered me.

I tried the first approach and adopted Bernarr McFadden's Health Food Restaurant, on Third Avenue near Thirty-sixth, as my one and only eating spot. Mr. McFadden had a similar restaurant on Sixth Avenue near Forty-eighth Street, but this was uncomfortably near Radio City and the theater area, and I didn't care for a potential associate to spot me there. The meal of the day, every day, was cracked wheat that sold for three cents a bowl. For something less than twenty-five cents a day, I ate in Mr. McFadden's Third Avenue emporium for six weeks. The truth is, I got fat on the stuff, and if the clientele had been of less questionable appearance, I might have been tempted to include it in a list I later kept of unusual restaurants in New York.

None of my theater auditions paid off: Guthrie McClintic, Norman Bel Geddes, Gielgud's *Hamlet*. I stood in line and it looked as if it were going to be a long wait. I could have waited as Vonny wanted and maybe have realized his dream of an acting career for me, but I got hungry, and as I learned at Cal, it's as tough to study on an empty stomach as it is to keep awake on a full one; and I knew radio had at least kept me existing for five years in Oakland and San Francisco, so I lit out in earnest to find the real end of my rainbow: a staff announcer's job on one of the big networks.

As the days went on, however, and none of the radio stations called me, for the first time I really thought I might have bitten off more than I could chew. One morning I stayed in my room and did lots of soul searching.

I felt almost defeated.

It was very near to the way I felt the day I lost the final election for Varsity Yell Leader at Cal, two years earlier. I deserved to lose the yell-leading job; I should have worked harder for it, I thought as I stood by the dresser looking at something less than five dollars in cash on it. I found some heart in the reflection of the earlier defeat, and was about to dress and go forth once more into the fray when the phone rang. I don't think I'd had half a dozen calls in New York. It was CBS. The audition of some sixty men for Del Sharbutt's old announcing job had been cut down to two candidates. I was one of them.

"Could you come in?"

"When?"

"Now."

"Yes, sir!"

I hung up. This was it. "If I were you, I would get to New York if I had to crawl." By golly, maybe I wasn't going to let Vonny down after all.

I threw on my suit. My only suit. It had a hole in the right elbow. The maid on my floor promised she'd sew it for me, but never had. Well, I'd just have to keep my hand over it, if it's in view. I blew five cents on the bus up Madison Avenue so I wouldn't be out of breath when I walked into the studio on the twentieth floor of CBS.

Ernie Bush handed me a Coca-Cola commercial and a Packard commercial, sixty seconds each. A two-minute test. It beat hell out of that English Comprehensive! I read the Coca-Cola commercial and was halfway into the Packard plug when I caught Ernie Bush out of the side of my eye, in the control room, on the interoffice telephone. I read on. A voice interrupted over the loudspeaker.

"Hold it!" Ernie Bush started to walk from the control room. Was this another Vonny? I unconsciously looked at my right foot. Mr. Bush said, "Come with me, please."

The vice-president in charge of summertime hiring, Doug Coulter, asked one question. "Ever do any radio before?"

"Yessir, six years—all through college—and before and after." I was holding my left hand on my right elbow.

"I like your work." He lifted a telephone receiver. "Hello—Burgess? I'm sending down a new announcer. Huh?—oh—Edwards. OK? Thanks."

A handshake and temporary exposure of the right elbow.

"Thank you, Mr. Coulter, very much."

I signed everything Mr. Burgess had to offer. I borrowed twenty-five dollars against my first forty-five-dollar-a-week paycheck from another Cal graduate, Roger Segure, and bought a new iron-colored, iron-textured suit, and that night I came back to the twentieth floor of the CBS building at Fifty-second and Madison. I stood on the fire escape in the Indian summer weather of October and looked out over the lighted skyline of New York. I had known this exhilaration only once before in my life: the day I walked up the marble stairs of Wheeler Hall to Cal's English Department and saw the B grade posted opposite my name.

*.   *.

Do entering freshmen today still have the challenges—the frontiers to conquer?

Three years ago I flew up to Berkeley to attend a meeting of the Board of Trustees of the University of California Alumni Foundation. I phoned my youngest daughter, Lauren, at the Theta house and asked her if she'd like to have dinner with her dad at Trader Vic's in Oakland.

As we were finishing up dessert, she turned to me and said, "Dad, tell me how you used to starve in New York."

I said, "Oh, come on. Quit putting me on."

"No," she said. "You've told Chris (my older daughter) and Gary (my USC son), but you've never told me. I want to hear the whole thing."

She really meant it. So I went into the full story—the sudden burst of New York's skyline, the church I slept in, the cracked wheat, the last two bits in the automat, the torn sleeve, right up to the final audition at CBS.

When I had finished, Laurie said, "You know, we just don't have opportunities like that any more."

By opportunities she meant the lack of them, or the Depression entrapment that forced us to develop opportunities.

I had never thought of it exactly in that light before, but the struggle back there in 1936 wasn't a struggle at all. It was an opportunity. And Laurie may have been right. Our nation's growing affluence has, to a certain extent, deprived kids of the struggle, or the opportunities as we knew them.

This throws more of a burden on our universities and colleges. The challenges, the struggles, the basic training field for life have more and more come to rest on the shoulders of the University. The revolts and discoveries, trials by fire that used to meet us when we stepped out of college now hit us when we walk in. If our college education has had effect, it will have given us the ability to understand this and to help our college administrators, faculty, and students to face this four-year crucible, to help meld raw material into productive maturity.

"I wanted to be a professional athlete, but Berkeley will not allow you to be educated simply in the discipline of your major. If you accept any of the many challenges Berkeley can throw at you, then you cannot simply be an engineer, or a chemist, or a professional football player."

JOE KAPP

Joe Kapp

I AM A PROFESSIONAL FOOTBALL PLAYER. This is not all I am, but it is certainly one of the important things I have accomplished. Professional football over the past decade has been built into a large and profitable industry. It has grown from twelve teams and one league to twenty-eight teams and two leagues. There is a series of play-offs and a "Super Bowl" interleague game worth many thousands to each player on the winning team. Pro football draws tremendous revenue and exposure from television. The games are played before capacity or near-capacity crowds in large stadiums. There are preview and review shows on TV; highlights of the games are even shown on cross-country airline flights. This exposure of the coaches, players, and others involved in this sport-business, places these individuals among the most widely known and influential people in the country. As an example, political candidates, even for the office of President of the United States, seek the endorsement of big-name professional athletes.

I signed a pro contract with the Canadian League after finishing my eligibility at the University of California (I later returned to get my degree), and received a bonus for signing. It was modest by present standards but it alone was equal to a first year's salary had I been, for example, a business administration major. I have played in the National Football League, an indication of having reached a highly regarded proficiency level in this profession. And, in addition to playing football, I am involved in several businesses and investments that will go a long way toward insuring my future and that of my family. All of this is noted to establish that professional football is a legitimate profession.

The preparation for this career started many years ago, in sports, principally football and basketball. I wanted my avocation to be my vocation. So sports has always had a major influence on my life. It influenced my wanting to attend college, my being able to attend college, my choice of major at the University and, of course, my life since leaving the University.

I was first exposed to the University of California when I was twelve years old. As a seventh grader in Salinas, I traveled to Berkeley to see a football game. The Golden Bears were playing Missouri and I had my first glimpse of the campus. Its setting on the Bay was impressive. It was immense; the eucalyptus trees, the buildings, the Campanile, Memorial Stadium, the students, the color—the whole scene captured my imagination. I wanted someday to belong to all this.

Upon returning to junior high school, I found out from my homeroom teacher, a Cal graduate, what the entrance requirements were. They were high, but since I wanted to go on to college to play football, I strained to qualify for admission to the University of California. Later I learned there were athletic scholarships available and I was relieved, because I could not see a way to go to college without some aid.

There was not much in my background to indicate a college future. I was, in fact, the first in my family to go to college. Money for rent and for food was the daily challenge facing my family. I was the oldest of five children; my father was of German descent, my mother Mexican-American. I was finally able to attend the University only because of the grant-in-aid offered to me by Cal on the recommendation of Coach Pappy Waldorf and Pete Newell, who thought I had enough talent to warrant this aid. What they saw in me was not readily apparent, evidently, because the University of California was the only major school to offer me a scholarship on graduation from high school in Newhall.

I wasn't one of the "name" high-school football players. I didn't have the reputation, but I did have potential and I needed the opportunity to develop it. There must be countless young people who are academically in a parallel situation: they may not have the grades, but they do have the potential and need the opportunity. These people come mainly from low-income groups, I believe, where the daily goal is to get enough to eat rather than to study to pass a classroom subject. I do not know where I would be today without the opportunity I was given. I feel strongly that the universities should search out these people and provide educational opportunities for them. I know that the University of California is doing this.

Though I was not taking money from my family while I was in school, I was not contributing to the family income either. This placed a hardship on my family and was a disturbing thing to me through my college years. Still, my mother always wanted the best for her children and she encouraged me to take college preparatory courses. I came within one B of qualifying for admission to Cal.

As is the case with most recruited athletes, I was invited to visit the campus during the spring of my senior year in high school. This was no unimportant event to a rural boy like me. I had to borrow a coat—you can't go visiting without a coat. I borrowed a blue one from a teammate; I had gray slacks, so I was all set to visit the Big U.

It was spring and hot. I carried the coat on my arm until I arrived at the San Francisco airport. I went into the men's room, slicked my hair a little, put on the coat, and confidently inspected myself in the mirror. Right in the back of the coat was a large L-shaped rip, which had been neatly but not subtly mended. I spent the next two days, when I was wearing the coat, with my back to the wall.

California had offered me the financial aid I needed. I was coming to a school with a great academic tradition, but this tradition, although important to me, was not as vital as the fact that its football team played in a major college league and that I might have a chance to play in the Rose Bowl.

I went to summer school to make up the B I was lacking. How I sweated through that summer; it took me both sessions to get the B and then I enrolled at Cal to play football and basketball and to get a degree. I was going to college specifically to prepare myself vocationally. This doesn't sound very high-minded, but sports was the major influence in my life.

In athletics, you advance in stages. I don't believe that during high school I counted on being a professional athlete, but I didn't discount it either. If you can excel or perform well at each level then you can make the next step. Following high school, the next step was college. Fortunately for me, the college I was entering was also a great educational institution, as well as giving me the chance to play against some of the best athletes in the world. It gave me training, by competent instructors, in the fundamentals and skills of a precise profession.

I remember after one game in my freshman year I was ready to give it all up. Those were the days of single platoon football, and even the quarterback had to play defense. A hurdler caught three touchdown passes over my head, and we lost to UCLA 38–0. I was ready to believe that there was no way I was going to be able to make it in college football. The coaches kept me from quitting, however, and for this I am grateful.

I majored in physical education. If I couldn't make it as a player, I figured, perhaps someday I could make it as a teacher and coach. As a freshman, in 1955, I believed the University was great. Berkeley was great, the times were great, but most of all, the people were great; and people, to me, are what life is all about. People were there from all over the world and from all types of social situations. I was delighted to be there.

That all these people were at Cal was not accidental, as it was perhaps accidental that I was there. I know other schools have exceptional people, but maybe not as many or in as many ways as Cal does. There were the rich and the poor. All my life I had known the latter, but I first met the former as a student at Cal. Down the hall from where I roomed as a freshman lived Earl

Robinson and Bob Tealer; for the first time in my life I met black people my own age. One of the things I learned at Cal was how much I didn't know. By meeting people whose capabilities were beyond the scope of my prior experiences, I learned how much I didn't know.

My first impression of Cal was its size. It has been said by its critics that the University is too big. This was what I heard all through high school. But to me, its size only increased the educational possibilities for the students. While I didn't take advantage of many of these opportunities—my own limited motivations held me back, the school didn't—California's impact upon me was tremendous. I am sure that today the challenges have increased, adding to what I feel is important about the University.

The environment brought me to a much higher achievement level within myself than I would have attained in a lesser school. Some students express themselves in their studies, and are motivated by them. It was through sports that I expressed—and am still expressing—myself. My limited motivation in the classroom is a matter of regret to me. But I cannot stress enough that to get by academically I was forced into self-discipline and had to develop a resourcefulness to survive.

I wanted to be a professional athlete, but Berkeley will not allow you to be educated simply in the discipline of your major. If you accept any of the many challenges Berkeley can throw at you, then you cannot simply be an engineer, or a chemist, or a professional football player. It is significant that of the players who were on our team, there are now four or five lawyers, three or four dentists, and many engineers and teachers. These men accepted California's academic challenge, as well as that of competitive athletics, and won. I returned to the University to get my degree. I needed six units to graduate, so I finished as I had begun, in summer school, sweating it out.

The work that goes into the making of a season of football is more than I have seen in any other walk of life, the severe challenge to develop the discipline of mind and body necessary to be successful in highly competitive football. You are constantly engaged in competition with yourself, with a teammate for starting position or with the opposition.

Engraved on the bench on California's side of Memorial Stadium are these words of Andy Smith:

> We do not want men who will lie down bravely to die
> for California, but men who will fight valiantly to live. . . .

When speaking or writing of reaching the highest limits, I always think of Jack Hart. We were teammates through four years. Jack wanted to win as much as any man I've ever met. This is why he played, while some men of perhaps greater physical ability sat on the bench. Jack came to California as a husband and father, to be a student and athlete; he succeeded on all fronts.

Football is pressure, ten pressurized Saturday afternoons, because winning is so important. There was pressure that summer in 1960; getting my degree was important. The degree was the badge of honor for four years of hard work. The diploma from Berkeley is a status symbol, because not everyone has one and not everyone who starts out in one succeeds. Because we had all fought, or were fighting, the same battle for this piece of paper, which Berkeley does not let you have easily, five of us celebrated my graduation. These men and I made our celebration at a little Chicano restaurant in West Oakland with tacos, tortillas, and maybe a beer or two. How sweet it was!

I went to Canada from Cal, mainly because of money, but also because I would be able to play right away rather than serve an apprenticeship on the bench. I played football in Canada for eight years. Canadian ball was good to me, but I always wanted to play in my native land. I stayed in Canada until we won the Grey Cup, the Canadian football championship. Success in football, as far as I am concerned, is measured only in championships won, not in yards gained.

If you accept Cal's educational opportunities, I believe you are training yourself to go for the championships. I feel it is important to try to be as big a person as possible, in terms of awareness, understanding, growth, and the desire to reach one's fullest potential. The development of these traits, I believe, is what I owe to the University of California.

The education I received was not accidental. Cal is the big time—it's where it is at! If what its students were doing didn't meet with the approval of the parental generation, it was nonetheless reflective of the most intelligent and articulate of America's future generations. Students all over the world are dissenting and are dissatisfied with the world they are about to inherit. Students are speaking out, challenging actively, and, of course, in America it happened first at Berkeley. I would have been surprised if it hadn't. I would expect the University of California's students to be leaders and challengers.

An old quarterback once told me, "My teams never lost any games . . . we just ran out of time." As quarterback of the Minnesota Vikings in 1970, time ran out on us in Super Bowl IV. Battling the system of professional football and the inequities of owner's rights versus player's rights, time ran out on my career as a professional player in the early seventies. I have learned over and over that athletic competition and the game of football are the most powerful teachers of the meaning and value of time. Crisis and chaos are part of the game, but learning how to deal with time is perhaps its most important lesson. You can imagine how I felt then, standing there on the sidelines as the coach of the Bears in the 1982 Big Game, behind by one point, with four seconds left! The most exciting place to be in the world for any old Bear. The truth of the situation was that our Bears had competed against a favored Stanford team. Our players, led by our quarterback Gale Gilbert, had played valiantly and well enough to win. Our defensive unit had risked greatly to stop the All-American, John Elway, but in the last minute John showed his worth and drove his team to take that one point lead. It looked grim! If the game was over, it didn't seem fair. But it wasn't over. There was life, and what happened in those four seconds has gone on to become part of college football history. "The Play" will be forever etched in my mind and in the minds of all loyal Golden Bears. I have personally met 1,987,000 Cal fans who saw it in person that day. Capacity at Memorial Stadium is 75,662 . . . that means there must have been over a million Golden Bear supporters up on Tightwad Hill that afternoon!

I have always felt that the *real purpose* of any athletic event is to provide a reason for celebration. I have never been to a bigger party than the one that started in Memorial Stadium that Saturday and spread throughout Berkeley to the rest of the East Bay, San Francisco, and the thousands of towns where Cal alumni of all ages resided. In fact, the events of that day, and "The Play" in particular, unified and energized the Bay Area, showcasing the value of athletics to a community. For weeks, even months after the game the "Bear would not die" attitude could be found reborn in companies, in families, everywhere where teamwork was necessary to defeat adversity. Successful athletic teams and seasons become milestones; visible memorable points of pride that become part of our tradition. Important lessons in learning about ourselves. Our Cal players refused to believe the Big Game was over. Those on the sidelines can participate in the game by supporting, rooting, hoping, and praying, but the power to make and take action is on the field. The leadership that Richard Rogers demonstrated in his cry "the ball will not fall," the unselfish positioning of Kevin Moen, he started and finished "The Play," the strength of purpose of Dwight Garner by not going down with two or three Stanford players on his back, and the confidence of Mariet Ford with his blind lateral back to Kevin who ran it into the end zone for the game winning touchdown are all actions by players who took control of their own destiny. These players and their teammates competed for the full sixty minutes and not one second less. Each of them accepted responsibility for achieving the goal with the full knowledge that the goal could not be achieved alone. Those four seconds of precious life demonstrated one of the greatest examples of TEAM-WORK in sports history (at least according to *Sports Illustrated*). They taught the value of team accomplishment through individual achievement.

Actually, most successful activities and accomplish-

82

ments involve group interaction. Individual success is achieved in direct proportion to the individual understanding and mastery of team dynamics. From birth to death, we are both voluntary and involuntary team members. Those who learn best . . . how we affect and are affected by our team involvements . . . are the people who live fuller, happier, and more successful lives. We all belong to "teams": the family, city, ethnic, gender, age, group, school, church, union, civic organization, profession. The average person is a member of twenty-six different teams. As many by accident as by choice. Team dynamics are an unavoidable aspect of everyday life. As a youngster the motivating force in my life had been competitive athletics, football, basketball, baseball, it did not matter. I worked hard academically and athletically and was then fortunate to team up with the University of California. As my career progressed, it became clear to me that most of life's lessons could be learned through sports. I began to write down the analogies, and when I realized that this material could help people develop the interpersonal cooperation they needed in their lives, I teamed up with an old Blue, Ned Averbuck (a college professor teaching communications since his Cal days) and formed Team Dynamics Inc., a company dedicated to the principles of teamwork. TD! delivers its messages in books, tapes, and workshops. Its focus on creating a winning process is an important supplement to the professional and experiential training most people receive. Whether you're trying to figure how to score a touchdown in four seconds, or achieve financial security for your family, the development of shared goals, team dynamics, is vital.

85

In athletics you choose up sides. Who do you want to play with, for or against? I chose to be on the University of California's side as a student in 1955. It was a privilege, and an honor to come back to Cal as the football coach in 1982. I used my persuasive skills on Bill Cooper, my old Rose Bowl teammate, a highly successful coach and administrator in Southern California, to join me in this labor of love. I remain an advocate and an ad hoc spokesperson for the University.

Much has happened in the past twenty-five years since *There Was Light* was originally published. The prevalence of getting a liberal education at Cal has given way to a more field-specific focus. The role of athletics has expanded to address all students as "student-athletes." We have larger physical education and intramural programs, a viable women's athletics program that basically didn't exist in 1969. We still field championship caliber NCAA teams in basketball, football, baseball, track, crew, swimming, water polo, gymnastics, rugby, tennis . . . the University presents its students with a greater variety of individual and team challenges. But winning and achieving at Cal is still not easy. Each accomplishment or victory is a hard fight. And failures are tough to take. But every Bear comes to know that level of toughness and tenacity required to succeed and takes it with them into their lives after graduation.

Not unlike its students, the University's role in education faces challenges that require the unifying force and spirit of "The Play." When coaching at Cal in the eighties, Coop and I made it a point to invite every professor and administrator on campus to our games. We embraced the local community, alumni, and students as teammates. Our focus was "we," not "me." That trust, cooperation and courage that made "The Play" successful have not always been evident in the University's actions in recent years. We are sailing into a larger world of competition as well as a multi-racial world of diverse customs and cultures. We live in a time of unprecedented change. We are confident the University will pull together, meet all challenges, and continue its leadership role in public education. There is no greater place to prepare yourself for life than the University of California, Berkeley. Thousands of graduates like myself will tell you so. We have a rich tradition to uphold and to look forward to in the future.

To get there we must learn from athletics and look to the power and spirit of TEAM to bring Cal into the twenty-first century.

"...I had always believed, and the years at the University had confirmed me in this, that the book is the most important tool that man has ever invented, more important than the wheel, cement, or running water."

IRVING STONE

Irving Stone

M Y MOTHER HAD NO EDUCATION. Her father, though he arrived in San Francisco just after the Civil War, when millionaires were in the making, preferred spending his days with his three brothers, playing pinochle. As a result, his children were forced into factories and shops of San Francisco around the age of twelve to help keep the family pot boiling.

But my mother had a mind. In a day before adult education, she craved books and knowledge but had nowhere to find them. From the first moment that I could understand the meaning of her words, around the age of five, my mother began drilling into me one passionate belief of her life:

"You must get an education. Only through education can you rise in this world."

Since I was not yet in primary school, I had no idea what my mother meant. But intuitively she knew what she meant by education, and it was her determination that I should learn this at the earliest possible moment.

She chose my twelfth birthday, for that had been the day she had been obliged to leave school and go to work. It also fell on a Sunday, which was her only day off.

We rose early, and packed a lunch of cold meat. We also had a bag of stale crumbs for the sea gulls. After breakfast we took the streetcar down Sutter Street to the Ferry Building where we caught the 8:10 *Southern Pacific*. It was one of those sparkling, brilliantly clear days which only San Francisco can produce. We leaned over the rail of the ferry, throwing crumbs to the screaming gulls while the boat made its slow, patient way toward the Alameda mole. From there we took the long train ride through the quiet city of Oakland. By nine o'clock we were in Berkeley.

My mother bought some powdered-sugar buns in the Shattuck Bakery, where she asked a few timid questions and learned the general direction of the college. It took us perhaps half an hour to find the first open, and hence to us official, gate. One or two steps inside and we were in fairyland: greenswards in front of classical structures; a running brook; magnificent shrubs and ferns; winding paths under tall, fragrant eucalyptus trees that led up a slight incline to a series of white stone buildings glistening in the sunlight against poppy-covered hills.

We walked slowly, hand in hand, a little frightened, past the building with the names of poets and humanitarians on it; and then past the majestic pile of the Library. There were few students around this early Sunday morning, nor would we have been so bold as to ask them for information even if they had sauntered by. Pearl and I were as though in a foreign land. We had no knowledge of how one got into a college, what the requirements might be, how much money it cost, or what one studied.

Our strongest emotion was that somehow we did not belong here, and if the authorities should come along they would promptly escort us out the sacred gate. We both had the uneasy feeling that college was only for the top layer of society and wealth, not for us.

After a couple of hours of wandering about the beautiful grounds and climbing through the golden poppies to the top of the hill to gaze down over the Bay, we returned to a small wooden bridge and sat by the side of the creek, eating our lunch. Then my mother turned to me.

"Son," she said, "you have to give me your word of honor. I may not be here to see it, and I may not be able to help you, but today you must promise me that no matter what happens to you, you will come to this college."

There was a burning intensity in her voice. Though I was

too young to understand the hunger and ambition behind it, I was deeply moved.

"I promise, Ma."

"Education makes a man grow." Pearl's voice rang out above the noise of the brook. "With it, he can be free. He will be his own boss. He will work at something he is good at, instead of the first job he can find."

I never doubted that I should go to this college; had I not given my word of honor? And that in some mysterious way it would free me. I never lost this conviction, not even in the difficult years that followed; for paradoxically, though I loved books and had an insatiable appetite to read, I was a poor student.

In my senior year I moved with my mother to Los Angeles and entered high school there. The teachers had a warm and interested attitude toward their students. I flourished to such an extent that I pulled straight A's. This accomplishment, along with make-up work, got me admitted to the University in 1920.

Riding to Berkeley on the train, I kept my saxophone, through which I then made my living, in the upper berth with me. I did not sleep all night because I had stuffed into the reed case my full savings of $246.

After dropping my bags at a boardinghouse, for the second time in my life I entered the University of California campus. It was the day before school was to open, and again there was not a student in sight. The chimes of the Campanile filled the warm and fragrant August air. I stood in front of Wheeler Hall, which I had learned would be the scene of many of my classes, realizing that I knew not a soul on the campus, that I had only enough money to put me through perhaps two-thirds of my freshman year, and that if the University required me to take mathematics and science, I should probably be in serious trouble again. My courage faltered; I had no right to be here. It was as though my mother and I, on that day five years before, had entered into a conspiracy to defraud the school.

Then, as I was about to turn away, feeling lonely, dejected, unwanted, an apparition appeared on the hill above me: a man on horseback, wearing a black hat and a loose black cape. I thought for a moment that the shock of entering the campus had created some kind of hallucination. As the figure rode slowly toward me, I perceived that it was one of the most beautiful human beings I had ever seen. There was a warm, gentle smile on his face; his cheeks were red, and his expression alive and excited; he was obviously of considerable age.

The man on horseback pulled up before me, took the black hat off his beautiful white hair, swept it before him, bowed to me from the saddle and said in a magnificently warm tone: "Good evening, sir."

With that, he smiled a broad welcoming smile, put his hat back on his head, bowed to me slightly again and moved on down the road.

I stood there literally transfixed. No one had ever called me "sir." It was not only that I had, by this one word, been transformed from a child into an adult, but also I had been promoted somehow from the lower middle class into a top echelon of gentlemen and scholars.

A student passed. I stopped him and asked who the man on horseback was. He replied, "Benjamin Ide Wheeler, president emeritus of the University. This building was named after him."

My mother had divorced my father when I was seven years old, just after my sister was born. She went to work selling gloves in S. N. Woods Department Store on Fourth and Market streets at four dollars a week. I was farmed out to my paternal grandmother. This was before the days of child labor laws, and an eager youngster could always find a part-time job: working in a milk depot on Haight Street, where I watched the owner pour buckets of tap water into his milk; driving a horse and wagon to deliver neighborhood groceries; folding and delivering men's suits for a clothing store; moving up to stock boy in a leather goods house. By fourteen I was ushering in movie houses, at fifteen spending my summers working on the pear and apricot ranches of Central

California. The hours were long; even while going to grammar and high school my part-time jobs involved up to thirty-five hours a week. The starting pay was fifty cents a week; it took years to work up to two dollars and then to three. Yet these sums were urgent to my mother's existence and to mine. When I was fifteen, and going about with a crowd of boys and girls from high school, I became so strapped for money that I dropped out of Lowell for an entire week, answered an advertisement in the *San Francisco Chronicle,* and took a job at Paul Elder's Book Store, unpacking crates of best sellers as they came in from New York, the chief of which was Blasco-Ibáñez's *The Four Horsemen of the Apocalypse.* The fifteen dollars I earned set me on my feet; and my cousin wrote an eloquent letter describing the near-fatal illness that had kept me bedded.

It was the saxophone that saved me. When I was fifteen my cousin and I bought the first two saxophones to be put on sale in San Francisco. I was clumsy with my fingering and could barely read a note of music, so I spent hundreds of hours developing a sweet tone, which paid my way through the next two years of high school and four years of college; playing for parties, dances, picnics. The highlight of my musical career came on a Sunday afternoon in a long hall of an upstairs building in Chinatown, where, our backs to an open lattice-work partition, we played for an Italian wedding, while a group of Chinese musicians sat with their backs to us against the lattice wall, playing simultaneously for a Chinese wedding.

Lowell High School was for me a rough passage. Though I did well in the subjects that I cared about: English, history, civics, it was only the heroic efforts of my classmates in chemistry, botany, and zoology, doing my experiments, making my drawings, that got me through. In two years of honest endeavor my algebra teacher never quite managed to persuade me that $2\pi r$ equals circumference.

I had written my first complete short story at nine; I remember it as a combination of a pulp western and a Jules Verne science fiction, the hero coming into a western town with a new invention attached to his pistol: a square box just behind the trigger into which he poured hot molten lead, which enabled him to shoot without noise or the show of smoke.

When I was fifteen I took a course in English and composition from a Mr. Morton, son of the principal. One Friday the assignment was to write a short story. The plot revolved around two men who met on a transcontinental railroad line and had a passionate argument about life and fate. Something was to happen on the journey which proved one of them to be right. On Monday morning Mr. Morton called up five of the students and had them read their work; at the end of each he said, "That is not a short story." I was the sixth to read my paper, for which I had invented a phrase: *The Eventualist.* My hero attempted to persuade the second man that fate determined each man's life and death; the second man upheld man's free will. A trestle buckled; the two men were caught between the cars, where they had been arguing. As the second man's head was about to go under the water of the river into which the train had fallen he ceded the philosophic point. When I had finished, Mr. Morton said, "Yes, that is a short story. It is a *bad* short story, but it is a story. It has a beginning, a middle, and an end." After class he asked me, "Do you write much?" I replied that I had been writing short stories for years, but that actually I had little time since I worked from three to six every school day and then ushered from noon until eleven on Saturdays and Sundays. Mr. Morton said, "Very well, take that last seat in the last row; and from now until the end of the year you will have one hour a day free for your writing."

At the end of the school year near-tragedy struck. My mother, who had remarried, was leaving San Francisco with the families of her sisters and brothers to settle in Southern California, where they saw greater opportunity for the future. I was to transfer to Manual Arts High School in Los Angeles. When I went to Principal Morton's office to ask him for a transcript of my record, he created a new phrase for his times. He said coldly, "Why don't you drop out? Since you're obviously not going on to college, get a job and start work as quickly as possible."

I stumbled my way upstairs to young Mr. Morton's office, crying. When he wanted to know what was wrong, I explained. He grabbed me by the elbow and hustled me down the stairs to his father's office, where he cried:

"You can't do anything as destructive as this! Young Stone is the most promising student I've had in any of my classes. I know he can't dissect a frog, but he's never going to have to. Give him his transcript and a recommendation to Manual Arts High School."

That summer, 1919, I worked as a desk clerk during the days at Hotel Tallac on Lake Tahoe, and at night played in the dance band. When I walked into the registrar's office of Manual Arts a beautiful young redheaded girl glanced at my transcript and said with a warm smile, "Mr. Stone, welcome to Manual Arts." This was the equivalent of the great gift that President Emeritus Wheeler had made me on my first day as a student at Berkeley; for no one had ever before called me Mister. When the young girl looked at my two years of English Composition, in which I had eight units of A's, she asked, "Mr. Stone, these are two different courses, are they not, English and Composition?" I told a whopper. "Yes, of course." Well then, the girl replied, "we have to add another eight units of A's to your record, don't we?"

With this benign beginning I had a magnificent time at Manual Arts, writing for the weekly newspaper, playing in a production of James M. Barrie's *What Every Woman Knows,* appearing with the Debating Team, playing in the school orchestra, and doing straight A work. There was a rule that a newcomer could not graduate from the high school until he had studied there for a full year. At the end of the first semester the principal called me to his office and said with a broad smile, "You're wasting your time here; on to college with you!"

My graduation came at the end of January, a full month after Berkeley had begun its second semester. The University of Southern California was about to begin its second semester. I was admitted. However I needed $120 for the tuition fee. The San Bernardino Orange Show was about to open; they needed a

93

saxophonist for twelve days in their dime-a-dance hall. The salary was ten dollars a day. We played from one in the afternoon until two in the morning. At the end of the twelve days I came back to Los Angeles, went straight to USC, and put down my $120 check.

☙ ☙

When I entered Berkeley on August 9, 1920, the administration had just passed a new set of regulations stating that every entering student must take two years of science and mathematics. I doubt that I could have passed those courses. Fate stepped in again: the administration had also ruled that anyone who already had fourteen units of university credit was exempt from these required courses. I had earned exactly fourteen units from USC! Now I could devote my college years to the subjects that I loved and did well in.

I assumed that when I registered early Monday morning I would be plunged so deeply into work that I would not have a chance to lift my eyes from the books for a solid four years. However, the faculty was not in that desperate a rush; there were few assignments given during the first week. Consequently by Monday afternoon I found my way into the Doe Library. There were no students yet at work. It was forbidden for an undergraduate to be allowed into the stacks. I fell into a conversation with a pleasant young librarian and asked him what the Berkeley stacks looked like. He offered to take me through and reveal some of the mysteries of library cataloguing. After he had spent an hour with me he agreed that it could do no harm if I sat on the stone floor between the narrow aisles of bookracks and read. I spent that entire first week on the stone floors, reading under a naked electric bulb. The first book I pulled out was Thorstein Veblen's *The Theory of the Leisure Class;* the second was Bertrand Russell's *Why Men Fight;* the third and fourth were Sigmund Freud's *The Psychopathology of Everyday Life* and *The Interpretation of Dreams.* I read all four of these volumes in one week. It came close to being the equivalent of a four-year college education.

The years at the University would be too precious for me to make of myself a grind. I neither wanted nor needed A's. I decided to be content with straight B's, and thus release myself for all of the days of reading in the library stacks, wandering the hills of Berkeley, carrying with me newly discovered volumes of plays, poetry, philosophy. In the evenings I went to Wheeler Auditorium, where a fine theatrical group, consisting of Sam Hume, Irving Pichel, and Mary Morris produced on a stage with absolutely no facilities, the world's greatest dramatic literature. Here I saw for the first time the plays of Ibsen, Shaw, Strindberg, Turgenev. After seeing a play, I would spend the following week reading straight through the dramatist's body of work. Somewhere along the line I had gained an impression that education meant self-education.

As a prelegal student I was a political science major. Our professors took us through the history of man's efforts to govern himself. In English there was a wide range of subjects, such as "The Age of Pope and Dryden." Kroeber introduced us to the fascinating world of anthropology, Prall to philosophy, Bolton to history: inspired teachers, all.

Part of today's turmoil on American campuses is charged to their enormous size and impersonality. When I entered the University of California in 1920 it already had 10,000 students, and was the largest university in the world. We were trained from the outset to compensate for size, to avail ourselves of the privileges that came from the extensive facilities and faculty. Passing each other on the campus, everyone nodded. It became an element of faith for every young man and woman at the University to participate in extracurricular activities. I made the boxing team by my sophomore year, was a member of the Senate Debating Society; was inducted into the honorary societies in political science and economics. Though there was cliquishness among the higher income levels and social backgrounds (60 percent of the men were working their way through Berkeley in part, 40 percent in toto), and the administration permitted its fraternities to write a clause into their constitutions which stipulated that they would admit only white Christians, in the classrooms, on the athletic fields, in all of the intramural activities, the University was a functioning democracy.

The professors were friendly and gregarious. Several hours each week we were welcome to gather in their offices, where we would smoke our pipes and have long bull sessions, not only about the subject at hand, but life in general. I was welcomed into many professorial homes for Sunday night buffet supper, as were my friends; we were taken along to the circus with their own children, and frequently to concerts or plays in San Francisco when extra tickets were available. It never entered our minds that the University was too big, or the faculty too remote or too pre-occupied to be concerned with our problems.

The first woman professor at the University of California, Dr. Jessica Peixotto, started sending my manuscripts around to the magazines with letters of recommendation just as soon as I began writing seriously. Professor Samuel May, whom I helped to found the first municipal bureau of research in the United States, recommended me for an important job in the St. Louis City Government.

There is a line in Carson McCullers' *The Member of the Wedding* in which a young boy, who has no mother, is playing out in the backyard with half a dozen playmates, says as each of this friends pedals off to go somewhere or do something, and he is left alone: "Everybody has a 'we', only I don't have a 'we.'"

Berkeley became my "we": my club, my organization, my political party, my church, my family; all the more so when my mother and sister died during my student years. I had been born on Telegraph Hill in San Francisco; but now I was reborn on this campus. The University became my loving and beloved parents. I enjoyed it all: Vachel Lindsay and Carl Sandburg reading their poetry in Wheeler Auditorium; Charles Mills Gayley reading from *The Widow in the Bye Street* at four of a Friday afternoon; the Saturday afternoon football games (our "Wonder Team" went undefeated for four straight years, giving many of us a severe success psychosis); the production of *He Who Gets*

Slapped; walking up Strawberry Canyon of a spring afternoon hand in hand with a pretty girl, to lie under the all-embracing oak trees and exchange kisses; the Saturday nights when I was not working and would take my girl to the College of Mining Ball or the College of Agriculture Ball, for which Harmon Gymnasium had been converted into the interior of a gold mine, or a huge barn with stalls for horses, cows, goats, chickens, and haylofts as well. I loved the Sunday afternoons in good weather, when at four o'clock I would drop down from the hills into the Greek Theatre to listen to a string quartet, or to watch a production of Aristophanes' *The Frogs.*

The University of California has frequently been great, but it has never been perfect. Its main liability during my student days was superimposed by the Regents: no political meeting could be held on campus, nor could aspirants for public office make speeches within its borders. I can still see the frustrated expression on the face of Upton Sinclair when he stood outside Sather Gate selling copies of his book *The Goose-Step* from an upended apple box. The meetings had to be held a full block away, on the corner of Telegraph and Bancroft. It was the refusal to allow this corner to be used, after the University had spread itself, that resulted in the first Free Speech upheaval on the Berkeley campus, and led to rioting on campuses all over the world.

The English Department turned a deaf ear to my pleas that they give writing courses. They said, "Writing is a trade. We are not a trade school." When I asked, "In what way is writing more of a trade than teaching, architecture, or agronomy?" I received no answer. Were they not worshipping at the altar of Shakespeare, Goldsmith, and Dr. Johnson, who in their times had, according to the department's definition, been practicing a trade?

There was only one activity I did not enjoy, and that was the theory aspect of the ROTC. I kept flunking my examinations because in the military maps we had to draw I had rivers running upstream. As a graduating senior I was still drilling in wrapped leggings and post–World War I uniforms on Tuesdays and

Thursdays with incoming freshmen. About ten days before graduation, when I received my final report of grades, I found that I
had, incredibly, flunked military science for the fourth consecu-
tive time! My roommate asked, "What are you going to do, go
out and get drunk?" I replied, "No, I'm going over to that military headquarters building and tear it apart plank by plank." I
started with a second lieutenant and worked my way up in a
shouting match to the colonel in charge. He proved to be a man of
eminent good sense; after a time he realized the futility of bringing me back to the campus for another year of military theory
when no one could ever teach me how to make a river run down-
hill. He changed my F to a C, and with a somewhat fatigued smile
congratulated me on my coming graduation.

Through these idyllic years (during the summers I
wrapped hams and bacon for the Armour meat packing plant in
Los Angeles, checked on gauges in a power plant on the Kern
River), there was one part of my life that was not right. I was being
dishonest with myself, or at least juvenile in my thinking, when it
came to the subject of my chosen profession. Although many of
my closest friends were going into Boalt Hall of Law, and I rea-
soned that I could do well there, the plain truth was that I did not
want to become a lawyer. I wanted only to become a writer. However, I had learned from a careful perusal of the facts that it took a
young writer anywhere from ten to twenty-five years to begin to
earn a living from his craft. I was going into law in order to have a
profession which would provide me with a livelihood until I
could become a successful author. In my sloppy thinking I rea-
soned that I would give my clients just barely enough time to
take care of them; the major part of my life, all of the great love
and passion and dedication that a man should feel for his profession, would be poured into my writing hours. Had I not been
blinded by necessity I would have realized that this would have
made me a very poor lawyer indeed, that I would have been
cheating my clients at best, and that before very long there would
be no clients left.

I was rescued from what could have developed into a

painful dilemma. In my last semester I was taking a graduate seminar under Professor W. R. Robinson, from whom I was also taking a senior course in economics. This senior lecture course also had two Quiz Sections a week, led by a graduate teaching fellow. One morning when I wandered into the nine o'clock Quiz Section unshaven, Professor Robinson came in to say that the teaching fellow had been operated on for appendicitis at five o'clock and would have to be out for three weeks. Then, without so much as a glance in my direction, he announced that I would take over the section in the interim. I stumbled up to the podium, sat down behind the desk, and gazed in consternation at the other nineteen students. They glared back at me resentfully. I said, "Look, you know that I don't know any more about this subject than you do. But I'm on a spot. Please help me." They did, and by dint of several hours of boning every day in this specialized field, I gave a respectable performance, finishing out the semester and emerging as a popular teacher by dint of giving every student in the class a grade one level higher than he deserved.

This experience earned me a teaching fellowship at the University of Southern California, where I taught for a year and took my master's. However, it turned me from political science to economics, a change which was to have repercussions. Then back to Berkeley, for two last years for the Ph.D., with a teaching fellowship again and a salary that was modest but sufficient to pay for my board and lodging at the Whitecotton Hotel.

It did not take me too long to find that I was trapped in a blind alley. I was interested in social economics, and quickly exhausted all the courses available: Labor Relations, Poverty Controls, Slum Clearance, the like. It took little perception on my part or that of my instructors in Marketing, Transportation, Statistics, Money and Banking, Taxation, to perceive that I had no interest in these technical fields. I grew bored, stopped working at my courses, returned to the stacks of the library to end up my University career just where it started: a kind of wild devouring of hundreds of books in every area that my imagination could carry me, trying to slake an implacable thirst: undisciplined, seemingly directionless. But I knew what I was searching for: the wellspring of human conduct; and an art whereby men could write true, strong, exciting, and meaningful books; for I had always believed, and the years at the University had confirmed me in this, that the book is the most important tool that man has ever invented, more important than the wheel, cement, or running water.

Had the modern science of sociology then been invented, I might have remained on the track; but it came to me that I had involved myself in the identical trap as that of planning to become a lawyer. I was not working for my Ph.D. so that I could teach for the sake of teaching; I wanted a teaching job, with security and a comfortable salary, because it appeared to me that the college professor lived about as amiable a life as there was to be had on the American continent, with almost four months off in the summer, three weeks at Christmas, and a sabbatical leave every seventh year. I guessed that I could very well get my books written during what I imagined to be a considerable leisure time.

But by now I had passed twenty-one and come into man's estate; it was possible for me to face up to a harsh truth: that I would be cheating my students, undertaking to become a cavalier and part-time instructor in the same way that I would have been cheating my clients as a lawyer. I had also learned by now that the good teacher studies, researches, and writes during his time off, so that he can bring an ever enriched mind and grasp of his subject to his classes.

There is a time to stay home, cherished, fed, comforted, and protected by loving parents; and there is a time to leave the nest. That moment had come for me; for I had at last realized that the only way to become a professional writer was to start writing, to write for twelve hours a day, seven days a week, three hundred and sixty-five days of the year. I was mildly encouraged at this last moment, just before my departure, by winning a prize for a one-act play to be put on by the University. The prize money was modest even for those days, twenty-five dollars, but since I had failed to place any of my writings over the years in the campus literary magazine, *The Occident,* the winning of the prize helped convince me that it was time to light out for Paris and the Left Bank of the Seine, where, said H. L. Mencken, art and culture were born.

What then did I emerge with, after five years at Berkeley? A couple of passing love affairs, which brought me more pain than pleasure. Exposure to a number of first-rate, disciplined minds, men whom I admired and who gave me of their friendship. The solid foundation of a science of research, which is still serving me honorably after the publication of twenty-one books. The intimate knowledge of the contents of one of the great libraries of the world; experience with the drama of the ages. The beginning foundations of an understanding of modern painting, sculpture, architecture, and of classical music as played in Harmon Gym by the San Francisco Symphony.

What forms an individual writer's values? Why does he think certain materials are urgent, and others unimportant? It lies in his character, some part of which he is born with (the "fertile soil" concept of the psychoanalyst), some part of which develops from the *ambiance* in which he is raised. What are a writer's greatest assets? A hunger for social justice; a compassion for all human suffering; a feeling of brotherhood for the neglected and abused of the earth; a will to stand at the side of those who suffer because they are willing to fight for what they believe to be right.

During my fifteen months in Paris, Antibes, and Florence, I wrote seventeen full-length plays, thirty-one one-act plays, several essays, and random chapters of novels that never got any further. The work literally poured out of my fountain pen; yet in some dim way I knew that this was an act of regurgitation rather than creativity. I would complete a four-act play at six o'clock at night and at eight o'clock the next morning start a new play. No one had told me that this could not be done; though I might have remembered that it took Henrik Ibsen two years and more to create each of his dramas.

During this period I made two urgent discoveries. While exchanging English and French lessons with a young student of the Sorbonne, I was asked to accompany him to an exhibition of Vincent Van Gogh's canvases. When I entered the large salon of the Rosenberg Gallery with some sixty of Vincent's blazing canvases from Arles, Saint-Rémy, and Auvers-sur-Oise, I stood literally transfixed. Summoning the strength to move slowly about the salon, I found myself undergoing my most intense emotional experience since reading *The Brothers Karamazov*. When I finally stumbled out to the sidewalk I asked myself, "Who is this man who can strip away all veils of illusion, and enable me to see man's part in the universe with such clarity and comprehension?" I read everything I could find about him, but there was not much. I had no intention of writing about Van Gogh, I simply wanted to know what forces and conditions had given him his voice. But when I returned to New York, and continued writing long, discursive plays which no producer wanted to produce, my mind kept going back to the Van Gogh story. I would have to write it to get it off my mind.

I was now earning a living by writing detective and murder stories one day of the week, leaving the other six days for what I considered my serious work; not a bad bargain to strike with the devil. Needing money to go back to Europe and get on the trail of Van Gogh in Belgium, Holland, and France, I wrote six murder stories and sold five of them. This gave me enough money to live in Europe for six months, providing I lived on two dollars a day, including transportation. I made my way on foot, with a rucksack on my back, working the coal mines of the Borinage, where Vincent had been an evangelical preacher; writing in his mother's wrangle room in Brabant, where Vincent had painted; living in the cell in the asylum in Saint-Rémy, where Vincent had been incarcerated after the first of his epileptoidal attacks; finally sleeping in the identical bed in which Vincent had died in a little hotel room in Auvers-sur-Oise in 1890. I worked my way back to the United States on an American President liner sailing out of Marseilles, scrubbing down decks at five-thirty in the morning.

I had not wanted to write the book as a fictional novel; who would believe such happenings if told in fiction form?

Neither did I want to write his life as a conventional biography. There was hardly any such thing as a biographical novel at the time. Merezhkovski had written a masterpiece called *The Romance of Leonardo da Vinci*; in America Gertrude Atherton had published *The Conqueror,* a biographical novel about Alexander Hamilton. With only these two examples to go on, I summoned the courage to tell Vincent Van Gogh's story as a biographical novel.

For the following three years *Lust for Life* was turned down by seventeen major publishers in New York. Their rejection notes were couched in almost identical terms: "How can you expect us to sell the story of an unknown Dutch painter to the American public in the midst of a depression? Besides, what is this manuscript? It's not a novel, it's not a biography, it's not a history."

They were difficult years. I wrote and published a novel about a group of students at the University of California, which had no success or acceptance. I went back to writing detective stories, but was not able to sell another one of them, even to my long-time editor friends. In the writing of *Lust for Life* I had lost this little plot talent. Broke, with no source of income, I went to the department stores seeking work; but when I filled out the questionnaire on education, and put A.B, M.A., I was quickly escorted out of the personnel rooms. The only job I could find was as an usher at the Paramount Theatre on Broadway and Forty-third Street; here at last I had a trade in which I was experienced. They fitted me out in a general's uniform with epaulets a foot wide on my shoulders. It was a culminating blow when I had to usher to their seats four of my former girl students in freshman economics at Berkeley!

At the beginning of 1934 the eighteenth publisher to read the manuscript decided to take a gambling chance. It had just been cut some 10 percent by my then fiancée, Jean, and still my editor-in-residence after thirty-five years of marriage. He told me, "We will print 5,000 copies and pray." The book not only swept through the reading public but dislodged the romantic idealizations of Maxfield Parrish from the walls of American homes and offices.

The other great discovery of this early European trip was that of coming upon Michelangelo and the Medicis in Florence. Fascinated by their intertwined lives, by the magnificence of the art and politics they had created, I determined that I would one day return to write a book about them. It took me exactly thirty years to get back, but for me at least it was well worth waiting for. The years of living in Italy and writing *The Agony and the Ecstasy* were among the richest of my life.

What effect did my years at the University have on my choice of subjects for my books, and on their content? A very sure and appreciable one. The subjects for my trilogy, Jack London (*Sailor on Horseback*), *Clarence Darrow for the Defense,* and Eugene V. Debs (*Adversary in the House*), were born and nurtured in the Berkeley years, when I read through and wrote early papers about their lives; argued, debated, and sometimes fought with my fellow students as to whether Clarence Darrow was correct in attempting to save Loeb and Leopold from capital punishment; whether Eugene V. Debs had lived the Christ story in America or had done labor harm by forming its first industrial union and the first indigenous Socialist Party; whether Jack London was as authentic a novelist as he was a revolutionary, and whether his work would one day be repatriated in America. The Darrow book was to a large measure condescendingly reviewed, one high-placed critic asking, "Why would Mr. Stone want to put in so many years of work on a totally unimportant figure on the American landscape?" Today we know the value of Darrow, a lone figure who stood up to fight for every unpopular cause, who defended those whom the rest of the world believed indefensible. Authentic folk heroes, all three men.

In 1925, while browsing through a copy of *American Mercury* in the University's periodical room, I came across an article called "Frémont and Jessie" by R. L. Duffus. This story seemed to me to unfold one of the most heroic and purposeful lives ever led by a woman in America. I not only vowed that I would one day write a book about Jessie Benton Frémont, but that I would also marry in her image. (I did.) However, it was not until twenty years later that I researched and wrote *Immortal Wife,* the biographical novel of Jessie Benton and John Charles Frémont, the first of a tetralogy of American women including *The President's Lady* (Rachel and Andrew Jackson); *Love Is Eternal* (Mary Todd and Abraham Lincoln); *Those Who Love* (Abigail and John Adams). Three of these women had been traduced and vilified by history.

Every writer worth his salt one day wants to repay his debt to the past, to acknowledge the strength he derives from his roots. During my years at Berkeley I read widely and with excitement the story of the opening of the Far West. Here were hundreds of colorful men: Sutter, Vallejo, Bidwell, Larkin, Frémont, Kit Carson; among the immortal women, Tamsen Donner of the Donner Party and Juliet Brier of the Death Valley Party. Here, too, were the fabulous stories of the Silver Kings of Nevada, the mining epic of Colorado as exemplified by H. A. W. Tabor; the inspired pioneering efforts of Brigham Young and his stout-hearted band of Mormons who opened the valley of the Salt Lake, turning it from a desert into a blooming garden. But each of these stirring tales was bound into the covers of its own little book or monograph. The conviction grew over the years that all of these larger than life-sized characters needed to be bound together in one integrated book which would not only tell the story of their lives, but bring out the meaning of the opening of this Far West Valley of the Nile. For years I searched for a central tent-pole for such a book. It was not until 1954 that the hunt came into focus, when I had an opportunity to write *Men to Match My Mountains,* which was neither a biographical novel nor history, but something which I believe can legitimately be called bio-history, in which the narrative is told in terms of the opening of a land and the building of a civilization.

Without my years at the University of California this

book could never have been envisaged, let alone written. The same is true of all of my books. Everything that I am, everything that I have aspired to, everything that I have managed to accomplish, either for myself or for the reading public, in terms of the joy of a great human story or the deepening of knowledge, I owe directly to my opportunity to attend a land-grant college, where a poor boy like myself could earn himself a fine education at the cost of twenty-five dollars a semester; but mark you! that twenty-five dollars included full hospital and medical care, a clean towel and gymnasium suit five times a week.

Has the writer served any purpose in the emergence of the American civilization? Has he been as valuable as an engineer, a businessman, a chemist, a dentist, or stockbroker? This is not an ideal question, for the creative writer has been downgraded in America. We have despised our writers as wasters, mystics, dilettantes, bohemians, posers, revolutionaries, serving no valuable purpose in first a frontier and later a bourgeois society.

What then is a writer? What did the University of California teach me that a writer should be? On March 22, 1968, I was invited to Berkeley to give one of the Centennial Lectures in Wheeler Auditorium. At that time I asked myself and my audience, "What is a writer?" I think it only fitting to stand on what I said at that moment, when the University of California was celebrating its first one hundred years of vigorous, purposeful life; and to speak in terms which would be indigenous to a writer who had been created by that University:

The writer is a seer, a prophet, an alchemist; he creates wisdom where none existed before. He is an entertainer, but hopefully not a court jester; a man who brings order out of chaos; creates new religions; new mentalities; new cultural and social patterns. He is a midwife, giving birth to new civilizations; an undertaker, burying old ones. The writer is an archeologist, uncovering layers of man's past. And then a sculptor, giving form to the unmolded and uncoalesced materials. The writer is a destroyer, putting to the Gutenberg sword and fire old shibboleths, ancient fears, tribal myths, falsehoods that have paraded as truths.

The writer is a warrior, fighting to possess men's minds, and at the same time a poet, trying to compress the complexity and confusion of a spent life into essence lines which scan, and perhaps even rhyme. He is a composer, attempting to capture the music of life for a tone-deaf world. The writer is an explorer, penetrating impassable jungles, traversing mountain ranges which start at the peak of Mount Everest as he searches for regions where men can live in dignity.

The writer is a philosopher, attempting to extract the meaning of life from the passing hurricane. A mirror in which mankind can see himself reflected—all too clearly. He is a seducer, attempting to break young people to pleasure; and an encyclopedia, which knows everything and understands nothing. He is a sieve, allowing all thoughts and ideas to pour through him.

The writer is a doctor, prescribing pills whose content he has not tested, for patients whose ills he cannot fathom; yet he is the catalyst bringing together people and visions who would otherwise not have bowed to each other while passing on the street. The writer is a scientist, searching for an antibody which will eradicate still another human disease, or human failing. A conservationist, trying to save a fresh-water lake or a giant redwood forest from the hands of human predators. A psychiatrist, going behind the insanity of the modern world to chart the trails whereby we have reached the sanitarium; and the paths out of it. The writer is a dinosaur, extinct for thousands of years yet believing because he has a shin bone and a piece of jaw he is still a monumental creature.

I write books because man is basically a lonely creature, a lonely animal. He has enormous difficulty communicating with other people. Confused and frightened, filled with anxieties, he has trouble finding focal points of assurance; he does not know who he is, or why he is on earth. I would like to write books which help people to speak to each other, understand each other, communicate. I would like to write books which in some way help people to be a little less lonely, a little less frightened, a little less anxious. And I should like to write books that would give man some indication of what his place is in this world and in the universe.

This is my heritage from the University of California.

"I was terribly anxious when I arrived at Berkeley. . . . I worked very hard. I remember sitting outside on the Griffiths Hall fire escape to study early in the morning so I wouldn't wake my roommate."

ZOË BAIRD

Zoë Baird

I T WAS THE RIGHT CHOICE FOR ME to go to Berkeley in 1970.
It was the center of political debate and activism for my
generation.

I'd grown up in the provincial—even isolated—town of
Bothell, Washington, which had a total population of less than
2,000 spread out over miles of forested countryside. Most residents were Scandinavians whose families had settled in this place
that reminded them of home. Our high school mascot was the
Viking, and Bothell crowned a Scandinavian princess each
Christmas with a crown of candles. But my family was different;
my parents were New York Jews who had come West to organize
for the CIO among the maritime workers. My father spent his
career as a labor union official. He created a huge retirement
home for union members which was a kind of arena for political
events of all types. The only time my mother worked was as an
administrator there.

Our home was full of vibrant political discussion which
we all took very personally, and of fundraisers for Senators
Magnuson, Jackson, Congressman Adams. Almost every summer we drove across the country to stay with relatives in New
York, and that was a political lesson too. I saw what people were
like in Idaho, Montana, North Dakota, St. Louis . . . and how different the grand city of New York was from my home town.

I was terribly anxious when I arrived at Berkeley. I'd
come from a rural high school, few graduates of which went to
a major university, to an institution that drew from the top 10

percent California high school graduates. I worked very hard. I remember sitting outside on the Griffiths Hall fire escape to study early in the morning so I wouldn't wake my roommate.

I relaxed a bit when I saw I did fine—and when my freshman English professor had a party at his house so we could all draw grades from a hat. Yes, it's true … the precedent had been set by professors the year before—during the student turmoil after the U.S. invasion of Cambodia—who had given out good grades for showing up at People's Park. There was an escape valve. You could see the professor privately if you "cared" about your grades so you could get into law or medical school. That provided my first awakening to my own politics: I strongly, enthusiastically strove for change but didn't feel it was necessary to tear down institutions and their values to achieve change: values such as caring about working hard to get good grades.

I sampled widely from the course catalogue's smorgasbord. I took rhetoric, history, the physics of music. I even took an ROTC course on military justice taught by a JAG officer who had prosecuted the officers involved in the Mylai massacre. But I found my home in the Political Science Department. I had a double major in Political Science and Communication and Public Policy, and both were important to me.

In a place as large and frenetic as Berkeley, it's necessary to find a center, and for me that was the Political Science Department. So many there were so good to me: Tom Blaisdell, Eugene Lee, Nelson Polsby, Sandy Muir, Ray Wolfinger, to name but a few. These men (and there were almost no women professors in the department) had national reputations as both scholars and political commentators. They combined careers of great respect by both the academy and government officials. I never seriously considered becoming a professor, but these men made me feel there were other ways I could combine a deep interest in ideas with a desire to better people's lives through government institutions. The ideal and the real. (I didn't think of going into business then—a place from which I now know one can have a hugely positive effect on people's lives—because I thought only

Republicans did that and not Democratic daughters of labor union officials.)

An adjunct to the Political Science Department as my center was the Cal-in-the-Capital program, which placed Berkeley students in summer internships in Washington, D.C. The support the University gave this program furthered my expectation that one could combine the pursuit of ideas and creative analysis with the real, practical workings of institutions. I roomed with women who were in this program the summer after my freshman year when I worked for a Washington State Congressman, Brock Adams. They were all older since only juniors and seniors were allowed in the program. We had a big house and great fun as our house was always open to crowds for late-night political debates and parties. We cooked elaborate meals, often planning and preparing them for days. But in addition to this development of my skill in a traditional female pursuit, I learned that summer that women could become lawyers because one of my roommates had been accepted to law school (when I was in high school my father encouraged me to take typing "in case I needed to work.")

Which brings me back to Professor Tom Blaisdell, my guide, my adviser, my dear friend. I still miss him terribly and have needed him often. Tom and I began having weekly lunches my sophomore year and they lasted right through my student years at Berkeley's law school. I helped him on his major project of those years, an exhibit of the American Presidency in political cartoons in celebration of the Bicentennial. Tom and his Catherine took me into their lives and told me of their early days in China, of working for Roosevelt, of Tom's administering the Marshall Plan in London, and serving as Assistant Secretary of Commerce under his good friend Averill Harriman, of their retreat to the restaurant atop the Hotel Washington to make decisions each time Tom was asked to consider a new appointment. Tom came to Berkeley to run the Institute for International Affairs. He was a kind and wise man who cared deeply about all kinds of people. He was a great thinker of his era who gave me a living sense of history.

Tom and I had long discussions about what was going right or wrong in Washington and who was to credit or blame. I pursued my commitment to citizen participation in government and he taught me of its limits and the need for leadership in those moments. I learned of his defense of a friend in the State Department against McCarthy and of the genius behind the social security system and the Securities and Exchange Commission. He taught me about the federal budget process. The centerpiece of a great education is often a single figure who becomes a mentor. Tom Blaisdell was that for me, and I will always be grateful to Berkeley for bringing us together.

I had the good fortune of staying at Berkeley for law school, just moving up the hill to Boalt Hall. This allowed me to continue to get a suntan at Cal football games as I was introduced to a surprisingly different discipline. I'd never thought before about contracts, property rights, constitutional law. I think I went to law school because it seemed necessary for a woman to be taken seriously. I found a way of considering social issues and relationships between people that was very satisfying to me. Today, I've concluded that we've become too much a "rights-oriented" society. People too often look to vindicate their rights, not to solve their problems. But then I was simply enthralled with the complexity of the legal framework that holds our public and private institutions together.

My second year, a professor asked me to teach some Contracts courses to first-year students. What a challenge to teach in the Socratic method where one develops the student's thinking through use of hypothetical scenarios. It certainly prepared me to respect my husband's work, as he does this every day on the spot in front of wise and wise-cracking students as Potter Stewart Professor of Constitutional Law at Yale Law School.

Boalt's student body was richly diverse in background, race and ethnicity, income level and age. I particularly was fortunate to be there at a time when many extremely talented women who had not considered the law an option had come back to school after staying at home or working in other fields. These more mature women were wonderful companions from whom I learned so much. Mine is a transitional generation of women, but many of them were challenging themselves to make personal transitions.

We were optimistic then about how fast things would change for women, how quickly opportunities would open up. I don't know how it would have affected the spirit of the women of my graduating class of 1977 if we'd known that almost twenty years later women would represent only 18 percent of partners in law firms, 3–5 percent of all senior executives, and 6.2 percent of directors of Fortune 1,000 companies.

As graduation neared, I was asked by the class leadership to invite Garry Trudeau to be our speaker. In his popular cartoon strip, *Doonesbury,* he had enrolled Joanie Caucus in our law school class and she had periodically surfaced struggling through with us. The problem was that Trudeau was thought to be an intensely private person who made no public appearances. Why they asked me, I don't know, but I gave it a try. I wrote a wild letter to Trudeau about his need to complete something he'd started, and to my surprise my phone rang one night with him calling to accept. He turned out to be an engaging, brilliant, serious person and a great graduation speaker. Last year, in what felt like private letters to me in return, Trudeau's strip had Joanie go to work with her old law school classmate who had been nominated to be Attorney General of the United States. Then, as now, I felt all the Berkeley memories, large and small, flooding back. It's a great and unique place.

"I cannot say what the University has become in these intervening years. I cannot guess what changes might have occurred in the relationships between faculty and students... I can only guess that there are still those warm and understanding teachers who will identify and nurture those of their students who have not become too callous, too impatient, too blasé to allow themselves to be genuinely influenced by their masters. So long as these teachers exist, the University will continue to exert its great lifelong influence on its graduates."

ANTONIA BRICO

Antonia Brico

BORN IN HOLLAND, I was brought to the United States by foster parents, Mr. and Mrs. John Wolthuis, at the age of five. I grew up with totally different values from other children of my own age. My contemporaries were always glad when weekends rolled around; I was miserable. They couldn't wait for vacations; I dreaded them. Others arranged their high-school schedules so as to have the maximum amount of time at home; I did all I could to have classes from the earliest period of the day until the latest possible in the afternoon. In those years children weren't trying to free themselves from the home influence, since most of them were happy there. With me, it was quite the opposite. At home I was unhappy, beaten, spanked, or scolded daily. At school I was loved and appreciated for my music.

My foster mother never adopted me. She said later she waited to see if she still wanted me as I grew older—and she didn't. She was a strong-willed woman, with a violent temper. Since according to her I was always naughty, she heaped physical abuse on me daily. At ten, I was exposed to the piano and fell so madly in love with it that I was at it every possible moment. When my foster mother became aware that I had talent, she sent me to San Francisco to vaudeville shows, where they had amateur nights. Since I played classical music, I won no prizes. After she had failed to get me on the vaudeville circuit, she forbade any more lessons, and I had to struggle on by myself, amid constant torture at home. At fourteen I discovered I wasn't an orphan, and after that my illegitimacy was cast up to me again and again: my mother was "no good" and I would also go "to the dogs."

My real mother, from a fine, Catholic family, fell in love with a nightclub pianist in Amsterdam. After her father forbade her to see him, she followed him to Belgium; he deserted her and she returned to her family pregnant. They sent her to Rotterdam to spare the family scandal. She lived there as a destitute domestic and it was there that I was born and abandoned at a convent. My mother advertised for a family to care for me and Mrs. Wolthuis agreed to take me for a certain sum of money. When my mother later tried to get me back, Mrs. Wolthuis declared she had never been paid for my room and board, and she would not release me. She took me with her to San Francisco, where her husband was working. I grew up in Oakland under the name of Wilhemina Wolthuis, under which name I graduated from the University of California.

My foster parents planned that I become a stenographer, since college was not for "the likes of me." When it was discovered that I had sneaked out to register at the University of California, I was thrown out of the house. They thought I would not be able to make the grade on my own, that I would quit college and return on their terms. But, to earn money, I worked at Woolworth's and waited tables in summer resorts. Though the labor law said one could not work more than eight hours per day, I labored from 9 A.M. to 10 P.M. Friends housed me and the University aided me with scholarships.

But the University helped me even more with understanding and friendship. Even in that large complex of colleges and people, I had friends on the faculty who understood my difficulty and helped in every way possible. The teachers were like parents; the campus was my home. I sought out older women, like Dean Lucy Ward Stebbins, who could represent the mother image, and men who were as fathers. I had worshipped such men as Dr. Karl Muck, the conductor of the Boston Symphony, for years before I met him, as well as Jean Sibelius and Albert Schweitzer. Dean Stebbins had the most extraordinary insight into the needs of women students. After my graduation, as I was leaving for study in Europe, she gave me a $100, on the condition that I would use it only after I arrived in Berlin. I complied, but the day came when I was completely out of funds—not even carfare. I received a notice that there was a cable for me at a certain bank. It was from Dean Stebbins, with a draft for another $100. The explanation arrived three or four days later in a letter. She had been worrying about me, and convinced several friends of the University to donate about $600 toward my Berlin studies. She wrote that it wasn't much, but "would it help?" Six hundred dollars plus the $100 draft amounted to 2,800 German marks. With great care and extreme economy I was able to complete two years of study. Should I not almost say that Dean Stebbins had made it possible? And after my debut with the Berlin Philharmonic, Miss Stebbins, along with Dean Charles Walter Lipman, head of the Graduate School, brought me back for a series of concerts in California, with Dean Lipman acting as my manager.

When I was a sophomore, I was constantly having to move because of my excessive piano practice. My French teacher, Miss Caroline Singleton, at once opened her home to an almost total stranger, and I was permitted to practice to my heart's content. Professor Clifford Bissell, another of my French teachers, also permitted me in his home for the purpose of practicing. Even University of California President David Prescott Barrows opened his home to me so that I might play on his beautiful Steinway.

When I was about ten years of age, there was a conductor named Paul Steindorff who directed band concerts every Sunday in Lakeside Park in Oakland. This was my first experience with conducting. I was so impressed with the magic of the baton that could control groups of people to make beautiful musical sounds that I then determined to be a conductor. Since Steindorff was also a teacher at the University of California, I was privileged later to study with him, and took my first lessons in serious conducting under his direction. Although he felt I would not have any chance as a symphony orchestra conductor simply because I was a woman, he nevertheless created opportunities for me. I was his rehearsal assistant and did some coaching for him in some of his big productions. This start he gave me early in life was a great deciding factor in my career.

When I was a student in Berlin, I was teased by my colleagues because I believed what the teacher taught. They said I would never develop independence of thought. Bewildered and confused, I consulted one of the great professors of Berlin, Dr. Max Deri, professor of art history. Would I not be an independently thinking conductor because I believed in the experience of the masters? Dr. Deri answered, "Michelangelo painted as had his master until he was thirty. If you are not an independently thinking artist by the time you are thirty, then you can afford to be worried."

After I had my American conducting debut at the Hollywood Bowl, and then in San Francisco, I was told that I should stay and form my own orchestra in California, with the help of sponsors. I turned this offer down, however, to the discouragement of my friends, but I felt that I was not free of the master, Dr. Karl Muck. Dr. Modeste Alloo, who replaced Professor Steindorff, was one of those who had originally made it possible for me to study with Dr. Muck. I leaned on him so much artistically that I knew I had to return to him for further study in order to be independent of him. After all, conducting a symphony orchestra required tremendous preparation in so many directions: languages, the psychology of handling groups of people, the study of all the instruments, music theory. In the Berlin University it was said the study of conducting began where everything else left off. And so I turned to Europe in 1930, where I conducted the Hamburg Philharmonic and the Berlin Philharmonic orchestras while continuing my studies with Karl Muck.

Then I entered into a period of great depression and poverty. Friends in Vienna, who themselves had very little money, fed and housed me as best they could. The contrast between the great success of Hollywood and San Francisco and the bleak outlook of no concerts made me wonder if I had made a grave error by not accepting the offer to conduct in some small city in California. All I knew was that I had wanted to continue to be a student, and the net result seemed a hopeless future.

After six months of worry and frustration, help came from the most unexpected source. Jewish friends from California were in Riga, Latvia, trying to get relatives out of Communist Russia. Mr. and Mrs. Ernest Feigenberg, and three children, were living in this small Baltic town. She was a singer who had coached operatic roles with me and liked my work. I asked if they could assist me to conduct some summer concerts. They tried and succeeded. I conducted a series of outdoor concerts in Riga and neighboring towns; the manager of the symphony was curious to see the California "lady" conductor (how I loathe that term!). The success of the concerts was so overwhelming that I became a guest conductor during the next several months for twenty concerts in Latvia, and Poland, including Warsaw, Lodz, Vilna, and Poznan. The orchestras, with the exceptions of Warsaw and Poznan, were not first-class, but the experience was tremendous, and I was accepted as a conductor, not a "lady" conductor. This went on until about January, 1932. I returned to Berlin with about 1,000 lats (Latvian currency), but when the Great Depression struck full force, the banks in Germany wouldn't accept the Latvian money and I was stranded.

Help came then in the form of a job playing for six opera singers. We performed at higher-quality cabarets in various seaport towns on the Baltic Sea, during the Hitler era. All the singers were foreigners—Russian, Austrian, Lithuanian, American, and one German girl who was Jewish, and, according to the Nazis, therefore not German. This caused us grave problems, resulting in fewer and fewer engagements. The troupe was finally stranded in Düsseldorf.

New York friends offered loans and the troupe sneaked me out of the hotel and onto a train bound for Holland. I arrived by ship in New York. From having conducted in Berlin, California, Latvia, and Poland, I was penniless again.

Then Mr. Ludwig Wielich, who worked for the periodical *Musical America,* showed my European review to Mrs. Sydney Prince, a patroness of the arts, whose husband had been president of the New York Stock Exchange. I became her protégé for the winter of 1932–33. Mrs. Olin Downes, wife of the dean of American critics of *The New York Times,* was putting on twenty symphony concerts at the Metropolitan Opera House, with an orchestra of 150 unemployed musicians. Mrs. Prince asked Mrs. Downes if I could conduct one of the concerts. If Mrs. Prince would guarantee the $1,000 the box office would lose on an unknown such as me, I could conduct. We each sold $500 worth of tickets. Mrs. Prince had my concert dress made for me, invited me to dinner to be sure I ate, and gave me an allowance on which to live. Three months to the day from the time I had my last cabaret appearance in Germany, I performed on the stage of the Metropolitan Opera House. The concert was enough of a success that I was engaged for a return appearance.

As a result, I was invited to conduct the Detroit Symphony and some operas in Manhattan. This was the era of the WPA and I became for some months the director of the WPA Symphony, which was sponsored by the federal government. In 1934, after a chamber music concert of several women musicians, I decided that if nine women could play together, so could ninety, and that became the slogan of the New York Women's Symphony Orchestra. Girls dusted off their trombones, horns, and drums and the orchestra found a place in New York musical circles.

To escape the dampness of the New York climate, I accepted guest concerts in Denver, Colorado, in 1940. Georges Enesco, the distinguished conductor, composer, and violinist, was scheduled to give a concert in Denver. At that time, Hitler would not allow him to leave Rumania, his native land, and I was engaged as a substitute. I was re-engaged for two more concerts the following year, and it was at this time that I decided to move to Denver, which I did in January of 1942. Though my concerts were successful and many people desired that I be the permanent conductor, the prejudice against women, which I was to suffer time and again, prevented my being accepted for this position.

Again my artistic life was at a standstill. In 1945, I conducted a rehearsal of about sixty-five members of the New York Philharmonic. Bruno Walter, the distinguished German conductor, Artur Rubinstein, and others were present. They wrote very enthusiastic letters, which resulted in engagements in London, Finland, Holland, and Yugoslavia. I am never so happy as with a baton in my hand. The orchestras, as well as the audiences, appreciated me, but boards of directors were loathe to engage a woman conductor. Probably one of the greatest moments of my life was when I conducted in Holland, where my own family was present.

As a student at the University of Berlin, I had studied Albert Schweitzer as an organist. I was surprised when he came to Aspen, Colorado, for a conference on Goethe. I was privileged to meet him, and he subsequently invited me to Alsace-Lorraine, his European headquarters. For fifteen years, I studied with him in Africa and in Günsbach, his childhood home. It was through him that I met that great and gracious lady Queen Elizabeth of Belgium, grandmother of the present King, at the home of Albert Schweitzer, where she had come incognito. She invited me to her Chateau Royale de Stuyvenberg in Belgium. For five days we played chamber music. The Queen was a violinist of distinction and invited members of the Brussels Symphony to join us. She ordered a command performance for me to conduct the National Radio Orchestra of Belgium.

What is there about music, and for me in particular about conducting, that grips one's being? Music is so intangible: you can't touch it, you can't see it; you can't even hear it, except for a second at a time. One anticipates a beautiful passage. One can hear it in advance and retroactively, but never can one hold the sound as one can read again and again a beloved passage in a book or gaze upon a Michelangelo work of art. Is this art so tremendous because it is so elusive?

Music is indeed an international language. I have conducted in many countries. There is no language barrier. The communication between the orchestra and myself was always instantaneous, whether it was in Yugoslavia, Italy, Holland, Germany, Austria, Denmark, Mexico, Japan, or Norway. Everywhere the unique feeling of togetherness was the same. In this world of stress, turbulence, and scientific advancements, a balance is needed, a balance between art and science. As for myself, I never need a sabbatical year away from music, or even an hour away from it. First thing in the morning I listen to it; the last thing at night I listen to it; I go to sleep with it. I have it at my meals; every spare minute that I'm not working, I need to hear music. I also need to make music, as a conductor or as a pianist, and at times as a singer, or through students. It is a spiritual as well as a physical necessity for me. Two years ago my Denver Orchestra flattered me by changing its name, after twenty years, to the Brico Symphony. Some of the same spirit I encountered so many years earlier on the faculty at the University of California lives on in the loyal orchestra members.

Had it not been for this great institution, so large and yet so willing to help develop the life and talent of one music student, I would have perished, artistically and physically, under the insurmountable obstacles. That I have been able to conduct in many capitals of the world is due in great measure to the help of countless people who for me came to personify the generosity and understanding of the University.

I cannot say what the University has become in these intervening years. I cannot guess what changes might have occurred in the relationships between faculty and students—relationships that made a true home of the University for me. I can only guess that there are still those warm and understanding teachers who will identify and nurture those of their students who have not become too callous, too impatient, too blasé to allow themselves to be genuinely influenced by their masters. So long as these teachers exist, the University will continue to exert its great lifelong influence on its graduates.

126

"I continue to be amazed at the depth of the loyalty and commitment so many graduates have to what some consider a large and impersonal state university. Through the years I have searched for an answer from others who share the same feelings. Certainly there is pride in having attended one of the finest teaching institutions in the world: in its outstanding faculty and curriculum and its adaptability to changing conditions. But there's something more that binds me to the University with a tie that is strong and unique."

WALTER A. HAAS JR.

Walter A. Haas Jr.

AVING ATTENDED a small "progressive" grammar school where each student was allowed to advance at his or her own pace, I entered Galileo High School in San Francisco a couple of weeks before my twelfth birthday. I was unprepared for the educational and social pressures of a large public school and was an easy target for the tough kids who were older, bigger, and wiser than I. After losing one semester to illness and staying on after graduation to take courses in shop, I was able to enter Cal when my age was almost comparable to that of my classmates. Nevertheless, because my life at home had been sheltered and because I was immature, I was overwhelmed by the size of the campus, the responsibilities I was expected to take on, and the experiences I encountered all around me.

My parents gave me an allowance to cover tuition, books, room and board, clothing, recreational activities, and charitable donations. It was my first experience with managing what were, for me, large amounts of money, balancing a check book, and living within a budget. All of this while I was adjusting to being away from home for the first time. I had to learn everything—how to find my way around, shop in the ASUC store, do what was expected from me in ROTC, use the library, try to keep up with my studies, and make the freshman tennis team.

Despite all this, my four years at Cal were among the most important and happiest time of my life. I grew in every way, made life-long friends, and developed an abiding pride and love for the University.

I continue to be amazed at the depth of the loyalty and commitment so many graduates have to what some consider a large and impersonal state university. Through the years I have searched for an answer from others who share the same feelings. Certainly there is pride in having attended one of finest teaching institutions in the world: in its outstanding faculty and curriculum and its adaptability to changing conditions. But there's something more that binds me to the University with a tie that is strong and unique.

I'm not the first Haas to feel this way. Cal is a part of our family history. Both my grandfathers attended Berkeley, though I'm not sure that either of them graduated. Dad was a distinguished alumnus; and our son, Bob, carried on and improved upon the tradition. Our daughter, Betsy, showed great courage by going to Stanford. Later, she atoned for this traitorous act by graduating from Boalt Hall and also earning her teaching credential from Cal. She and I still have an annual bet of one dollar on the Big Game, which at this writing appears to be a foolish wager on my part, albeit a sensible amount.

During my first two years I lived comfortably at Bowles Hall, and then I was invited to become a member of Alpha Delta Phi. As their first Jewish member, I hoped that by joining I would help open the doors of other fraternities as well. Doing this has become a pattern in my life, helping to broaden the membership policies of several private clubs.

In my years at Cal, few of us challenged authority. I had been brought up to respect and follow the traditions and values of our elders. Teachers, policemen, or people in positions of responsibility were not questioned. In 1934, at the height of the Depression, there was a general strike in San Francisco. Absolutely all services were closed down for the first and only time in the city's history. It was a major economic struggle; but many of us on the campus were indifferent, and unaware of the basic issues. We believed what we read in the local newspapers, that this work interruption was caused by "that communist," Harry Bridges, and his followers. A few of my more socially conscious classmates volunteered to help the thousands who were out of work. A close friend, Jean Haven, skipped classes and spent hours in a soup kitchen to assist strikers. We couldn't understand her motivation.

I remember certain professors with fondness: Ben Lehman in English, Robert Kerner in History, Ira B. Cross in Economics. Provost Monroe Deutsch was admired by all the students. But classes were large and impersonal. I was in awe of my professors and rather shy about taking the initiative to meet with them or get to know them, which was my loss. I did get to know Scott Wilson, the resident manager of Bowles Hall, and Garff Wilson, who worked in Administration.

My most meaningful experiences at Cal came in nontraditional ways, not through classroom learning. I had been an honor student in high school without having to study too hard. When I moved into the dorm, I quickly discovered how much I enjoyed the social life and the extracurricular opportunities on the campus. I attended classes regularly, but didn't apply myself. My report card at the end of the first semester was about 50 percent C's and 50 percent B's which seemed okay to me. When my father saw my grades, he blew his top. He said he wasn't going to spend his money on my education if I didn't want to receive one, and he would take me out of school if I didn't show improvement. Lesson learned. I raised my grades and managed to graduate as an Honor Student.

One day a group of seniors visited me in my dormitory room telling me a great injustice was being done to a fine professor who was being disciplined. They assured me that the professor was an excellent teacher, admired by his students, and was being penalized for political reasons. They presented a petition for me to sign on his behalf, and I complied.

Some weeks later, I received a call asking me to come to President Robert Gordon Sproul's office. He was most cordial in greeting me, and the visit began quite pleasantly. Then he asked me to tell him my impressions of a particular professor. I told him I wasn't in any of the man's classes and had never heard of him.

When he showed me my name on the petition on behalf of this same man, I was mortified. Lesson two: I've never signed anything of importance since, without reading it first.

I also remember an incident involving a close friend of my father's, Professor Henry Grady, a great teacher who later became Under Secretary of State and author of our international free trade policy. I had enrolled in one of his courses in my sophomore year. When I took the final, I put a self-addressed card in the blue book we used for final exams. In those days, the reader would mail out the grade well in advance of official notification from the University. I thought it would be fun to tease my father by making him think I had failed the course, so I mailed another card to myself—with an F—knowing it would arrive before the real card could be received. Again my father was sad. "How could you embarrass me by flunking a course given by my best friend?" he asked. He railed and ranted and was so upset that I regretted what I had done. And of course the joke ended up on me, because I began to worry about how I had really done on that damned test. Would I end up with a D or an F? I fretted and fumed for two weeks, and blamed myself for a stupid prank. You can imagine my relief when the official card arrived with a B in the course, but I don't think Dad ever forgave me. Lesson three: don't play uncaring pranks.

During my sophomore year I decided to try out for the *Daily Cal.* Without any journalistic aptitude, it seemed my best chance would be to secure a position on the business side of the student paper. My first assignment was to get ads. It seemed to me that my best prospects were the landladies with available rooms to rent near the campus. I had expected the work to be tedious, but it proved depressing as well. I found myself soliciting from people in obvious economic need while I was not sure that the ads would produce results. I was uncomfortable whenever I succeeded in making a sale because I felt I might be taking badly needed money to no avail. I quit the paper after only a few weeks, but I have never forgotten that you can only sell a product if you believe in it and can only succeed if you are comfortable with what you are doing. Another lesson learned.

I was part of one other adventure while at Cal—my investment, with four others from Bowles Hall (Bob Coop, Bob Millen, Stan Brunsten, and Stan Blush), in an old 1916 Pierce Arrow Phaeton. It was beautiful and provided us transportation, as well as fun. We bought it for twenty-five dollars, but it was difficult to keep it operating, especially to keep it in repair. The model was already twenty years old, and dealers had no parts. We had to go to the junk yard to find even tires. When we needed money for expenses, we'd bank a roulette game in one of our rooms. We rotated the "bank" among the five of us, while the other four would knock on dormitory doors to get players who favored the bank. We also used the car to conduct a limousine service, with driver and footman (equipped with blinders) available to other students wanting to make an impression on their dates. This small business was successful for several months until the Pierce Arrow just broke down and couldn't be repaired any more. It was a sad day when the car was hauled away to a junk yard. We were paid fifty dollars for the aluminum in the chassis, however, the first capital gain for all of us!

I was obsessed throughout my four years at Cal with trying to make my Big C in tennis. I was something of a jock, and tennis was my best sport. I had won a few minor club championships and even a junior city title in San Francisco, so I was reasonably confident about my prospects, not realizing how limited my exposure had been to real competition. I did manage to earn my freshman sweater by winning a doubles match against Stanford and proudly wore it throughout my sophomore year. But reality set in when I tried to make the varsity; there were several players with considerably more ability than I possessed. I practiced long hours year round, yet there were fellows with whom I could barely compete. What a glorious time it was, however, as I struggled to become a participating member in intercollegiate matches. My mood was tempered by the fortunes of the team, with some of whom I still maintain occasional and happy communication. But my heart was broken during my sophomore year when I was asked to play a practice match against a senior to determine who was to make the traveling squad to go south to play USC and UCLA. At the time, making the trip was the most important thing in my life. I won the crucial contest in straight sets and savored not only the great achievement, but the likelihood that I could be a member of the varsity for the next two years.

It's difficult to describe my deep disappointment when the next day our coach took me aside, put his arm around my shoulder, and told me he had decided to take the fellow I had beaten instead! He explained that my rival was a senior, it was his last chance for such a trip, and that I had two more years remaining. It seemed like a very unfair decision to me, and I came close to quitting. It was a long time before I could re-dedicate myself wholeheartedly to the team and its success. Remarkably, the coach and I remained good friends.

I continued to be a marginal member of the squad, calling lines and matches, and occasionally getting to compete when the outcome was already decided. Our final match of the season was against Stanford; and when I learned I was going to play second doubles, I realized that the Big C was mine and that all the hard work and determination had paid off! Actually we had a remarkably fine team, winning both the Pacific Coast Championship and the Intercollegiate Championship during my sophomore and senior years. In a 1937 edition of *Life* magazine, listing universities nationwide who were noted for excellence in different sports, Cal was recognized for having been preeminent in tennis. It made me proud to have played a small role in earning that distinction for our University.

I have always had a great interest in sports of all kinds. They build character and help individuals cope with difficult situations. Some of my friends, however, have questioned this enthusiasm and judged it to be misplaced. I used to commute to work in San Francisco from the Peninsula, always sitting next to one of these people. On the train we'd each read our newspapers. He constantly criticized me for looking at the sports page first, saying that someone with my responsibilities should begin with the front or the financial page instead. I said that I didn't think it made a difference since by the time we got to our destination, I completed reading the entire paper. For some reason this didn't satisfy him. Then one day I came across a quotation which ended the discussion. It said, "The sports page is an account of man's triumphs while the front page is an account of man's failures." Perhaps that's why I'm so intrigued by sports.

I continue my great interest in Cal sports to this day— with seats in the press box to the football games (with former Chancellor Roger Heyns) and season tickets with classmates to the basketball games. Except for the years I was in the service during World War II, I believe I have attended every Big Game since 1923, a 9–0 Cal win, when I was seven years old.

It is a joy to reflect back on my years at Cal and try to recapture the highlights of a happy, growing, and learning experience, the struggles the first year and the increased maturity and confidence as the months passed. Senior Week and graduation came much too fast, and with them a major wrench.

From Cal I went to Harvard Business School where I met Evelyn Danzig, who was attending nearby Wheaton. We were married fifty-three years ago and now have a wonderful family of children and grandchildren who make us proud.

After fifty-two months in the army, I joined the family business, Levi Strauss & Co., and participated in its phenomenal growth from a small Western wholesaler and manufacturer to the largest apparel company in the world. I also sought to honor a family tradition of helping the company be a model employer and an exemplary corporate citizen. What we accomplished to improve the work life of our employees and to serve our communities are proud memories of my many years in business.

For my second career I bought a professional baseball team, the Oakland Athletics, to keep them from moving to Denver. My son and son-in-law took what had been a troubled franchise and built it into one of the finest organizations in baseball, winning our division four times, the American League three times, and the World Championship once in the past four years.

Through the years I have also served on the boards of several major corporations, government commissions, and civic and philanthropic organizations. My twelve years as a Trustee of the Ford Foundation gave me an awareness of the world's problems and how difficult it is to make a difference, even with large infusions of money. The experience that really changed my perspective, however, came when President Lyndon Johnson appointed me Regional Director and Executive Committee member of the newly formed National Alliance of Business in 1968. Our role was to find jobs for 500,000 virtually unemployable people, those who had been in prison, had substance abuse problems, or poor education. We accomplished our goal through the unprecedented collaboration of business, labor, and government. Lesson: through dedication and ingenuity business can help solve major societal problems that until then I had thought were primarily the responsibility of government.

I have received honors and awards, but the ones I treasure most were being chosen Cal Alumnus of the Year in 1984 and receiving the Berkeley Medal in 1991. There is no doubt in my mind that my four years at Cal helped form the values and aspirations that made this possible. I suppose that's as close as I can get to explaining why my heart skips a beat every time I hear the Cal marching band strike up "Our Sturdy Golden Bear" and why I will always be a loving, loyal, and grateful Cal alumnus.

"After the seminar was over I walked the streets of Berkeley for hours, alternately exhilarated by the beauty of the discovery, despairing over my lack of insight, and intrigued by the import of this exciting new fission reaction."

GLENN T. SEABORG

Glenn T. Seaborg

ONE SUNNY MORNING in September of 1929, I walked across the ravine on the bridge which served as the entrance to UCLA from the Hilgard Avenue side. This was the opening year of the Westwood Campus and the total facilities consisted of four buildings: Royce Hall, the Library, the chemistry building, the physics building, and a couple of temporary structures, including a student bookstore and gymnasium facilities. This opened a new world of opportunity for me, one which would not have been possible if a tuition-free state university had not been available. I well remember my first class that morning, which was the freshman chemistry lecture of William Congor Morgan. Professor Morgan strode into the lecture hall—a tall, powerful, and impressive-looking man—and glowered at the class. Among his opening words was the frightening admonition, "Look at the person on your left. Now, look at the person on your right." And then, after an impressive pause, he added with great authority, "One of you three will not be here at Thanksgiving time." This prognostication had a very salutary effect on my study habits.

In 1929 UCLA offered unique opportunities for undergraduates in chemistry. In addition to Professor Morgan, Professors William R. Crowell, G. Ross Robertson, J. Blaine Ramsey, Hosmer W. Stone, Max S. Dunn, and, a year or two later, William G. Young and Francis E. Blacet offered an extraordinary curriculum. The absence of graduate work in those years was probably the reason our able professors gave us a taste of graduate-type research by the time we had reached our sophomore or junior years. My experience was further enriched through my service as a reader and laboratory assistant for Professor Crowell's quantitative analysis courses. In addition, the precious funds received from this work made it possible for me to stay in school from the second semester of my sophomore year until I received my degree.

I had almost no exposure to science in my early years. I was born of Swedish ancestry in Ishpeming, Michigan, a small iron-mining town on the Upper Peninsula. My mother, a girl named Selma O. Erickson, came to the United States from Sweden in 1904, when she was seventeen, and my father, Herman Theodore Seaborg, was born of Swedish immigrant parents in Ishpeming. His father had worked at the iron works at Hallefors, Sweden, at the same time as the grandfather of the Swedish Nobel prize winner The Svedberg, so I suspect that the name The and my middle name Theodore have a common origin. I attended the Ishpeming public schools until I was ten years old and starting the fifth grade.

Then my family, which included my younger sister Jeanette, moved to Home Gardens, now a part of South Gate, California (near Los Angeles). This move was made largely at the urging of my mother, who wanted to extend the horizon for her children beyond the limited opportunities available in Ishpeming. However, unlike in Ishpeming, where he would have had guaranteed employment for life, my father never found permanent employment at his trade in California, and our family found itself in continuing poor circumstances. Since the new subdivision of Home Gardens had no schools, my sister and I during the first year traveled by bus to attend the Wilmington Avenue Grammar School in the Watts district of Los Angeles. I completed my grammar school education through the eighth grade in the newly constructed Victoria Avenue Grammar School in Home Gardens, skipping a couple of semesters on the way to my eighth-grade diploma.

My father was a machinist. He had worked for iron-mining companies, as had his father and grandfather, but it didn't take me long to realize that I had no aptitude for my father's craft. I think I was a good student in grammar school, but I had no special scholastic interests. When I entered David Starr Jordan High School in the Watts district of Los Angeles, I had to choose between a commercial and a college preparatory curriculum. My mother urged the commercial course; to her this was the road to a respectable white-collar job. But I started down a different road and chose the college preparatory program, with literature as my major subject. During my freshman and sophomore years, I studied the usual college preparatory subjects such as English literature, oral English, and world history, as well as algebra, geometry, and a foreign language.

141

    In my junior year I was required to take a laboratory science. Because my high school was small, chemistry and physics were offered in alternate years, and chemistry was the offering in my junior year. It was fortunate for me that my first science course was taught by Dwight Logan Reid, an outstanding teacher who exerted a strong formative influence on me. Mr. Reid not only taught chemistry, he preached it. He related some fascinating experiences he had as a chemistry student in college, and, when he lectured, his eyes would light up. His irrepressible enthusiasm, obvious love for the subject, and ability to inspire interest captured my imagination almost immediately. Early in Mr. Reid's course I decided I wanted to become a scientist. As a senior I took physics, also from Mr. Reid, and since then my interests in physics and chemistry have been inseparable.

    After I finished high school in June 1929, I was very fortunate to find employment during the summer as a laboratory assistant, working as the lone control chemist on the graveyard shift at the Firestone Tire and Rubber Company in their South Gate plant. This provided me the money that made it just barely possible for me to enroll at the University of California at Los Angeles in the fall. I lived at home and commuted by car with friends a distance of some twenty miles to UCLA. I knew I wanted to major in either physics or chemistry. My preference was physics. But I believed that a physicist could make a living only by teaching in a university, and during those Depression years university faculties had few openings. On the other hand, a chemist unable to find a university teaching position could go into industry. So I chose chemistry, hoping to become a university teacher, but knowing that if I did not, other career opportunities would be available. While majoring in chemistry, I took the maximum number of courses in physics. In my senior year at UCLA I had a course in modern physics given by Professor John M. Adams, who talked to us of the exciting discoveries in nuclear science. And these lectures fixed my sights on this new frontier.

For my graduate work there could be no place but the University of California, Berkeley. The very name, Berkeley, was magic, a distant and almost unattainable mecca. The chemistry staff at Berkeley was legendary, having written the textbooks from which we took our courses at UCLA. There were names such as Joel H. Hildebrand, Wendell M. Latimer, William C. Bray, C. Walter Porter, Gerald E. K. Branch, and, of course, the great Gilbert Newton Lewis, dean of the College of Chemistry. The name of the rising young nuclear physicist, Ernest O. Lawrence, was beginning to ring through the world of science. I wanted to work as near as possible to Lewis (the great "G. N."—"The Chief") and to Lawrence. And again the absence of a tuition fee was consistent with the state of my finances.

Reaching this mecca was not necessarily simple. Not everyone was admitted, and so the custom was to apply to a number of graduate schools. Moreover, I had not only to be accepted but also to be granted a teaching assistantship (at a salary of fifty dollars per month) to support me through graduate study. Professor Ramsey, who had done his graduate work at Berkeley, assured me that there was no need to apply to alternate institutions, that Berkeley would grant me both my wishes. And so it did, to a lingering disbelief on my part, despite Professor Ramsey's reassurances.

It is difficult to describe the exciting, glamorous atmosphere that existed at the University of California at Berkeley when I entered as a graduate student in August 1934. I took formal courses in chemistry from such eminent men as Professor Axel R. Olson and William F. Giauque, and in physics from Raymond T. Birge and Robert B. Brode. As a teaching assistant in freshman chemistry my instructor colleagues in the laboratory sections included such men as Hildebrand, who always gave the main lectures as well, Latimer, Bray, Giauque, and Ermon D. Eastman. Probably the high point of each week was the Tuesday afternoon Research Conference held in Gilman Hall, at which graduate students presented a research paper on a current topic from the literature, which was followed by a faculty member, postdoctoral scientist, or advanced graduate student describing his own recent research. This latter was always in the forefront of scientific research in an interesting area. Here we saw G. N. at his best, sitting at the head of the table which dominated the center of the room, chain-smoking his huge black cigars. He asked questions and stimulated discussion over the whole wide range of chemistry and physics in a manner which I have never seen equaled.

143

Another high point was the weekly evening Nuclear Seminar, covering recent articles from the scientific literature and the current work in the College of Chemistry in the area of nuclear science; this seminar was run by Willard F. Libby and Robert D. Fowler, who guided my research until he left. G. N. also always attended these seminars, which added considerably to the excitement. In Le Conte Hall on Monday evenings, there was the Physics Journal Club, presided over by Lawrence, including the brilliant galaxy of J. Robert Oppenheimer, Edwin M. McMillan, Luis W. Alvarez, Philip H. Abelson, Martin D. Kamen, and John J. Livingood, just to mention a few. It was in this atmosphere that I was privileged to carry out my doctoral research in the company of such fellow students as David C. Grahame, who worked with me as my research partner, Kenneth S. Pitzer, Samuel Ruben, and many others.

I made a good start toward realizing my ambition to become a nuclear scientist when I completed my graduate thesis on a nuclear physics project, the inelastic scattering of fast neutrons. After starting this project with Fowler, who moved to Johns Hopkins University, I completed the work with chemistry professor George Ernest Gibson. Grahame and I carried out this research in the cavernous auditorium of abandoned East Hall, an ancient building which had been moved from its original site at the present location of Le Conte Hall to a then vacant spot just to the south of Faculty Glade at about the present location of Hertz Hall. We were forced to perform our experiments during the graveyard shift because Lewis required the use of the Chemistry Department's sole radium-beryllium source of neutrons during the daytime and evening hours. Our experiments provided what was probably the first unequivocal evidence for the phenomenon of inelastic scattering of fast neutrons. We established a minimum probability (cross section) for this type of reaction in the region of lead and bismuth, an observation that was beyond theoretical understanding at that time but was explained years later as due to the closed nucleon shells of 82 protons and 126 neutrons.

When I obtained my Ph.D. degree in May 1937, I stayed on, continuing my research even though I had no immediate prospect of a job. This was a Depression year and satisfactory positions were very difficult to obtain. Yet such was the atmosphere at Berkeley and my preoccupation with my research that I was only vaguely worried about my future. Then one day in the middle of the summer, G. N. called me in and asked whether I would like to serve as his personal research scientist. Because of his reputation and standing, he was almost unique in having such an assistant, and the position at $1,800 per year happened to be open at that time. I was overwhelmed at this opportunity and immediately accepted, after first expressing some genuine doubts as to my adequacy. In this role, I published several papers with "The Chief" in the area of generalized acids and bases, which was his current interest and rather far from my own area and aptitude. It was also during this period, 1937–39, that he started his famous work on the absorption of light and the determination of energy levels (i.e., the triplet state) in organic molecules.

Some time before I began my work with G. N. I entered almost by accident the mainstream of my career as a nuclear scientist. One day in 1936 I was suddenly confronted by Jack Livingood, a physicist who was favored by ready access to that nuclear horn of plenty, the thirty-seven-inch cyclotron. He literally handed me a "hot" target, just bombarded by the machine, and asked me to process it chemically to identify the radioisotopes that had been produced. Naturally, I jumped at the chance. The facility he offered in Le Conte Hall was hardly luxurious. My best recollection is that it was the custodian's closet and that the resources consisted of tap water, a sink, and a small workbench. With some essential materials bootlegged from the Department of Chemistry, I performed the chemical separation to Jack's satisfaction. In the course of my collaboration with Livingood, covering a period of five years, we discovered a number of radioisotopes which proved useful for biological explorations and medical applications. Among the isotopes that we discovered were iodine-131 and iron-59 and among the useful isotopes that we characterized was cobalt-60.

The discovery of iodine-131 has given me special satisfaction. On one occasion during this period, in 1938, the late Dr. Joseph G. Hamilton, one of the outstanding nuclear medical pioneers, mentioned to me the limitations on his studies of thyroid metabolism imposed by the short lifetime of the radioactive iodine tracer that was available. He was working with iodine-128, which has a half-life of only twenty-five minutes. When he inquired about the possibility of finding another iodine isotope with a longer half-life, I asked him what value would be best for his work. He replied, "Oh, about a week." Soon after that, Jack Livingood and I synthesized and identified iodine-131, with a half-life, luckily enough, of eight days. This isotope is now used some half million times a year for the diagnosis and treatment of thyroid disease and the diagnosis of other disorders. I have the added satisfaction that my own mother had her life extended by many years as a result of treatment with iodine-1 3 1.

My experience as a radioisotope hunter led eventually to the transuranium elements, a nuclear field that was to become my life work. My interest in the subject had been aroused soon after I arrived at Berkeley. In the fall of 1934, at the evening Nuclear Seminar presided over by Libby and Fowler, we learned of the experiments by Fermi and his group in Italy. They reported that they had bombarded uranium with neutrons and produced what they thought were radioactive isotopes of transuranium elements, i.e., elements in the periodic table that were heavier than and beyond the heaviest natural element, uranium. Somewhat later, this work was taken up in Germany by Otto Hahn, Lise Meitner, and Fritz Strassmann. I read avidly all the reports on these so-called transuranium elements. I even chose this as my topic for the Tuesday Research Conference, using one of the papers by Hahn and his associates as the basis for a complete description of the chemical properties of these transuranium elements, a non-subject on which I considered myself already a minor expert.

Then, at the Journal Club meeting in the Department of Physics on a Monday night in January 1939, my mastery of the "field" vanished in a moment. The information had come through by word of mouth that Hahn and Strassmann in Germany had identified some of the radioactivities as isotopes of barium and lanthanum, and that what actually happened upon the bombardment of uranium with neutrons was the splitting of the uranium nucleus into two approximately equal-sized fragments, with the release of a large amount of nuclear energy. Nuclear scientists had been looking at fission products, not transuranium elements.

I cannot possibly describe either the excitement that this produced in me or the chagrin I felt in realizing that I had failed to interpret correctly the wealth of information I had studied so assiduously for a number of years. After the seminar was over I walked the streets of Berkeley for hours, alternately exhilarated by the beauty of the discovery, despairing over my lack of insight and intrigued by the import of this exciting new fission reaction.

The following year, McMillan and Abelson identified the first real transuranium element, with atomic number 93, which they named neptunium, produced as a result of the bombardment of uranium with neutrons produced in the new sixty-inch cyclotron. Following a start by McMillan in a search for the next transuranium element, No. 94, I received his permission to carry on this work when he was called away to perform important war research in the East. I had already asked Arthur C. Wahl, one of my graduate students, to begin studying the tracer chemical properties of element 93 with the idea that this might be a good subject for his thesis. My other co-worker was Joseph W. Kennedy, who by that time was a fellow instructor in the Chemistry Department. We were able to produce and identify the element, No. 94, to which we gave the name plutonium (symbol Pu), in experiments involving the deuteron bombardment of uranium in the sixty-inch cyclotron. The critical chemical identification that constituted the discovery of this important element was performed on the stormy night of February 23, 1941, in Room 307, Gilman Hall. That room was dedicated as a National Historic Landmark just twenty-five years later.

Almost concurrent with this was the search for and the demonstration of the fission of the isotope of major importance, that is, plutonium-239. Emilio Segrè joined Kennedy, Wahl, and me in this experiment. (I had been collaborating with Segrè for several years in several areas of nuclear research, which included some fundamental discoveries concerning nuclear isomerism and the discovery of the chemical method of separating nuclear isomers.) After production of half a microgram of plutonium-239 from uranium irradiated with neutrons from the sixty-inch cyclotron, we demonstrated on March 28, 1941, that this isotope is fissionable with slow neutrons, produced with the thirty-seven-inch cyclotron. This demonstrated the utility of plutonium as the explosive ingredient in a nuclear weapon and, I hope, more important, opened the use of uranium as a nuclear fuel for breeder reactors to meet the future energy needs of the world. I placed the sample used for this historic experiment in one of G. N. Lewis's cigar boxes. It gathered dust during the ensuing years but was finally found in an old storeroom in time for the twenty-fifth anniversary of the crucial experiment. It was presented by Segre and me in a ceremony on March 28, 1966, to the Smithsonian Institution and is now on display in the Museum of History and Technology.

In February 1942, John W. Gofman, a graduate student, Raymond W. Stoughton, a young research assistant, and I were able to say that we had created and identified a second major source of nuclear energy, the isotope uranium-233, which is the key to the use of the abundant element thorium as a nuclear fuel. The sample upon which this measurement was made was also stored in one of Lewis's cigar boxes, has been found and will be placed on public display in the Lawrence Hall of Science at Berkeley.

The demonstration that plutonium-239 was fissionable played a central role in the decision to pursue a crash program to develop the nuclear reactor for plutonium production. I was called to the University of Chicago Metallurgical Laboratory in 1942, to direct the work on the transuranium elements and, in particular, the work on the chemical extraction of plutonium from the uranium and fission products of the fuel elements in which the plutonium would be produced in the uranium chain reaction. I was granted a leave of absence from my position as assistant professor of chemistry at Berkeley and arrived in Chicago on my thirtieth birthday, April 19, 1942. I returned briefly to Berkeley in June to pick up my bride, Helen L. Griggs, a University of California, Berkeley graduate of the class of 1939 and at that time Professor Ernest Lawrence's secretary. In my visits to Lawrence's office, I had become enamored of her; we were married on June 6, 1942, at Pioche, Nevada. (Incidentally, some of our six children are already students at the University of California, and I suspect others will follow.)

Among those who went to the University of Chicago with me were Isadore Perlman and Burris B. Cunningham, now professors of chemistry at Berkeley, and Stanley G. Thompson and Albert Ghiorso, now senior research scientists in the Lawrence Radiation Laboratory at Berkeley. We succeeded in developing a chemical separation process for the extraction of plutonium which operated successfully first in the pilot plant stage at Oak Ridge, Tennessee, and then at the Hanford Engineer Works in the state of Washington, where the plutonium was produced during the war. Among the accomplishments of our Chicago group was the first isolation of a visible amount of a plutonium compound on August 18, 1942; this also constituted the first isolation of a visible quantity of any synthetic element. This was followed immediately, on September 10, 1942, by the first weighing of a compound of plutonium; Room 405 in the George Herbert Jones Chemical Laboratory at the University of Chicago, in which this occurred, was dedicated as a National Historic Landmark on the twenty-fifth anniversary of this event. The sample upon which the weighing was performed was preserved and will be put on public display in the Lawrence Hall of Science. The chemical properties of plutonium were investigated rather completely by subsequent work in our Chicago laboratory on the ultramicrochemical (microgram) scale.

Also, while at Chicago, Ghiorso, Ralph A. James, Leon O. Morgan, and I succeeded in synthesizing and identifying the next two transuranium elements, Nos. 95 and 96, americium and curium. Our group discovered numerous isotopes of the transuranium elements. It was during this period, in the summer of 1944, that I evolved the Actinide Concept for identifying the position of the heaviest elements, including the transuranium elements, in the Periodic Table; this was the key to the subsequent discovery of a number of transuranium elements.

After the end of the war, in May 1946, I returned to Berkeley as a full professor of chemistry and brought with me a number of my associates at Chicago, including Professors Perlman and Cunningham. In the following years up to 1958, my colleagues, particularly Ghiorso and Thompson, and I succeeded in synthesizing and identifying the next six transuranium elements, those with the atomic numbers 97 to 102, inclusive. For elements 97 and 98 we suggested the names berkelium and californium, respectively, in honor of the city of Berkeley and the state and University of California. These two and element 101 (mendelevium) were the first synthesized through the use of the sixty-inch cyclotron. Elements 99 (einsteinium) and 100 (fermium) were discovered in collaboration with scientists of the University of California's Los Alamos Scientific Laboratory and the Argonne National Laboratory (the successor to the wartime Metallurgical Laboratory) as the result of their production in the first thermonuclear test explosion conducted in the Pacific Ocean area of Eniwetok. The element with atomic number 102 (nobelium) was first produced by the use of the Berkeley Radiation Laboratory's Heavy Ion Linear Accelerator (HILAC).

Also, during this period, while I served as director of the Nuclear Chemistry Division and beginning in 1954 as an associate director of the Radiation Laboratory, Berkeley, we carried on a number of other researches in the fields of nuclear structure and nuclear reactions (including the first observation of "spallation" reactions, using the 184-inch cyclotron). The work of our group on alpha particle radioactivity and nuclear energy levels furnished the bulk of the data needed to evolve, by the Copenhagen school, the modern and very successful theory of nuclear structure. Our group discovered several dozens of radioactive isotopes of transuranium elements and a large number of radioactive isotopes of other elements. In the field of chemistry much progress was made in the investigation of the chemical properties of the transuranium elements, especially by the use of the microchemical and ultramicrochemical techniques. I believe that this period (1946–58) was a very productive one and that our laboratory was and continues to be one of the leading centers in nuclear chemistry and low-energy nuclear physics.

My introduction to national public service came when I was appointed by President Harry S Truman to serve on the first General Advisory Committee (GAC) to the Atomic Energy Commission for a term extending from January 1947 to August 1950.

This first GAC played an important role in helping to establish a number of the basic policies of the AEC.

The real beginnings of diversion from my scientific career began in the fall of 1952, when Clark Kerr, who had just been appointed the first Chancellor of the Berkeley campus, called me to his office. Would I like to serve as Faculty Athletic Representative to the Pacific Coast Intercollegiate Athletic Conference? I was taken by surprise and unable to give him an immediate answer. However, I had a lifelong interest in athletics and had been an avid follower of the University of California's athletic teams. I soon decided to accept Kerr's offer. I served as Faculty Athletic Representative from January 1953 until July of 1958, attending all of the meetings of the Pacific Coast Conference (PCC) and several meetings of the National Collegiate Athletic Association (NCAA). My duties included ruling on the eligibility of the athletes and presiding over the Berkeley campus Athletic Advisory Board meetings. During the latter half of this period, I served as the press spokesman for the Pacific Coast Conference at its semiannual meetings. This was a lively responsibility since during this period the rather widespread rules violations in the conference were discovered. The violations led to the ultimate breakup of the conference. I was then cast in a leading role in putting together the successor to the PCC, that is, the present Athletic Association of Western Universities (AAWU), which has in the meantime been expanded to eight members or the so-called Pac-Eight.

In the summer of 1958, Chancellor Kerr became President of the University. Once again, Kerr called me to his office. Perhaps because of our close association in weathering, somewhat successfully, the highly publicized and difficult PCC affair, he and the Regents wondered if I would be a candidate for the chancellorship. The decision was a difficult one to make. I was reluctant to step out of science to the extent that this position seemed to require; yet the larger challenge was appealing. When I was allowed to continue as an associate director of the Radiation Laboratory and to direct graduate student research in the laboratory and the College of Chemistry, I accepted.

The two and a half years I served as Chancellor was a period of extensive development for the Berkeley campus on many fronts. The campus academic plan was first put into effect. Important academic developments included the establishment of the College of Environmental Design in July 1959, combining the College of Architecture, Department of City and Regional Planning, and Department of Landscape Architecture; the development of the Space Sciences Laboratory; the conception and planning of the Earl Warren Legal Center and the Laboratory of Chemical Biodynamics; and the establishment of a variety of new research institutes, centers, and facilities in diverse fields. My concern over the need to strengthen the humanities, to provide some balance with the sciences, led to my suggestion for the creation of an Institute for the Humanities; this later culminated in the establishment of the Humanities Research Committee with its Humanities Institute and Humanities Research Professorships. A major academic development, having an important impact on the University starting in 1959, was the provision of sizable new federal funds for student loans, graduate fellowships, and language institutes under the National Defense Education Act. The exploitation of television for teaching was launched. Among honors that came to the Berkeley campus was the award of Nobel prizes to Berkeley faculty members—to Emilio Segrè and Owen Chamberlain, in physics in 1959, and to Donald A. Glaser, in physics in 1960.

During my chancellorship, continuing work started by Clark Kerr, we implemented and extended the long-range physical plan of the Berkeley campus. It was a time of prodigious construction and further planning for updating the academic and student facilities. Completed in this period were Kroeber Hall and the Lowie Museum, Campbell Hall, the first eight residence halls, the Strawberry Canyon Recreational Complex, and a large addition to Cowell Hospital. The Student Union came into use shortly after my departure. Construction was started on the Earth Sciences Building, Tolman Hall, Latimer Hall, and the married students' apartments. Meanwhile, a careful landscape program was undertaken to preserve the beauty of the campus in the face of rapid development.

We initiated a number of efforts to raise the level of teaching in the lower schools, which was then recognized as being seriously deficient. The Chemical Education Material Study (CHEM Study) (I accepted the chairmanship and have served as chairman of the Steering Committee) was undertaken by our College of Chemistry in collaboration with Harvey Mudd College in 1959; this program has since revolutionized the high-school curriculum in chemistry on a national basis. The Lawrence Hall of Science was conceived and planned to do research in science teaching and to disseminate knowledge of science to the public.

Berkeley seemed to be unusually successful in athletics in those years. The 1958 football team won the Pacific Coast Conference title, went to the Rose Bowl and, as the last titlist of the conference, stands as the permanent champions of the PCC. In 1959 the basketball team won the PCC title (thus also the permanent champions of the PCC) and went on to take the National Collegiate Athletic Association play-offs, becoming national champions, a first for Berkeley in basketball. In 1960 the basketball team won the championship of the new conference, the Athletic Association of Western Universities, and was the runner-up for the NCAA title. Berkeley won the Intercollegiate Regatta Association championship in 1960. The California Intercollegiate Baseball Association championship came to Berkeley in 1960 and also the AAWU water polo championships in 1959 and 1960. It was a halcyon period for rugby; in 1959 the team went undefeated for the first time in modern rugby history and repeated this remarkable performance in 1960; the titles included the World Cup series in both years, the PCC Southern Division championship in 1959, and the AAWU Southern Division championship in 1960. Control of athletics was transferred from the Associated Students University of California to the campus administration during this period.

While Chancellor, I was appointed by President Dwight D. Eisenhower, in 1959, to be a member of the President's Science Advisory Committee (PSAC), on which I served until January 1961, and to the National Science Board of the National Science Foundation (1960–61).

In January 1961, I was called by President Kennedy to serve as the chairman of the U.S. Atomic Energy Commission, a position that I have held for about nine years while on leave of absence from the University of California, a period longer than that of any previous chairman and spanning the terms of three presidents, John F. Kennedy, Lyndon B. Johnson, and Richard M. Nixon. In this capacity I also serve on such bodies as the National Aeronautics and Space Council, the Federal Council for Science and Technology, the Federal Radiation Council, and the President's Council on Marine Resources and Engineering Development.

These years with the AEC have been an extension of my experience at the University of California, from freshman at UCLA in 1929 to Chancellor at Berkeley ending in early 1961. I have continued my associations and friendships with University Regents, leaders of the administration, and colleagues on the faculties. In my travels around the country and the world, there are few places where I do not find an opportunity to renew acquaintance with former colleagues, students, and alumni friends in many walks of life. To me these experiences are a continuing symbol of the great and diverse contributions the University has made, not only to the nation but to the world.

Perhaps most rewarding to me has been the opportunity to participate in the development, for man's considerable benefit, of many major discoveries in pure nuclear science made years ago at Berkeley and in other laboratories. As I see at firsthand the amazing growth of nuclear technology for man's use, I am occasionally bemused by recollection of Professor Adams opening the vista of nuclear science to me at UCLA in 1934; of hours of intense concentration at the Geiger counter in 1937 during the eerie hours before dawn in old East Hall; of pacing the streets of Berkeley in 1939 after hearing for the first time of the discovery of fission; and of the exhilaration when plutonium was born in 1941 during the early, stormy hours under the eaves of Gilman Hall.

The University can take considerable pride in its contributions, both past and continuing, to the rather dramatic changes that have taken place in the U.S. nuclear energy program since 1961. The program has progressed from a largely government-financed and -based program to a broader, more varied program with increased industrial support. Tremendous strides have been made during this period in the peaceful uses of nuclear energy.

Perhaps of first importance is the progress in the civilian nuclear power field. When I first came to Washington the prospects for the early attainment of economic nuclear electric power seemed to be so slight that it was difficult even to defend the program in the budgetary process. In contrast to this, we find today that nuclear electric power is economic in comparison with the competitive source generated from fossil fuel. In fact, nuclear plants now account for more than half of the new steam-generating capacity contracted for by the utilities in the United States during the past three years. Today more than 75 million kilowatts of nuclear power are either in operation, under construction, or committed, and we forecast an installed nuclear power capacity of 150 million kilowatts by 1980. An important step toward placing the nuclear power industry in the domain of private enterprise was the enactment of legislation in 1964 which provided for the private ownership of nuclear fuel.

The future prospects of nuclear power are even rosier than this present picture might imply. The Atomic Energy Commission has turned to the development of more advanced types of power reactors, including breeder reactors (a development rising from the discovery of plutonium and uranium-233 at Berkeley), which will greatly increase the efficiency of the use of nuclear fuel and substantially lower the cost of nuclear power.

It will be possible in the future to apply nuclear power to

the desalting of ocean water, to the production of fertilizer together with desalted water for the operation of "food factories" on many desert coastal plains of the world so as to help alleviate the world's food shortage, and ultimately to huge agricultural-industrial complexes, termed the "nuplex," which should revolutionize the industrial economy in our country and abroad. In fact, I believe nuclear power will radically change our relationship to our environment—to our production of food and the use we make of our water, air, minerals, and other natural resources. Nuclear electric power is a clean source of power, alleviating our burden of air pollution, and offers an almost limitless supply of energy for generations to come.

156

This tremendous growth in nuclear power led to the establishment of a very vital separate branch in the Atomic Energy Commission, devoted entirely to the regulation and the issuance of licenses for nuclear power plants and the manifold uses of radioactive isotopes.

Another area in which nuclear energy made great progress, with the technical leadership of the Lawrence Radiation Laboratory, Livermore, California, is that of the peaceful uses of nuclear explosives—the Atomic Energy Commission's Plowshare program. In this form, nuclear energy gives promise for the economic conduct of huge excavation projects, such as canals and harbors. In addition, nuclear explosives for underground engineering purposes give promise for the recovery of natural gas from low-grade gas wells, oil from oil shale, valuable metals from low-grade minerals, and for the underground storage of water and natural gas.

Also, under my chairmanship, the Atomic Entergy Commission made large advances in the application of nuclear energy to space for propelling rockets on long, heavy payload (i.e., manned) missions to the moon and planets. Similarly, significant progress was made in the development of long-lived compact auxiliary nuclear power to be used in space missions, including colonization of the moon and planets, in earth satellites for world-wide TV communications purposes, and for the production of long-lived energy in remote and inaccessible places on earth.

The applications of radioactive isotopes in medicine, agriculture and industry have made tremendous strides in these years. In medicine, radioactive isotopes are used in the United States on some three to four million persons a year in the diagnosis and treatment of diseases of all kinds, which has made a tremendous contribution to the alleviation of human suffering. The Atomic Energy Commission even has under development, in collaboration with the National Institutes of Health, a radioactive power source for a completely implanted artificial heart.

In agriculture, radioisotopes are used for the development of more efficient fertilizers and plant foods, the production of new crops through mutations, the eradication of pests, the deinfestation of grain, and the preservation of food.

In industry, there is a broad application of radioisotopes in quality control processes and in the production of new products, which leads to savings of hundreds of millions of dollars per year.

Nuclear science is also used in investigations in the fields of the humanities, including dating of historical events, and in non-destructive analysis for the validations of coins, jewelry, and art masterpieces, just to mention a few of the applications. It is also finding widespread use in crime detection.

One of the prime efforts of the Atomic Energy Commission, of course, has been and continues to be the development, testing, and production of nuclear weapons, which remain today as our main strategic deterrent. Although I cannot elaborate on this important aspect of my responsibilities as chairman of the Atomic Energy Commission, I can say that we have developed very efficient methods for carrying on this part of our responsibility.

I am particularly proud of the role that I was privileged to play under President Kennedy in connection with the attainment of the Limited Nuclear Test Ban Treaty, which prohibits signatory countries from testing nuclear weapons in the atmosphere, in outer space, or underwater; I was a member of Secretary of State Rusk's delegation to Moscow in August 1963, for the signing of this treaty. And I have been privileged to collaborate with President Johnson in reducing the level of production of fissionable material for our nuclear weapons production program as part of a concerted move toward arms limitation in this important field. Most recently, under the leadership of President Johnson and President Nixon, the Atomic Energy Commission has played a significant role in the attainment of the Non-Proliferation Treaty (NPT), perhaps the most important step in arms limitation since the advent of the Nuclear Age. We have also taken a stronger and more aggressive stand in the need for and implementation of effective safeguards, both nationally and internationally, to assure that nuclear materials intended for peaceful uses are subject to appropriate inspections and controls to insure that they are not diverted to weapons purposes.

During this period the AEC has become more and more involved in international affairs. I have visited forty-one countries and in each country where nuclear programs exist I have visited nuclear facilities and discussed these programs and their implications. I have attended each year since 1961 the annual General Conference of the International Atomic Energy Agency (IAEA), the agency that will administer the vital inspection safeguards to assure compliance with the NPY and which is assuming an increasingly important role in world affairs. These General Conferences have been held in Vienna, Austria, the headquarters of the IAEA, with the exception of the Ninth General Conference, which was held in Tokyo in 1965. In September 1964, President Johnson designated me as chairman of the U.S. delegation to the Third United Nations International Conference on the Peaceful Uses of Atomic Energy, held in Geneva, Switzerland, where I delivered the summary lecture at the conclusion of the conference.

Also, during my tenure as chairman, I have seen our support for basic research in the physical sciences and in biology and medicine more than double. The Stanford Linear Accelerator was successfully completed and put into operation during this period, and the 200 Bev accelerator was initiated. During this period the Atomic Energy Commission increased its support of its on-campus laboratories (Berkeley, UCLA, Notre Dame, Princeton, Harvard, Iowa, etc.) and of many smaller research projects at universities and colleges in the United States. These have led to many fundamental advances in physics, chemistry, mathematics, metallurgy, materials science, medicine, and biology. Of special satisfaction to me is the increased use for research and educational institutions associated with the Argonne National Laboratory, the Oak Ridge National Laboratory, and the Brookhaven National Laboratory. In addition, we now have co-operative arrangements for both nearby and somewhat distant colleges and universities to take advantage of the unique facilities of the commission's Lawrence Radiation Laboratory at Livermore, the Pacific Northwest Laboratory in the state of Washington, the University of California's Los Alamos Scientific Laboratory in New Mexico, and the National Reactor Testing Station in Idaho.

During the last ten to fifteen years I have become quite interested in the improvement of the teaching of science, the need to interest young people in careers in science, the impact of science on society, the necessity for greater scientific literacy among the general public, and the need for scientists to understand social problems and the humanities and to help bridge the gap between the two cultures. Thus I have served, as mentioned earlier, as chairman of the Steering Committee of CHEM Study. I had the privilege of serving on the Commission on the Humanities (1962–65), whose report played an important role in the establishment of the National Foundation on the Arts and the Humanities. I am also serving as president of the Board of Trustees of Science Service, a Washington-based organization with a strong national program for the popularization of science which includes country-wide sponsorship of the high-school science fairs, and as a member of the Board of Directors of the National Educational Television and Radio Center (NET).

This developing interest in the broad implications of science led to an increasing regiment of public speeches covering this subject, which has expanded to even broader areas. Although I had made many speeches on scientific subjects at seminars and meetings of scientific societies, I did not feel myself capable of venturing beyond this domain for a long time and then I approached it gradually. Actually my first speech in such a broader, philosophical vein was not made until I had passed the age of forty; this was entitled "Dawn of the Nuclear Age" and was delivered at the Charter Day Banquet of the Alumni of the University of California, Riverside, in March 1953. This was preceded by a number of talks to University of California, Berkeley, alumni groups, including an alumni tour in 1952 with President Robert Gordon Sproul up and down the state of California, on the "Peaceful Uses of Atomic Energy"; and followed by a similar alumni tour in 1956 with Chancellor Kerr, on which I spoke on the shortage of scientists, and by numerous talks to Berkeley alumni groups on these topics and other topics such as athletics and the Berkeley campus. These beginning attempts were followed by an escalation of topics and number of speeches, including the period of my Berkeley chancellorship, culminating in my Washington period, which has resulted in hundreds of speeches beginning in 1961. Such activity led to my election in 1967 as a member of the Board of Governors and in 1968 as the president of the International Platform Association, an organization of professional speakers.

Despite these other responsibilities and interests I feel that I have managed to stay abreast of the field of research of special interest to me, namely the transuranium elements. I have continued to keep in rather close touch with the research work in this now broad field, to write a number of articles, and to author or co-author a number of books.

Implicit in all that I have written here is the critical role that the University of California played in my development. The young man who entered UCLA in 1929 and went on to spend the major part of his life in association with the Berkeley campus was molded, I believe to an unusual degree, at various stages of his development by that environment. Obviously he would have developed in a much different way had he cast his lot with another institution, but, I sincerely believe, he was fortunate in finding the environment that led to maximum development of his limited potential. He was lucky to be at the right place at the right time.

In retrospect, I can see my stepwise progress, how each phase of my career prepared me for the next. The extraordinary, I called it magic, Berkeley atmosphere of the 1930s offered unparalleled opportunity. My close association with G. N. Lewis showed me firsthand how the world's best chemist worked and thought, and gave me, a young chemist rather lacking in self-confidence, the confidence that was essential to future progress. The association with the Radiation Laboratory, and the amazing Ernest Lawrence, made possible the discoveries with which I was involved before the war. This experience made it possible to carry out my subsequent responsibilities at the wartime Metallurgical Laboratory of the University of Chicago. These experiences, in turn, made it possible for me to carry out my research role in the Radiation Laboratory during the productive period 1946 to 1958. All of this experience, and especially my experience as the Faculty Athletic Representative to the PCC, prepared me for the Berkeley chancellorship. And the administrative experience gained in the latter position, together with all of my research experience, prepared me for the chairmanship of the AEC.

My plan is to return to the University of California when my period of service as chairman of the Atomic Energy Commission comes to an end. It is obvious that I owe my career and whatever I have succeeded in accomplishing to my education at and nurturing by and connection with the University of California. My entire life since graduation from high school has been as a member of the University family in one capacity or another, on two occasions on a leave of absence. I hope to continue my career in one capacity or another in that environment.

"When we honor UC, we celebrate with good reason its academic renown and achievements, its impressive list of Nobel laureates, its contributions to science and the humanities. But we need to recall as well those who struggled through the years to make UC a free, open, and pluralistic campus, a true marketplace of ideas, a University tolerant of a diversity of views and expression within its faculty and students, a place that would become synonymous with this nation's most cherished right—the right of dissent."

LEON F. LITWACK

Leon F. Litwack

MY GRADUATION EXERCISES IN 1951 were held in Edwards Field, the track stadium. I was not present. Some weeks earlier, I had shipped out from San Francisco as a messman on a freighter, the President McKinley, heading for Hong Kong, the Philippines, and Japan. Having grown up in Santa Barbara, having eagerly devoured the sea stories told by Howard Pease, Richard Henry Dana, and Jack London, among others, this was the realization of a boyhood dream. And few academic courses or commencements could have been nearly as instructive.

Thirty years later, a history professor at Berkeley, I was asked to address the Class of '81. I thought it might be instructive to learn more about my own graduation. The University Archives supplied the answer—the full texts of the commencement speeches I had never heard. Robert Gordon Sproul, completing his twenty-first year as President of the University, gave the main address. It was the stuff of which commencement speeches are invariably made: facing the world, limitless horizons, and bold new challenges. We were told that our class belonged to a unique generation. (That we already assumed.) We were told to conduct ourselves as "straight thinking, right acting men and women." (We had been taught what that meant.) We were admonished to avoid both "misguided" conservatives and "insane" radicals. (We knew who they were, and that it was better to be misguided than insane.) We were warned of the stormy world we were entering: "Society everywhere is in revolution.

Western civilization is being challenged by a hostile, militant, fanatic ideology." Such a world, we were told, needed "a generation of clear thinking, well trained youth, capable of strong, enlightened leadership." (That was us.) Finally, we were urged to unify behind the struggle that had to be fought, and to be loyal to our government and ready to serve our country. (My draft notice arrived less than two years later.)

The student speaker, who had distinguished himself on the gridiron, reminded us of the war in Korea, that some of us were bound to serve there, and that our enemy—being Asian—had no concept of the worth of human life. "In the Orient this concept has not yet come to acceptance." Finally, he left us with the immortal words of Andy Smith, the great Cal football coach, the same words inscribed on the Andy Smith bench in Memorial Stadium. "We do not want men who will lie down bravely to die; but men who will fight valiantly to live." To make the point, he repeated those words three times during his brief talk.

What was not said at my graduation was as instructive as what was said. One would not have known that the University of California had just experienced a divisive, destructive, demoralizing controversy over the imposition of a faculty loyalty oath. In the usual accolades to Berkeley as "the truly great University," no one thought to mention the exodus of world renowned scholars who found the intellectual atmosphere too repressive and stifling, or the thirty scholars (none of them Communists or even ex-Communists) dismissed for refusing to sign the oath. In the tributes to the University of California as the marketplace of ideas, no one mentioned the ban on political speakers and on Communists as faculty members. Nor did anyone speak to the national obsession with internal security, the criminalization of dissent, the unquestioning unity demanded for the conduct of a bi-partisan foreign policy, the debasement of intellectual life, the corruption of culture and discourse, or the impoverishment of public life.

But these were the 1950s, the decade we move through rapidly in history courses as we can find so little to say about it.

The Fifties had about it the smell of suburbia and a relatively comfortable, complacent middle class which saw no reason to question its assumptions or beliefs. We were learning to live with The Bomb (the first backyard underground atomic bomb shelters hit the market, and $1,995 would get you one with beige-painted concrete walls, green carpeting, and storage space for canned food.) The music we danced to at the proms was adult, white pop, sing-along, toe-tapping music that spoke of self-contentment and reinforced traditional values. Suzy Parker graced the covers of *Vogue*, *Life*, and *Harpers Bazaar*. ("I come from an average Ku Klux Klan family," she said of her Texas background.) Creativity in this decade was best summed up by the popularity of kits for amateur painters with color-coded canvases. ("The Last Supper" was a favorite at $11.50, including a "beautiful antique gold frame.") Captain America, the Marvel Comic hero, switched from battling Nazis to exposing Communists, a mission he shared with a variety of congressional committees. Television made an auspicious debut, along with Howdy Doody, Mickey Spillane, and the Playboy Bunny. The Class of '51 found its literary inspiration in Herman Wouk's *The Caine Mutiny*, with those immortal words addressed to our generation: "The idea is once you get an incompetent ass as a skipper, there's nothing to do but serve him as though he were the wisest and the best, cover his mistakes, keep the ship going, and bear up."

But for me Berkeley managed to make the Fifties tolerable, even as the University itself was embracing intolerance. As early as junior high school, I had dreamed about coming to Berkeley. It was not only my first choice but my only choice. Santa Barbara, my home town, not only seemed small but conservative and intellectually narrow and stultifying. By comparison, Berkeley had come to symbolize in my mind liberation, openness, and political, cultural, and intellectual ferment. My first glimpses of the campus in the fall of 1948 exceeded my expectations. The place throbbed with energy and excitement, student political activity was extensive and diverse, and my commitment to social and political activism (which had begun in unreceptive Santa Barbara) quickly flourished on a number of fronts. Active in the ASUC, I ran for the office of student representative on a platform calling for voluntary ROTC, a one dollar minimum Fair Bear wage for student workers, more and less-expensive student housing, and an end to racial discrimination. In a subsequent race for the same office (like my hero Eugene Debs, I was a perennial loser), one of my opponents (also a personal friend), Zulfikar Bhutto, endorsed me in the runoff race, saying that "the only difference between our platforms is that he is opposed to excluding Communists from the faculty." (The Regents had barred Communists from the faculty in 1940, an act the faculty did not oppose.) My position was that the competence of any professor should be based on his scholarship and performance in the classroom, not on his political affiliations or beliefs. (Bhutto would return for a visit to the Berkeley campus in 1973 as the Prime Minister of Pakistan.)

Despite Berkeley's reputation as a campus open to a variety of politics, the old mechanisms of repression and surveillance were always very much in place, along with overly protective and vigilant administrators. Robert Gordon Sproul, for all of his unquestioned devotion to UC, assumed a paternalistic attitude toward students and viewed the free exercise of dissent on campus as a source of potential contamination. Students in these years were not said to be influenced by radical ideas; they were said to be infected by them. The FBI made its presence felt on campus, compiling names and affiliations, seeking out information on faculty members as well as students. The Berkeley Police Department had its own "Red Squad." The familiar figure of Inspector O'Meara, notebook in hand, with his photographer nearby, graced nearly every student political gathering at Sather or West Gate.

Administrators expended an inordinate amount of time and energy in searching for ways to contain "subversive" influences. Only in recent years did a student bring to my attention some revealing materials in the University Archives, including a letter from W. A. Brownell, Dean of the School of Education, to President Sproul regarding my admission to the student teaching course required for a secondary teaching credential. Armed with information supplied by the Berkeley Police Department and the FBI, these administrators tried to find "some basis for excluding Mr. Litwak [sic] from [the] program in teacher education.... All agreed that Mr. Litwak should be discouraged, but none was able to provide us grounds for doing so that would stand up in court....[W]e can do nothing other than allow Mr. Litwak to register in the credential program." He did suggest that students assigned to practice teaching be required to sign the loyalty oath. "Whether we may safely take any further steps to defend the University I cannot say; but I should appreciate any suggestion which you [Sproul] or other administrative officers may be able to give us." (Unaware of any of this, I did my student teaching at El Cerrito and Oakland Technical High School and secured the credential.)

169

The contradiction seemed clear enough. Even as the University displayed its motto, *Let There Be Light,* it found various ways in these years to dim or obliterate that light. In our political science and history classes, we studied the Constitution but outside the classroom we were advised to be cautious and prudent in practicing the individual freedoms the Constitution guaranteed. Sproul talked about combining "liberty with order." He embraced the idea of "moderation in all principles." But neither concept was deemed incompatible with surveillance of students' political thoughts, activities, and associations. Controversial speakers were excluded from the campus, and University rules forbade using the college grounds for partisan political activity. Dean of Students Hurford E. Stone, along with local authorities and the FBI, carefully monitored radical and liberal student activism, and they claimed to find alien ideology everywhere they looked—an obsession they shared with many in the 1950s. Dean Stone detected Communist subversion in the opposition to racial discrimination in fraternity charters. Addressing the National Interfraternity Conference, he thought it no accident that racial bars to fraternity membership had been challenged. What he called "new race pressures and the opposition to secret, selective associations" stemmed from a philosophy of social action deeply rooted in Marxian concepts. The first move of a leadership bent on communism or fascism, he subsequently told Provost Monroe Deutsch, in defending his address, "is to control the conditions of membership in secret societies."

Fear, intimidation, repression, and careerism would take its toll. By the mid 1950s, after I had served my two years in the army and returned to Berkeley to enter graduate school, the campus had become quiet and secure, with a student body that was increasingly cautious, passive, and fearful of any ideological contamination. Curious pollsters circulated a petition containing the Bill of Rights—nothing more; most students refused to sign it. It became difficult to find a rebel or a reformer on campus, let alone a Marxist, and increasingly difficult to find anyone who felt very strongly about anything. If students gave their elders no clear sense of who they were, it was because they were very much like their elders. If they made a fetish of noninvolvement and the avoidance of controversy, they were much like the faculty who taught them and the administrators who managed them. One observer thought it a clear case of the bland leading the bland. Students had few gods or heroes, not even Ike. McCarthyism and HUAC taught students and faculty to be careful in choosing their ideas, friends, affiliations, endorsements, and publications. The mass of college students, a teacher observed in 1957, "lead lives of quiet enervation." Predictably, the war in Korea provoked little discussion and virtually no dissent, only a determination to avoid military service.

Whatever dissidence managed to surface in the Fifties seemed somehow illegitimate. The most profound social critic of the era turned out to be a standup nightclub comic who played regularly in the Bay Area—Lenny Bruce. He found his society rational but no longer sane, and he insisted in exploring this madness to its very roots. University administrators in these years expressed pride in their master plans for expansion and consolidation; they liked to talk about their physical plants, their input and output, and they could, in fact, take much pride in their products: easily adaptable, noncontroversial, essentially conventional young men and women who clearly preferred security and the good life to risk and self-assertion, who were ready and willing to subordinate their personal values to those of the institution. "These men do not question the system," an economics professor said approvingly of my generation. "They want to get in there and lubricate the machinery. They're not rebels; they'll be social technicians for a better society." In 1959, not long after he had become President of the University of California, Clark Kerr said of its students, "The employers will love this generation. ... They are going to be easy to handle. There aren't going to be any riots."

Throughout my years at Berkeley I managed somehow to balance my political activism with a continuing fascination for history. My political and social commitments (around such issues as racism, trade unionism, the loyalty oath, and the Cold War) had no doubt influenced both the way I looked at the past and my decision to specialize in the history of African Americans and race relations. The study of history, on the other hand, had also helped to inform and shape those commitments. Since high school in Santa Barbara, I had come to be moved by an awareness of the uses and abuses of the past and of the fundamental contradictions between my country's often proclaimed ideals and its practices, between its professed egalitarianism and deep inequalities in wealth and in conditions of work and life. Clearly, as my studies at Berkeley confirmed, history was more than the dead past; the way in which it was written and taught had consequences, and black Americans, in particular, had seen how it might be used both to explain and sustain their repression.

A chance meeting in my junior year at Berkeley proved memorable. A friend called and asked me to come over to his apartment; he said someone wanted to meet me. I was ushered into the living room, and I recognized his guest immediately—it was W. E. B. Du Bois. I had read his books, and one of them I had used to write a report refuting my high school textbook. But why had he singled me out? He wanted, he said, to meet an undergraduate in history. He wanted to know what I was learning in particular about slavery and Reconstruction. My response was in two parts: the textbook (by John D. Hicks) reflected familiar distortions and biases; the course lectures did not, and their content impressed and astonished Du Bois, as they revealed new ways of thinking about both slavery and Reconstruction. The person teaching the course was a young assistant professor, Kenneth M. Stampp, who would have a profound impact on my thinking and with whom I would ultimately write my dissertation.

I left Berkeley in 1958 to teach at the University of Wisconsin. When I returned here as an associate professor of history six years later, the harmonious political, intellectual, and social system characteristic of the past several decades was coming apart, and the legitimacy of our institutions, our dominant values, and assumptions were being disputed as never before. Within a year, Berkeley symbolized around the world a new spirit of dissent, in which students thought to question and confront the insensitive and faceless bureaucracies that made the most critical decisions affecting their lives, including the programmed brutality being visited upon Southeast Asia.

The sight of the massive rallies, some 5,000 or more students filling Sproul Plaza, recalled the pitiful handful present at Sather Gate only a decade earlier. I caught a glimpse of Inspector O'Meara, standing on the balcony of the student union overlooking the huge throng below him. It must have been for him an awesome and intimidating scene, well beyond the reach of his notebook, his photographer, and perhaps his comprehension. Within a year or so, he had retired, along with the Red Squad.

Historians, like others, would be very much affected by the domestic and campus upheavals, the civil rights movement, and the war in Vietnam. Growing numbers of scholars, white and black, turned their attention to groups long excluded from historical study, to people who had spent their lives in relative obscurity, who had never shared the fruits of affluence, who had never enjoyed power—the very people who had initially inspired my interest in history. In seeking to capture their historical experience, I now found myself with plenty of company. With the inclusion of new voices and a greater sensitivity to the complexities and varieties of cultural documentation, the study and teaching of American history would never be the same again.

I entered history in the hope that my work would make some difference, not only the books and articles, the public lectures, and the films, but most important my teaching, the nearly 30,000 students I have taught at Berkeley over the past thirty years, mostly in the survey American history course (which I continue to teach) and in the course on the History of African Americans and Race Relations (first taught at Berkeley in 1968). The challenge is to force students to see and to feel the past in ways that may be genuinely disturbing, to overcome cultural illiteracy, and to bring into their historical consciousness the perceptions and experiences of people ordinarily left outside the framework of history.

The University of California thrives on challenging the conventional wisdom. And our students, as in the 1960s, have often insisted on participating in the shaping of history, rather than being passive and complacent objects. That is a fine tradition, though it has led at times a precarious existence. When we honor UC, we celebrate with good reason its academic renown and achievements, its impressive list of Nobel laureates, its contributions to science and the humanities. But we need to recall as well those who struggled through the years to make UC a free, open, and pluralistic campus, a true marketplace of ideas, a University tolerant of a diversity of views and expression within its faculty and students, a place that would become synonymous with this nation's most cherished right—the right of dissent. The time to be alarmed about a great university, after all, is not when its students are exercising publicly their freedom of expression but when they are quiet, when they despair of changing society, even of understanding it.

Few universities of any standing have not come under suspicion of subverting the society around them. What defines the university is its receptivity to the new, the untried, even the alien. The University asks the most uncomfortable questions. It is the place where we question, even undermine old dogmas and values, where we force students to reexamine their assumptions and to see and feel in ways that may be genuinely disturbing. And the University sometimes pays a heavy price for its intellectual hospitality and diversity. The University of California has been denounced for godlessness, free thinking, debauchery, subversion, coddling Communists and radicals, and for exposing students to radical and unconventional ideas. Whenever I hear those charges, I am always most proud of my alma mater. That means the University is doing its job.

When I spoke to the history graduating class of 1981, I expressed the hope that it would produce its share of dissidents, rebels, and disturbers of the peace, for whom personal commitment to social and racial justice will be nothing less than a moral imperative, men and women who will choose to question our sanity and values, who will opt for the highest kind of loyalty to their country—a willingness to unmask its leaders and subject its institutions and ideology to critical examination. History teaches us, as I have told my classes, that it is not the rebels, it is not the curious, it is not the dissidents who endanger a society but rather the accepting, the unthinking, the unquestioning, the docile, the obedient, the silent, and the indifferent. That lesson Berkeley has not always heeded, but it remains timeless.

Dissent and disturbing the peace, like Oski and the Golden Bear, have become a Berkeley tradition. It is a legacy each new class inherits, along with a recognition of the underlying fragility of the freedoms we enjoy. Unlike some traditions, this one is worth preserving. The health of the academic culture, the vitality of the campus, the sanity and survival of the nation depend on it.

174

"[By the end of the 1930s the National Park Service] had a large bureau with areas from coast to coast and in Hawaii and Alaska, and our responsibilities for protection of them were so different from those of any other agency that there could be no danger of the National Park Service being absorbed by some other bureau."

HORACE MARDEN ALBRIGHT

Horace Marden Albright

I HAVE BEEN ENGAGED IN ACTIVITIES relating to the conservation of the natural resources of America, with emphasis on
national park establishment, administration, and protection
since leaving the University of California in 1913, at the end of
undergraduate work and one graduate year in the School of
Jurisprudence. Now as I approach eighty years of age, I find
myself the chairman of a group of men and women who are planning the Pacific Tropical Botanical Garden under a charter from
Congress and with an initial grant of $1 million by the late Robert
Allerton of Kauai, Hawaii.

The University's officers, scientists, and alumni have
been advisors and aides and allies in many projects, and able
alumni have been associates of mine in and out of public service.

I was fortunate in having opportunities to help establish
and manage a new federal government bureau in twenty years'
service in the Department of the Interior, and subsequently to
head an industrial enterprise which built and operated the first
successful potassium (potash) mine in the Western Hemisphere.
As a member of organizations outside of government, I have
taken part in many movements concerned with historic site and
structure preservation, and resource conservation causes involving national and state parks, wilderness forests, seashores, recreation areas, mineral and water resources.

My education at the University of California prepared
me for these activities and my opportunity to engage in them
came to me at the University. So did the inspiration for interest

in public service.

I went to Berkeley in August 1908, to enter the University as a freshman. I came from the village of Bishop in the Owens Valley, near the California-Nevada state line in Inyo County. My high school, only seven years old when I was a senior, had not been accredited by the University, but Dr. W. Scott Thomas of the Department of Education had personally examined the four seniors and had reported that we should be admitted on probation with the provision that we pass the first semester exams creditably or be required to pass the regular entrance examination for readmission. Only two of the four went to Berkeley and we had no difficulty in passing the tests at the end of the first semester.

I was a mountain boy unfamiliar with city life. Our high school had so few students that we had no supervised competitive sports, nor training for them. Our games were some baseball and basketball, in which girls often had to be drafted to complete teams, and foot races on festive occasions. However, I camped, fished, hiked, and climbed in the Sierra and rode saddle horses, followed pack animals and camped with forest rangers on patrols in wilderness regions, had jobs haying on ranches and worked a summer in a sawmill. I quit my mill job and rode horseback forty miles to take the train to Berkeley.

On the train in Nevada, I met Beverly Clendenin, also on his way to enter the University, and we became close friends. At Berkeley as a freshman on probation I was very shy, introspective, and lonesome. I knew only five people at the University: Dr. Thomas, three friends from Bishop, and Beverly Clendenin. My father, who had emigrated from Canada at the age of twenty-two and whose education had ended with the sixth grade, had worked in mines in Nevada until the 1893 slump in silver. He wanted me to be a mining engineer and hoped I would seek admission to the new Mackey School of Mines in Reno. My mother had been reared in mining camps and had an understandable aversion to the thought of her three sons spending their lives in them. Besides, she thought her oldest son was not engineering material; I was concerned with the mountains, lakes, streams, trees, fish, and animals, and with history. She favored the University of California.

My maternal grandfather, who had quit mining and was in the logging business when I was growing up, spent two winters with us. He favored better forest management, was a progressive Republican, and a strong Roosevelt adherent. From him I heard much conservation talk, pro and con, about the new management policies which reduced livestock pasturage on the high summer ranges in the mountains and was beginning to enforce better methods of timber cutting on government lands.

All of this was leading me away from mining. At the University I registered in the College of Commerce, believing I was taking a middle route between mining and the lumber industry. My courses for my first two college years were in English, economics, political science, math, languages, and, of course, military drill and physical education. Having no training in athletics, and very little in dramatics and debating, my activities outside the classroom were on the social side—bleacher enjoyment of sports, rallies, dances, and Greek Theatre musicals and dramatics, both amateur and professional. I tried out for a place in a college production of *Caesar and Cleopatra,* but drew only a part as a Roman soldier who walked behind the Queen's chief nurse and fanned her with a palm frond. I was a soldier in Sothern and Marlowe presentations of two Shakespearean tragedies in the Greek Theatre, and nearly froze both times when cold fog enveloped us in our tin armor over thin underclothes. Some soldiers deserted, but most of us did not, for we needed the modest compensation promised us.

By the end of my sophomore year, I had many new friends, as I had made it a rule to do everything possible to break away from the shyness and to make friends. I joined the Del Rey Club, a local fraternity, and managed it as an upperclassman for two years. I worked at miscellaneous jobs during the school year and vacations since my home was too far away for holiday or vacation visits and the rail fares too expensive. So the University was an all-year-round residence for me.

In my junior year, a girl invited me, along with two boys from my club, to a dance at her home in Berkeley. I enjoyed the party very much, dancing twice with a classmate whom I thought was a lovely, charming girl, a vivacious brunette with big brown eyes. Over the weekend I dreamed of taking her to various college affairs, if she would go with me! On Monday afternoon, walking up the central path toward North Hall, she passed me with an armful of books and gave no sign of recognition. When I was working in the Recorder's Office, I peeked at her scholastic record. It was so much better than mine that I was further disheartened. I realized that she was too pretty, too charming, too smart for me. Eventually, as graduate students, we became acquainted. In 1914 we became engaged and were married in December 1915.

In the autumn of 1910, many of us took an active interest in politics. Hiram Johnson was the Republican nominee for governor and the Southern Pacific Railroad was the whipping boy of the campaign. It was loudly and widely proclaimed that California had to be rescued from the railroad's heavy hand, which was controlling the state, dictating legislation in Sacramento, and even dominating the governor. I was enjoying my economics and political science courses and Professor Thomas Reed, the head of the poli-sci department, influenced some of us to take a special interest in politics that year. Johnson won in November and with my pioneer grandfather I witnessed his inauguration at Sacramento on January 2, 1911.

At the end of my junior year, I decided to major in jurisprudence. I changed registration from the College of Commerce to Social Sciences and planned to take only law courses in my senior year. Near the end of my senior year, I was seeking employment in the University to carry me through my two graduate years in the School of Jurisprudence and I applied for a job as reader in economics. Professor Adolph C. Miller, the chairman of the department, employed me at fifty dollars per month and outlined duties enough to frighten away a law student, for the courses in jurisprudence were tough and required an enormous amount of reading. Professor Miller occasionally suggested that I forsake the law for economics and work for higher degrees with a view to college teaching. How great was his interest in me suddenly appeared shortly after Woodrow Wilson was inaugurated and Franklin K. Lane was appointed Secretary of the Interior. Lane and Miller had been in the University together and had continued their close friendship through the years. A week or so after the inauguration, Secretary Lane invited Professor Miller to Washington as assistant to the Secretary, to have general supervision over the Bureau of Education, the territories of Hawaii and Alaska, and the national parks, for which there was no central organization. Dr. Miller accepted and promised to report early in the summer. He asked if he could bring me along and was told he could. Miller told me he wanted me to go to Washington with him for a year, saying it would be a good thing for me to see something of the United States besides parts of California and Nevada. He argued that a year in the Interior Department would give me sound experience useful in my practice of law. I had only one more year of law study before finishing my courses and had been appointed assistant in economics for the next year at seventy-five dollars per month and was perfectly situated to finish the requirements for my degree, so I declined his invitation.

Dr. Miller guaranteed me pay of $100 per month, although he had no idea what the Secretary had in mind, as well as funds for my rail ticket and other expenses for the trip from Berkeley to Washington. After consulting with several other professors, a few friends, and of course, my family, who all advised me to accept, I told Dr. Miller I would go with him. I loved the University and was not happy to be leaving it. It had been home to me for five years and given me a sound foundation for a career, as well as opening up this new opportunity.

I arrived in Washington on a hot Saturday morning in May 1913, and walked to the Interior Department. All offices were open on Saturdays, and I reported to Mr. Lane's office, where I was administered the oath of office as "confidential clerk to the Secretary." I was dumbfounded by the salary of $1,600 per year.

Professor Miller arrived in mid-June. Neither of us knew very much about the department, so we did considerable reading about the affairs of our department and spent time in getting acquainted with our associates in the offices of the Secretary and the solicitor, and the chiefs of the various bureaus and other agencies.

Most of the supervisory duties of Dr. Miller's office were routine and only involved conferences with executives and signing of official papers. The important objective to which Dr. Miller had to address himself was securing legislation for the establishment of a bureau of national parks, bills for which had been introduced in previous sessions of Congress.

When the Federal Reserve Board was formed, Dr. Miller was appointed one of the first governors. He asked me to go with him to the new board, but I preferred to stay in the Interior Department.

During my first year in Washington I attended Georgetown University Law School at night, graduated in June 1914 with the Bachelor of Laws degree, and was admitted to the bar of the District of Columbia. On vacation in California that summer, I was admitted to the bar of California after passing examinations in Los Angeles. At the Interior Department I carried out many routine assignments and managed Dr. Miller's affairs there as best I could with the help of the permanent civil service staff.

In December 1914, Secretary Lane persuaded another Californian to take Dr. Miller's place, Stephen Mather, and I was assigned to be his secretary. Mr. Mather made it plain that the national parks would be his primary interest and lost no time in outlining a whole year's activities. His tentative plan called for extensive travel for him and for me, especially in the West. He increased his staff by employing a few people whose salaries he paid personally. He thought the American people knew little about the national parks, and he wanted them to be informed. And he wanted to help advance legislation for a national park bureau. He planned a conference of national park superintendents to be held at Berkeley.

The Berkeley conference was a great success, with members of the faculty, classmates of 1887, and William E. Colby and other Sierra Club leaders, participating in discussions. The conference of March 1915 broke up after a day at the San Francisco Exposition. Mather and I returned to Washington. With the adjournment of Congress, Mather managed to join a subcommittee of the House of Representatives Appropriations Committee in the West. For mid-July he planned a trail trip across the Sierra from Giant Forest in Sequoia National Park. Already he had decided to obtain, if possible, a large extension of the Sequoia Park. His Mountain Party, as we called it, was designed to develop support for this vast park enlargement, and for a national park bureau in Washington. The Mountain Party was a gratifying success. Before leaving the Giant Forest, Mather learned that the beautiful area of enormous sequoia trees was privately owned. At once, he secured an option on it for purchase at $50,000, and when Congress convened in December he asked for an appropriation to complete the transaction. Congress delayed in making the funds available, and the option expired. The new option price was $70,000. The trustees of the National Geographic Society made a grant of $20,000 and the Giant Forest passed into government ownership.

Mather and I covered several park areas in 1916, but concentrated on legislation for the establishment of a bureau to be called the National Park Service. The President signed the bill on August 25, 1916.

Hawaii and Lassen Volcanic national parks were authorized that year and the Mount McKinley Park legislation was being advanced in the Pubic Land Commission. Mather, working feverishly, organized concessions in Yellowstone Park, which had been opened experimentally in 1915 and permanently in 1916, helped a new concession company in Mount Rainier, personally bought land for the headquarters of Glacier Park and just before the election of 1916, studied the Indiana Sand Dunes between Gary and Michigan City, Indiana, a superb area of national park quality. In 1917, Mr. Mather collapsed in a nervous breakdown and had to spend several months away from Washington. I had to pick up the reins he had dropped and carry on his program, provide funds for the establishment of the National Park Service, defend the budget for the next fiscal year, direct the day-to-day operations, and plan for the organization of the new bureau.

When it was finally established, I was appointed acting director, the position I was to fill for the remainder of the year. As acting director, I had to organize the bureau by filling positions authorized by the act creating the agency. I had to go to Yellowstone Park to supervise the installation of the new bus transportation system, supplanting the horse-drawn stages, and inspect most of the national parks. I went to Utah and visited the colorful and scenic region of the upper Virgin River and what was called Little Zion Canyon. Out of that exploratory tour came Zion National Park.

Perhaps the most difficult task in managing the national park system in wartime was to prevent opening some of the parks, especially Yosemite, Glacier, and Mt. Rainier, to pasturage of livestock and other commercial objectives. The pressures for the use of the forage resources of the wild areas of the parks was great, often supported by political allies. I resisted these demands with the support of the Sierra Club, the Mountaineers of the Seattle region, and the Mazamas of Oregon.

In 1918 the Save-the-Redwoods League was formed, whose goal was to acquire outstanding groves of old-growth redwood trees to be preserved as state or national parks. The first officers were all connected with the University of California and its immense success is a University achievement.

About this time, we created a Division of Landscape Architects for landscape protection in the management of the national park system. It developed master plans for the national park areas, including improvements such as roads, trails, buildings, telephone and power lines. All construction and mainte-

184

nance operations had to be supervised by its technicians. The architects designed new buildings for the government and approved plans for concessionaires' tourist facilities. The division's work was so highly regarded in professional circles that several executives in the agency were made honorary members of the American Society of Landscape Architects.

In June 1919, Director Mather appointed me superintendent of Yellowstone Park, which had been under military protection and administration since 1886. While I had my headquarters at old Fort Yellowstone at Mammoth Hot Springs, after the winter snows closed the roads and trails, my assignment called for inspections of other western parks, conferences with other field superintendents and technicians, and the writing of reports back to Washington. We built a field organization with headquarters in San Francisco, and worked closely with the new School of Forestry at the University.

My assignment to Yellowstone was an exciting challenge. The park, created in 1872, was the first national park created in the world. It is a huge rectangle astride the Continental Divide, embracing well over two million acres of wild mountain and forest territory lying in three states: Wyoming, Montana, and Idaho. It is nearly twenty years older than these states, hence was and still is an exclusive federal legal entity like the District of Columbia.

With the end of World War I, Americans began to travel by automobile, even though there were very few miles of paved roads in the West, and none in the national parks except for four miles of experimental pavement in Yellowstone, put there by the army engineers. The park roads had to be widened for automobile traffic, although several important sections could be kept open only for one-way travel for years.

There were no campgrounds for visitors coming with their own equipment, no sanitation facilities, no garbage disposal equipment. Only people coming by rail and traveling in buses via the hotel and lodge systems could be adequately cared for, and soon the concessionaires' facilities became overcrowded and had to be extended. Travel to the park increased rapidly. There were over 200 miles of roads to be maintained, about half of which had to be sprinkled with water twice a day to control the dust. There were 1,000 miles of trails and about 500 miles of telephone lines, a few small power plants, and one large one to provide light and power for our headquarters at Mammoth Hot Springs, one of the four or five principal visitor objectives. Principal points of interest where there were hotels, lodges, and stores were long distances apart—fifteen to fifty miles.

186

To meet the new travel patterns following the war, every feature of Yellowstone's facilities had to be modified, extended, or rebuilt, and for the rapidly increasing camper population entirely new facilities had to be constructed. Naturally we had to await appropriations for these improvements and they came very slowly.

We never made any plans for opening new sections of the park as we thought the untouched regions should be kept as wilderness. Today less than 10 percent of the total park area is accessible by highways. My Yellowstone organization contained a protective force of thirty rangers, increased in summer by sixty temporary seasonal men, all college boys; about twenty road maintenance crews, telephone, sanitation, trail, and such construction gangs as our improvement programs demanded. At times there were several hundred men and women employed in the summer. Being executive head of a completely federal area, I was chief prohibition agent, and all my rangers were also agents. We successfully enforced the law, considering the conditions under which we had to work.

We had visitors from all over the world, occasionally including high government officials and even royalty. Our American visitors came from every state and territory, officials from local administrators and legislators to governors, senators, and congressmen. We entertained Presidents Harding and Coolidge and Secretary Herbert Hoover just before his election as Chief Executive. We usually had ceremonies on the day in June when we opened the park to visitors coming by train and bus, and sought prominent men as speakers for these occasions.

From 1919 to 1928 the National Park Service, under Stephen Mather, moved ahead rapidly, adding new parks, extending old ones, providing for visitors in ever increasing numbers, receiving as much favorable consideration of Congress as could be given within the limits of the Coolidge economy policies. We sought to enlarge Sequoia National Park by adding the Kings River region after securing the Kern River country in 1926. We tried hard to secure 800,000 acres as an addition to Yellowstone to include the Teton Mountains and other Jackson Hole lands. We planned entirely new parks. We tried to have transferred to us the battlefield parks and historic sites such as Gettysburg, Shiloh, and Appomattox from the War Department, and the parks and memorials of the District of Columbia, which were also under army supervision. Local opposition, however, prevented us from having this done at that time.

In 1926, after a trip to Yellowstone Park, John D. Rockefeller Jr. undertook to acquire the private lands which stood in the way of a Grand Teton National Park. He acquired over 30,000 acres, which he then donated to the federal government.

In November 1928, Director Mather suffered a stroke of paralysis and had to resign. I was appointed to succeed him. As his assistant in the field, I had been in charge of Yellowstone for nearly ten years, had covered the western parks year after year, had spent weeks and sometimes months in Washington every year, had many friends in Congress, and knew every part of the Interior Department. I had served under five Secretaries of the Interior.

As director, I endeavored to carry on Mr. Mather's activities and his general policies. Congress created a small Grand Teton National Park early in my administration and some other parks and national monuments followed.

In 1929 I was part of a committee to help President Hoover select a site for his weekend retreat and vacation spot.

The place we chose was eventually to become part of the Shenandoah National Park.

About this time Congress authorized the appointment of a commission to arrange for a celebration of the anniversary of the Battle of Yorktown, and soon, another to plan a national commemoration of the bicentennial of the birth of George Washington. In the development of programs by these commissions, I saw opportunities to expand the National Park Service in territory and responsibilities into the field of historic preservation. We found a way to acquire the birthplace of George Washington and built a memorial home which architects had planned and regarded as one that would be in the spirit of the colonial times when Washington was born. It was dedicated on February 11, 1932, Washington's birthday under the old calendar.

We worked on a plan to acquire Jamestown, then an island in the James River, and the battlefield of Yorktown, and connect them with Williamsburg by a parkway. Legislation for this project followed in 1930, together with authority for appropriations of funds to purchase lands and rights of way. Thus we began what is now the Colonial National Historic Park.

In the meantime, three national parks to be established in the East were being acquired by the states involved— Great Smoky Mountains in North Carolina and Tennessee, Shenandoah in Virginia, and Mammoth Cave in Kentucky. I had to spend considerable time on problems of acquisition and boundaries.

Early in 1933 Secretary of the Interior Harold L. Ickes was made chairman of the Public Works Administration, and he assigned me as a sort of temporary assistant to work on public construction programs. My job was to consult all Interior Department bureau chiefs, and help them compile data for projects in their jurisdictions. Of course, the Park Service already had many sound national park projects in master plans, thanks to our engineering and landscape divisions. I had to argue in the PWA executive sessions for projects for the whole department. At the same time, President Roosevelt secured legislation for the employment of young men in conservation work, authority for what was called the Civilian Conservation Corps. It was organized by a council of four men, each representing a cabinet officer. We were to put 200,000 men to work in camps by early June. The President added new contingents such as unemployed veterans seeking the bonus from Congress and others, and so it was that we established 1,400 camps and had about 300,000 men in camp by early summer, and within the appointed time.

It was about this time that we got the long-sought transfer of all War Department battlefield parks, memorials, and cemeteries, even Arlington—which we had re-transferred to the War Department. We were awarded the parks and memorials in the District of Columbia. This reorganization gave the Park Service one or more areas in many eastern states, and we were now involved deeply in the preservation and administration of historic sites. We had a large bureau with areas from coast to coast and in Hawaii and Alaska, and our responsibilities for protection of them were so different from those of any other agency that there could be no danger of the National Park Service being absorbed by some other bureau.

With my organization expanded and thoroughly entrenched in historic preservation, and with our participation in the new emergency agencies—CCC, public works, and other lesser ones—I felt I could accept an offer to leave the government after more than twenty years in the Interior Department and accept the position of chief executive officer of the United States Potash Company, which had just completed a mine and refinery in New Mexico. I resigned in August 1933 and entered the business world.

I came into the mining business prepared for the work ahead of me. I had a mining background from boyhood, a legal education, long experience in Washington, and wide knowledge of the West and its leaders. We were mining largely on lands leased from the state of New Mexico and the federal government, and operated under the observation of the United States Geological Survey as to mining plans, ore analysis and exploration, extraction of ore and royalty payments, and were subject to the United States Bureau of Mines as to mine safety. We were in reality carrying on a conservation enterprise, involving a natural resource necessary to the nation's welfare. My own staff was an exceptionally efficient one and our company prospered. The British aspect of our operations required an occasional trip to Europe, and I had opportunities to inspect potash mines in France, Germany, and Spain. We greatly expanded our mine production and the output of our refineries in order to meet our country's needs for potash in wartime, since all European imports were stopped during the war. After the war, the Secretary of the Interior organized the National Minerals Industry Council to advise on postwar problems of the mining industry. Donald McLaughlin was its first chairman, and I succeeded him as the second and last, as the council dissolved itself when there seemed to be no more need for it.

In the field of conservation I continued my interest in parks, wildlife, and recreational areas, and spent time on historic preservation as a trustee of the American Scenic and Historic Preservation Society. In 1949 I was one of a group of men and women who helped in securing a charter from Congress for the National Trust for Historic Preservation and was a trustee until 1962.

Other conservation activities were in the National Audubon Society, the Theodore Roosevelt Association, the American Forestry Association, the National Parks Association, the Wilderness Society, and, of course, the Sierra Club, which had an Atlantic Charter.

In 1956, when the United States Potash Company merged with the Pacific Coast Borax Company to form the United States Borax and Chemical Corp., I retired and became a business consultant. Then I was able to enter more intensively into conservation of resources activity through organizations.

In October 1952, I helped organize Resources for the Future, Inc., a non-profit enterprise which the Ford Foundation undertook to finance in our initial program of research and education in the development, conservation, and use of natural resources. I became chairman of the Board of Directors and served from 1952 to 1961. Grants by the Foundation since 1953 have totaled over $10 million and a new grant for $8 million to extend well into the next decade has just been made.

The National Park Service is now a large and internationally respected agency of the United States Government. It administers over 220 areas and will soon take over more with the recent authorization for a Redwood National Park, a scenic trail system, and a wild river system. Visitors each year total well over 100 million. Always an ally of the National Park Service, the Sierra Club, now an association with chapters in many parts of the United States and with 60,000 members, continues to be influential in resource conservation. California alumni have from its organization in 1892 been leaders in its various fields of activity.

I have had a wonderful life, whose groundwork was laid on the Berkeley campus and which since college days has been constantly enriched by association with the University's alumni, faculty, and affairs.

191

"I found a wonderful life at the University. It was as if the whole world had opened up for me after the sheltered years at home and in a girls' school. Cal gave me the opportunity to be my own person."

RHODA HAAS GOLDMAN

Rhoda Haas Goldman

Y FIRST MEMORY OF CAL is going to the football games at Memorial Stadium with my father, probably in the late 1930s, when we were living at the corner of Pacific and Lyon streets in San Francisco. It was a Saturday morning ritual during the season. We often picnicked at the Hearst Mining Circle and then walked to the game. I was in my early teens when this weekly fall routine started.

I had an extra interest in cheering the football team to victory. These were the years the Lewis brothers played. They were the sons of my father's classmate and friend, Louis "Windy" Lewis, from Southern California. Cal was synonymous with Berkeley then. My background was pure University of California! My grandfather on my mother's side, Sigmund Stern, had attended in the 1880s. So had my father, Class of 1910; my two brothers '37 and '40 respectively, my husband a 1941 graduate, and his father, Class of 1909. When my two brothers were in college, we would often meet at our picnic spot before the football game. My loyalty to Cal has never wavered to this day. We're "Old Blues."

In 1940, with encouragement from my parents, my grandmother, Rosalie M. Stern, donated a much-needed dormitory to the school. It was designed by her friend, William W. Wurster, a world-renowned architect and Berkeley professor, while the furnishings were the creative work of Francis Elkins, a noted interior decorator. Granny originally decided that this would be a residence hall for men. My mother pointed out, tactfully, that there already was a residence for men, Bowles Hall, and that I might be attending Berkeley. As a result, Stern Hall, located in the northeast corner of the campus, became a dormitory for women. My years at Berkeley were largely influenced by this innovation.

I graduated from the Katherine Delmar Burke School in San Francisco in June 1942, and considered going to college in the East as my grades allowed me to be admitted without taking the college boards. How different the admission procedures were in those days! Because of World War II, my parents did not want me to be so far away. It wasn't the time of rebellion by children. I agreed to attend the University of California, vowing to myself, however, that I was going to act as if I were 3,000 miles away. I became one of the first ninety residents when the dorm opened in fall 1942, and Stern Hall became the very center of my campus experience.

Initially, I had a single room, but after one semester there was a vacancy in a double room, and a new friend, Natalie Burdick, asked me to become her roommate. All the dorm rooms were furnished with simple individual wood desks, bureaus, and beds; the closets had ample hanging and shelf space. The bedrooms formed a squared-off U shape with a bathroom at each right angle. The entrance and small parking lot were on the upper side of Hearst Avenue, which meant the public rooms, living room, small library, and beau parlor all faced the Bay and had wonderful views. The office, which comprised switchboard, mail slots, desks, and a private office for the housemother, was opposite these rooms. An outside balcony ran across the length of the public rooms. A handsome curved staircase provided access to a lower floor. On one side was the dining room and kitchen and on the other the game room. We also used the back entrance for our exit to classes and the lengthy walk from our perch on the hill. It was said that Stern girls could always be defined by their muscular legs. We moved into #314 and we decorated it with light blue bedspreads with white stars sprinkled in the fabric. We also found stickum-stars for our ceiling that glowed at night when the lights were turned off.

Governed by strict curfew rules, freshmen and sophomores could be out one night during the week until 1:00 A.M., and until 2:30 A.M. on weekends. Upper classmen could stay out until 2:30 A.M. on weekends. Our best-known house- mother, Mrs. Florence Greene, would stand by the door while everyone was saying her fond goodnights and lock it promptly at 2:30 A.M. There were severe penalties for rule-breaking ranging from grounding for a number of days to expulsion from the dorm for flagrant disobedience. Tales of keys thrown down or other help so friends would not be locked out were numerous. Mrs. Greene had an apartment on the top floor of Stern. There was also a graduate student in residence who had an adjoining single room in the middle of the third floor. No one had a telephone in her room: we would be paged by a buzzer system and pick up the extension at the end of the hall. In the basement there was a laundry room as well as the loading area. An extra-wide door led to this space since most of us came with trunks holding our clothes and other possessions when we moved in.

We could only meet our boyfriends in the public rooms. However, when male relatives visited or there was the occasional necessity to have a young man in the residential area, we would have to shout as we came into the dorm, "Man on second" (or third, or whatever the case may be).

We were served three meals a day by student hashers who were residents. Breakfast was buffet, but lunch and dinner were sit-down affairs. There was a late cold lunch for those who had noon classes. I guess it was fairly natural that we tried to avoid sitting with Mrs. Greene, a fate that was left to the latecomers. On Saturdays, a home economics class practiced by preparing the lunch. I remember some weird concoctions, including a purple apple dessert. On Sundays, only two meals were served and a varying group of us would get together to create something simple but edible such as crackers and cheese, plus soup or anything else that came from a can, that we could warm up. Hot plates were frowned upon.

In a sense, all ninety of us were pioneers in a new venture. A house council was formed and residents served in this as well as in many other necessary capacities. Stipends were given for office and switchboard duty as well as for bussing tables. Because we had all started together—freshmen, sophomores, juniors, and seniors—we became close friends. Whatever your class, you were allowed to remain at Stern until you graduated, unless you broke the rules or flunked out. Most of us shared a number of years together. A fiftieth reunion was held in October 1992, and it was great fun to catch up and renew friendships with the many former dorm mates who came.

A word about my three roommates. Natalie Burdick was a junior at the time we first got together. She ran for student body president in her senior year and was the first woman to hold that office. She was not studious and her cramming consisted of writing notes on the palm of her hand before exams. However, I never knew if she used them or not. I was fortunate that my background had prepared me for bluebook exams. I kept up with my work, yet still crammed at the time of semi-finals and finals. At this time of the year, coffee was always available and I recall drinking three to four cups in an evening so I could stay awake past midnight. Natalie was the recipient of my good nature, as I loaned her some of my clothes and my class notes. We had different philosophies and that, plus her appearing in one of my favorite dresses at a get-out-the-vote rally without prior permission, cooled our relationship. We had not seen each other since her graduation until the reunion. By then, my animosity had disappeared and we were happy to catch up on the years that had intervened. Gloria Henderson, my roommate during my sophomore year, was exotic looking and spoke with an accent best described as "sultry." She was wise in the ways of the world and had plenty of dates. She taught me lessons on makeup; however, my naiveté kept her from divulging more of her secrets. My roommate for the next two years was Marie Laws. We had fun together and have maintained our friendship through all these years. Several more of us who lived at Stern those years have maintained a close connection.

My first year at college, 1942 to 1943, had a full enrollment of students, approximately 13,500. With the draft, that
number dwindled to 7,000. The males on campus were either
NROTC (Naval Reserve Officer Training Corp), ASTP (Army Student Training Program), or those who had, for various reasons,
been classified as 4F. With the war, a Pacific Coast black-out was
enforced and women were told to travel in pairs in the dark. We'd
adhere to this rule whenever possible, but as time went on, I
found it hard to do, as often I was the only one going to a particular meeting or activity such as Prytanean and Mortar Board, a
senior class honor society with only ten members. One advantage was that I lost my fear of the dark! This is also education!

The war had other effects on us. We had to turn in our
ration cards to a central office, but the purchasing agent for the
college dorms must have been a whiz because I don't recall any
real deprivation as far as our meals were concerned. We would
sign up to fill in for farm labor and to harvest crops where and
when it would be helpful. One day we were sent to harvest wal-
nuts. Our hands were stained green and even black. When we
arrived back at Stern, I tried every remedy, including Lysol and
bleach, to return my hands to their normal color. It was particularly important since there was a dance scheduled at the dorm
that night, and I had a blind date. Everything went fine until a
"friend?" said, "Let's see the palms of your hands." I don't think
my date asked me out after that.

I took advantage of a course being presented on campus
and became a Nurse's Aide. At first we worked at Cowell Hospital, the college infirmary. There were few patients there, and I
don't recall any of them having a serious illness. After a short
while, a group of us were bussed each Thursday afternoon to and
from the University of California Hospital in San Francisco. We
worked on various wards carrying trays, helping patients to eat,
and doing the necessary with bedpans.

Gas was rationed, but only a handful (if that) of friends
owned or had the use of a car. I used the Key system train that

went across the Oakland–San Francisco Bay Bridge to commute home, when and if I went, either for a special occasion or for a weekend every couple of months.

I recall my first activity was to join the ASUC (Associated Students of University of California) Housing Board. In my senior year, the semester of 1944, I was vice president and subsequently president of my class. Men were scarce so all of us women held higher positions than would have been usual. I met monthly with the Dean of Women, Mary B. Davidson. There was also a Dean of Men. These positions were abolished later; instead there was a Dean of Students. I was having fun making many new friends in Stern Hall and among the other students, particularly classmates, meeting boys (we were "girls" and the opposite sex were "boys" in those days). Most personally important was my feeling of an independent life.

One action the University took during these war years was to have a summer term the same length as the other two semesters—fall and spring. Since I felt it wouldn't be patriotic to take time off during the summer, I kept going to school throughout the year. As a result, I graduated in June 1945 instead of, as I normally would have, in June 1946. Between this speed-up and the GIs returning to study, the graduation dates during the war years became very confused as we find when we plan our fiftieth year reunions.

I remember very few professors from that period. I was one student among hundreds who gathered in Wheeler Hall to listen to Ira B. Cross and his economic theories. I enjoyed a couple of anthropology classes from a teacher who himself bore a close resemblance to Cro-Magnon Man, but the courses I liked best were those given by John Hicks in American history. I chose a major that gave me many elective courses. What appealed to me most was teaching nursery school, known today as preschool. No teaching credentials were required to teach nursery school then. Therefore, I had an individualized major composed of certain required courses in education, home economics, and psychology. But there was plenty of time to take my beloved history courses and anything else I desired. I taught for a year at Presidio Hill Nursery School after graduation and before marriage. As a matter of fact, my marriage took place on the day I would have normally graduated, June 23, 1946.

Because my husband also graduated from Berkeley, and because we have always lived in San Francisco close by the University, our ties to our alma mater have remained strong. We root for the Blue and Gold at basketball games, track and field, and football games, especially the Big Game. Both Richard and I have been involved in class reunions and fundraising. I've served on the Alumni Council and on the UC Berkeley Foundation. Many Chancellors and some Presidents have been good friends throughout the years. Each of us has received the honor of the Wheeler Oak Award and are Berkeley Fellows.

There have been many changes since my days as a college student. Stern Hall has tripled in size; the hills where I and a date cut classes to picnic are now covered with buildings. Sather Gate is no longer the outer southern border of the campus, and LSB, the Life Sciences Building where many of my large classes were held, has been modernized and two new large science buildings have been added. But the dedication to excellence in education remains, as does the devotion of the University's "Old Blues" who serve their alma mater in a variety of ways.

I found a wonderful life at the University. It was if the whole world had opened up for me after the sheltered years at home and in a girls' school. Cal gave me the opportunity to be my own person. I had the chance to meet, live with, and interact with a variety of people. It also gave me a flying start on involvement with community service that has guided my activities ever since, and brought me a sense of fulfillment, often termed "psychic income," throughout my life.

Go, Bears!

"The University of California is the
engine which drives the economy of the
state. For decades it has generated a
worldwide brain drain into California.
We have attracted the best minds in
every field."

NICHOLAS C. PETRIS

Nicholas C. Petris

L
IFE AT THE UNIVERSITY OF CALIFORNIA at Berkeley began
for me in January 1940. I was a bewildered sixteen-year-old
from McClymonds High School in Oakland, the only student coming from a tiny class of 100 and going directly to
UC with an enrollment of over 16,000! A few others did go later,
after working for a year or two. One of them became a doctor. I
am grateful to my high school classmates who went to work
immediately. Their taxes helped put me through UC.

Today I still think of UC with a great deal of gratitude
and affection. As a student I benefited greatly from the stimulating, meaningful application to me of its motto: Let There Be
Light. Apart from that, I am grateful as a citizen and senator of
California for the magnificent contributions of the University to
our state, our country, and, indeed, the whole world!

My parents, Chris Petris and Mary Kakouris Petris,
were immigrants from Greece. They had a better than average
education. Both of my mother's brothers who remained in
Greece became educators. For several decades my father worked
at the Southern Pacific round house in West Oakland, servicing
the steam locomotives. He saw the world from a wet, noisy, and
greasy pit, underneath the engine. He inspected and repaired the
"truck," the bed of wheels on which the locomotive is cradled.

I have a younger brother, Gus, and a younger sister,
Katherine. Our parents became naturalized citizens when we
were in grammar school. From that time until their deaths, they
never missed voting in an election. I have seen them get up out of

a sickbed and walk to the polling place on a cold or wet day in November. Good citizenship and a good education were top priorities they emphasized for us. To be a good American, they felt, we must first be cognizant of our Hellenic heritage. Thus, they lectured us on the wonders of ancient Greece, the cradle of Western civilization, the birthplace of democracy. If we combined the best features of Greek and American history and traditions, we would become the best of Americans. These lessons, and my UC years, prepared me for election to public office.

My parents had great respect for teachers and appreciated the importance of education. There was never any doubt that we would go to college. Unfortunately, our father insisted that this did not apply to our sister who should learn secretarial skills. It was a bad decision which I deeply regret to this day. (She has been using those skills for many years in the Office of the President of Merritt Community College.)

Like other members of the Greek Orthodox Community of Oakland, our parents paid tuition for the three of us to attend Greek school three afternoons a week. We learned the language, recited poetry, and acted in plays. This was to prove invaluable to us throughout our lives. For example, in 1946 Gus and I were two of the six liaison officers to Greek officials while we served under Ambassador Henry F. Grady (of UC) on the Allied Mission for Observing the Greek Elections. The U.S., England, and France participated. In 1966 I represented Governor Edmund G. "Pat" Brown and the University at the inauguration ceremonies in Delphi, Greece, for the UC Graduate Study Center in Ancient Greek Drama.

For me, UC presented a golden opportunity to expand the horizons of the mind. UC meant the chance for knowledge, for an understanding of the past, for dreams and visions of the future. I remember President Robert Gordon Sproul's welcome to the freshman class. He urged us to pay close attention to our professors. "We have a great faculty—but the progress you make will be up to you." He urged us to get acquainted with one of the leading libraries of the world, which was at our disposal. He also said that the professors were at their best when they wrote their books. So I read and read and read.

I never had a bad or indifferent teacher. I learned from the professors and the teaching assistants. I plunged into the "extra" reading lists recommended by the professors. I took more and more courses until, in my junior year, I was packing 22 $^1/_2$ units. When I tried to increase it to 25, my faculty counselor stopped me. At the same time, my parents became concerned and made me quit one of my three part-time jobs.

Life at Cal provided precious memories: President Sproul's oratory, his booming voice and great wit; the graciousness and kindness of Vice President and Provost Monroe E. Deutsch, who always took time to counsel the students and listen to us; the lectures of Professor Smyth in European history; former General David P. Barrows in political science; Robert Nisbet in sociology. I spent a lot of time in the library stacks. It seemed to me that nine times out of ten he was there, pulling down books.

In the School of Journalism, my major, we had experienced journalists teaching us. They were always accessible, helpful, and encouraging. The dean, Professor Robert Desmond, led a very competent group. Among them was the late Scott Newhall, who was editor of the *San Francisco Chronicle* for many years.

I enjoyed the tranquility of a beautiful haven, the A. F. Morrison Memorial Library. Textbooks and note papers were not allowed. It was strictly for pleasure. No pressure. No exams to worry about. It was beautifully decorated with luxurious chandeliers, comfortable couches and sofas, and wood paneling. There I read books totally unrelated to my courses.

I spent hundreds of pleasant hours in the Doe Library. When the voice announced that the library was closing at 10:00 P.M., I wondered where the time had gone. I was impressed by the man after whom the Charles Franklin Doe Library was named. He was born in Maine in 1833 and died in San Francisco in 1904. After all these years I am still deeply moved when I read the inscription about him at the entrance, among which nestle the following lines:

> He was a quiet man of simple tastes and orderly life. Dili-
> gent in business, he dealt honorably with all men. Charity
> for divergent views and a gentle tolerance toward the
> beliefs of others tempered the native sternness of his
> convictions.

I remember the foyer of the Doe Library with its four impressive tall marble columns. On one side, two are adorned with the busts of Homer and Hermes (a copy of the famed Praxiteles' sculpture of 300 B.C.). Opposite them, on the other two columns, are the busts of two Roman emperors, Caesar Augustus and Marcus Aurelius. I remember these as symbols of our Graeco-Roman civilization—our roots which are now under heavy attack on many campuses throughout the United States.

These columns, standing like sentries in defense of our civilization, call to mind the admonition of my parents to become good Hellenes in order to be good Americans. They embellish the academic atmosphere of the University. These and the Greek ceilings and key architecture of several of the buildings on campus help me to reach back to those illustrious beginnings: Socrates' admonition to "know thyself"; Plato's first days as a teacher in that garden in Athens where he sat on one end of a log and his student at the other. This eventually became Plato's Academy which lasted for 900 years.

As the University celebrates its 125 years, my fervent hope is that it lasts much more than 900 years and that those columns will still be there and the students will still be receiving the Light beamed through the centuries from the ancients.

More memories . . . Campanile's carillons; sitting in the Cal rooting section at the football games; the amazing enthusiasm and "school spirit" of Geology Professor Norman E. A. Hinds, who invited the Cal marching band to burst into Wheeler Auditorium going full blast during his lectures on Fridays; commuting daily from West Oakland by streetcar, with my books and a big brown bag containing both lunch and dinner lovingly prepared by my mother; the wondrous magical effect on me of reading—especially in history, political science, philosophy, journalism, sociology; students of Hellenic descent forming Epsilon Phi Sigma, the Hellenic students' club . . . with Paul Christopulos, Georgia Changaris, George Nicholau, Ted Efstratis, Gus and John Nichandros, and many others.

Then there was ROTC. By mistake I got steered into the Coast Artillery Corps instead of the Infantry unit. I was out of my league, with a lot of engineers, scientists, mathematicians, but the error probably saved my life. The Infantry units were called up for active duty long before us. Not only did I have a difficult time with mathematics, the circular slide rule, sines and co-sines, parallax, computations of the speed of the airplane targets, the velocity of the 90 millimeter projectile, the powder temperature, I wasn't even marching properly. One time our army instructor raced all the way across Edwards Field to shout at me to straighten out my rifle!

That changed after Pearl Harbor. We were all bucking to become officers when called up. My whole attitude changed. I forced myself to learn and ended up as the commanding Cadet Colonel of the Coast Artillery unit of the ROTC!

My fervent hope is that the University will never again be subjected to the attacks and the painful cuts which it is suffering these past few years.

Since 1959, I have been in the Legislature. For the past several years I have chaired the Education subcommittee of the Senate Budget and Fiscal Review Committee. I have fought consistently against student fee increases, and I have watched with much pain the severe wounding of the greatest public University in the world.

We have lost some of the nation's finest professors in this process because we did not have the courage to communicate frankly with the public about the needs of the state. We should have asked them to support a tax increase to solve the problem.

Justice Oliver Wendell Holmes described taxes as "the

price of civilization." Today *taxes* is a dirty word to be avoided at all costs. So, we protect the private comfort of our wealthiest citizens, at the expense of good public policy—especially in higher education.

The University of California is the engine which drives the economy of the state. For decades it has generated a world-wide brain drain into California. We have attracted the best minds in every field.

Sadly, the direction of the brain drain has been reversed in the last few years—resulting in irreparable harm.

"Homecoming was another Berkeley watershed for me. In 1958 at the age of twenty-one I discovered my lifelong propensity to make everything more unique and larger than what anyone had done before. I decided Homecoming would be the biggest extravaganza the campus had ever seen."

KEN KRAGEN

Ken Kragen

THE IMPACT THE UNIVERSITY OF CALIFORNIA at Berkeley has had on my life goes beyond that of most students who enroll there: if it weren't for the University, I might not ever have been born. In October of 1928 my father, Adrian Kragen, a sophomore student at Berkeley, met my mother, a new freshman, on a blind date and took her to a sorority dance. They were married in 1933 while Dad was still in law school at Boalt Hall. I was born in Berkeley's Alta Bates Hospital in November of 1936. So I was a California Bear right from the beginning.

My love of California athletics started early too. One Saturday in 1937 my grandmother put me out in a playpen in the front yard to get some sun. We were living at that time on Parker near Warring not far from the football stadium. As the crowd streamed by on their way to the game, I decided I didn't want to be left out and crawled out of the playpen heading up the hill to the stadium. I had gotten less than a block away when some nice person decided I was a bit too young for football (at least on my own) and carried me back to a somewhat panicked grandmother.

In the early 1940s, after my dad did a stint as deputy attorney general of the state of California under Earl Warren, we moved to Los Angeles. There dad became a senior partner in the USC law firm of Loeb & Loeb. However, the University's pre-enrollment influence on me was far from over. One of the most significant events occurred in 1952.

Dad made the decision to leave his highly lucrative and star-filled life as a Hollywood lawyer to take a teaching position at Boalt. It brought him back to one of the true loves of his life—the University. My father loved the law, he also loved teaching, and he loved UC Berkeley. I was an impressionable fifteen-year-old at the time, and it was a lesson that has influenced the decisions I have had to make in my own life. By significant example, my father had taught me the importance of doing what I enjoyed doing, those things that would make me truly happy. I am very sure that he feels he made the right decision, as reflected by the many wonderful years he has enjoyed there.

With dad now teaching at Berkeley our family was involved once again in the University life. Of particular significance for me was a trip we made to the University's summer camp, the Lair of the Golden Bear in Pine Crest. While we were there for two weeks, one of the student dishwashers got sick and had to leave. I was asked to fill in, and when my parents left for home, I stayed on for the rest of the summer. Being nearly six feet tall, I didn't look quite as young as I was, although it took a little time for the other students to fully accept me. I enjoyed the job so much that I spent the next six summers working at the Lair.

I remember the competitive softball games between the staff and the campers, Mike Koll's vision and constant drive for perfection, and the stunning beauty and wonderful warmth of his wife, Jane. I also remember how in those early years the students all played bridge, a game I had yet to learn. My parents were expert bridge players and taught me so well that by the time the summer rolled around I was a pretty good player. Ironically, that year no one played bridge. Instead, they paired up and went off on their own. Once again I was somewhat left out of the social circle.

But I don't remember ever considering any other possibility than enrolling at Berkeley.

Shortly before I left high school my mom took me to a presentation being made by industry to encourage students to become engineers. There was apparently a shortage of them. I'd always been curious about the way things worked and so, ignoring the fact that I'd often skipped out on my math classes in high school in order to make basketball practice, I enrolled in Berkeley in engineering.

I promptly got in over my head. That first year I was taking eighteen units, was elected president of my freshman class, and went out for varsity basketball. I also pledged a fraternity. This lifelong pattern of taking on more than I could possibly do and then finding some way to accomplish most of it was set then. My real skill, however, promotion, brought out the largest group of students ever to attend a freshman class meeting (400). When it developed that there was little for them to do, the numbers dropped dramatically. Then Pete Newell, the basketball coach and a close friend of my family's, reluctantly cut me from the team, a move thoroughly justified on the basis of my lack of basketball skills. He did, however, allow me to participate in a lot of the team's activities and to go on some of the road trips.

My participation in fraternity life was equally marginal. I was devastated during my pledging when they stood me up in front of the entire fraternity and asked me to name every member. Under that pressure I couldn't even remember the fellows I knew well! The trauma of it kept me from fraternity gatherings during my years at Berkeley.

But the most significant failure of that first year occurred in my weakest area, math. I failed my calculus course. I promptly took some career counseling, and an aptitude test. I'll never forget that counselor's words, "You can be an average engineer if you work at it, but you'll be much better in a field that requires people skills." I transferred into a little-known major called communications, a course really designed to make things easy for student athletes. In my case it was the perfect opportunity for satisfying my curiosity about areas that interested me. I signed up for sociology, anthropology, and journalism. Since my major required only twelve units of study, I perused the catalogue for another area of interest—history. It was education in a more classic sense, broad-ranged and thoroughly engaging. My participation improved immediately.

It was the mid-50s and while I was at the University,

215

across the bay in San Francisco a musical phenomenon was incubating that was soon to sweep the nation: folk music. On the East Coast it was spearheaded by Pete Seeger and the Weavers. On the West Coast a group had formed called the Gateway Singers. Flamboyant entrepreneur Enrico Banducci opened a club called the "hungry i."

It became the crucible for a whole generation of entertainers, as well as a popular hangout for many UC students. When I went to see the Gateway Singers perform, I was immediately mesmerized. In high school I had produced concerts and dances and been elected president of my high school club as a result of my success doing these shows. A friend of mine named Barry Sherman and I went with dates one night to the hungry i. While the Gateway Singers were performing Barry leaned over to me and said, "Why don't we bring this group to the Berkeley campus?" I began to work on it immediately. Somewhere along the way "we" became "me," but Barry had certainly laid the seeds for my future career.

I arranged to bring the Gateway Singers to the University's Wheeler Auditorium and worked around the clock to promote the show. The night of the actual performance, I was sitting in the office of the *Daily Cal* editor Bob Steiner, fretting that probably no one was going to show up. I still have the poster from that concert, and it shows that the price of the tickets was seventy-five cents with no advance sales. It was first-come, first-serve on the night of the show. Bob and I walked out of his office and down to Wheeler. There to our amazement was a line of people stretched all the way around the auditorium. It was a sell-out, and suddenly I was a college concert promoter. Now every weekend I would hang out at the hungry i or the Purple Onion across the street, the clubs that were hotbeds of hip activity, watching new talent like Mort Sahl, Phyllis Diller, Lenny Bruce...

One night at the hungry i, I was approached by a young man named Nick Reynolds. Nick wasn't much older than I was, and he later confessed to me that his real reason for coming up to me was to meet the very attractive young lady I was with. In any event, he introduced himself as a member of a group called the Kingston Trio, and told me they were performing across the street. Lou Gottlieb, the leader of the Gateway Singers and by now a friend, intervened to tell Nick that I was the Bay Area's leading concert promoter—an easy statement since I was probably the only concert promoter in the Bay Area at that time. Impressed, Nick urged me to come over and see the Trio perform. Very simply, I was knocked out. I was the target audience for this group and I had never heard anything quite like them. I marched back to the tiny dressing room just behind the stage and predicted with great bravado that within the year they would be the biggest group in the country. (This wild prediction came true, exactly one year later, when the Kingston Trio's first record, "Tom Dooley," became the number one record in the country.) That first night I offered to produce a concert in Berkeley for the group. They were delighted and I went to work. This time I decided to produce the show as a commercial rather than a University venture, and I rented a small auditorium at my alma mater, Berkeley High.

Despite my school schedule, I got busy on advertising and promotion. When all was done the evening came close to selling out, making the Kingston Trio the exorbitant figure of $360 (more than they had made in a week at the Purple Onion) and me a profit of $82. However my tax expert father informed me that I owed $80 in amusement taxes. So the profit of this first commercial venture ended up being just $2, but my career as a concert promoter and ultimately a life in the entertainment business was sealed.

My senior year on campus was rapidly approaching, and I decided to run for student body president. I enlisted the help of a cheerleader named Bill Bell, who was one of the best yell leaders the campus had ever had. There were several other candidates, among them Roger Samuelson and Scott Sherman. Despite Bill Bell's support, I came in dead last. Roger Samuelson won. All my life I have believed everything happens for a good reason, that for me things work out the way they should. On the ballot that year was an organization named Slate with a leader named Mario Savio. Poor Roger had to deal with the problems an emerging student movement brought with it. I, in turn, was asked to run the Homecoming show. I had a ball, while Roger sweated out the student council meetings.

Homecoming was another Berkeley watershed event for me. In 1958 at the age of twenty-one, I discovered my lifelong propensity to make everything more unique and larger than what anyone had done before. I decided Homecoming would be the biggest extravaganza the campus had ever seen. Towards that end I resurrected an old Berkeley tradition of the 1930s and 1940s. I asked the fraternities and sororities to decorate their houses for Homecoming and set up a competition between them. It garnered lots of participation and a considerable amount of publicity.

I remember other moments connected with the Homecoming event. One was the election of a Homecoming Queen. I held it in Wheeler Auditorium, the site of my earlier important triumph. This time it was almost a disaster but became a learning experience. I had asked comic Professor Irwin Corey, whom I had seen many times at the hungry i, to entertain while the votes were being counted. The problem was that I couldn't get him off the stage! He went on and on. Finally in desperation, I went out in front of the stage and handed him a note saying, "*Please* get off of the stage." He took it, looked at it, turned around with his back to the audience and made a motion like he was zipping up his pants. Then he turned, thanked me . . . and continued on with his act. By the time I finally got him off, there was barely time to announce the nominations. I had not known about comics; they were nowhere on my curriculum.

I remember the show for its hosts, one a young fellow named Bill Bixby, and the other a cheerleader named Larry Stuart. They were sensational. Bixby went on to a terrific career in television. All I knew then was that I had the best two hosts any Homecoming had ever seen. I can't remember whether Cal won that Big Game, but I do know that I basked in the glory of that hugely successful Homecoming week for a long while. If the University was supposed to prepare one for life on the outside, Berkeley was certainly doing that for me.

At Berkeley I also got a memorable nickname that took me years to shed. It was during an intramural football game between my fraternity and one of the others. The star player for the other team had been making great catches and I commented, "What terrific hands he has." When I got my chance to play and made a diving one-handed catch in the end zone for a touchdown, my friends came running up to me crying, "Hands, hands, great hands!" The name stuck, "Hands." It took considerable explaining to my dates why my friends called me this.

Yes, the classrooms, too, held memorable experiences for me. I particularly liked history, a subject that has fascinated me to this day. I took an advanced history course from a wonderful professor named Armin Rappaport. At the end of the first session, he called me aside and asked me to participate in an experiment. He suggested that I not take any notes during the lecture, but listen carefully to whatever he said and then retire immediately to the library to write out everything I could remember. I did this faithfully throughout the semester. It was a terrific idea, and forced me to really concentrate on what he said. However, it was my *short-term* memory that was good enough! I could keep almost everything straight as long as I went immediately afterwards to write it down. I was crushed when he gave me a B in the course, for I had loved the subject matter, his lectures, and the fact that I was participating in an experimental way of studying.

Another particularly important course I took was from the leading theorist on socialism, who was a visiting lecturer on campus. He implanted in me many strong concepts of how workers had lost control of the workplace as society evolved and how such control must be reengaged for true productivity and happiness. This reengagement is happening today, as more and more people are working for themselves, and employees are actually buying and controlling large corporations such as TWA and United.

One particular anthropology lecture also stands out in my mind. The professor was riotously funny, while being fascinatingly good at his subject. One day the window happened to be open and a strong gust of wind came in and blew all of his papers off the desk. The course was being given in the science department and the desk was a long solid one. The professor immediately got down on his hands and knees underneath the desk where we could not actually see him. Every few seconds a hand would come up and place another one of the pages back on the desk but the lecture itself never broke stride. The class completely broke up. This incident seared into my mind the fact that nothing is better than spontaneity in any kind of public performance, including lectures. That it is taking advantage of the things that happen unexpectedly that makes for successful entertainment as well as instruction.

Not only was I a student, I was also the son of a renowned Berkeley professor, an expert in taxation law whom President Eisenhower actually tapped to help revise the U.S. tax structures in the 1950s and whom President Reagan later tried to get to do the same thing in the 1980s. This made the University experience for me multi-dimensional, and also created its own interesting moments. There was the time during a pick-up basketball game when one of the players was swearing up and down about his professor, who of course turned out to be my dad. I didn't say anything, I simply played a little harder.

So . . . Berkeley not only provided the impetus for my birth, it provided the crucible for my skills. The University helped set me off in a professional direction which has been both fulfilling and rewarding.

For the Kragen family Berkeley is a three-generation tradition. My sister Robin, like my mother before her, met her future husband, Robert Merritt, on the campus and two of their children, Kim and Kevin, have recently graduated from there. Robin's oldest daughter, Kim, is now engaged to a young man she met at Berkeley. The University's influence on our family is well into its sixth decade.

May it continue to be so.

"There is no question in my mind that our generation has had a profound impact on the University. In our era, the University moved a step farther from the isolation of the ivory tower. As students we fought to play new roles; we were not content to be scholastic sponges, absorbing and regurgitating academic information; we responded to the need for greater participation in the affairs of the University and our society."

ROBERT DOUGLAS HAAS

Robert Douglas Haas

A RRIVING ON CAMPUS IN SEPTEMBER 1960, my class was greeted by a *Daily Cal* editorial which described the University as "an educational slot machine. You are not going to do anything without an investment of your own effort; if you pull the right lever, you can fall heir to the richest educational experience of your life." Slightly over four years later, Mario Savio was to describe the University as a "machine"—but with a very different emphasis: "There is a time when the operation of the machine becomes so odious, makes you so sick at heart, that you can't take part.... you've got to put your bodies upon the gears and you've got to make it stop."

These quotes, which bracketed my undergraduate years, illustrate the enormous changes which shook the University. Change and growth were the hallmarks of that period.

The physical growth is easiest to describe. Enrollment in the fall of 1960 topped 21,000; by the time I graduated the student body was approaching the present limit of 27,500. Even when we came to Cal the University's size was an issue. We had been warned by high-school counselors and friends that, "Cal is such a big, impersonal place," and the housing shortage which greeted our arrival as well as all-night vigils in pre-registration lines for English 1A and Edward Teller's Physics 10 tended to confirm these warnings.

For many of my classmates Cal seemed like four years of waiting in lines: lines for a hamburger at the Bear's Lair, for basketball tickets, for a "must" book in RBR; lines to hear Frank

Wilkinson, Fulton Lewis III, Gus Hall, and other controversial speakers in Wheeler Auditorium, Pauley Ballroom, Dwinelle Plaza, and Stiles Hall, and even all-night lines to rent a print from the Morrison Room collection in the library.

The most obvious index to Berkeley's rapid growth in the period was the number of new buildings which transformed the campus skyline: towering residence halls, the student union, Tolman Hall, the Earth Sciences Building, Wurster Hall, Barrows Hall. Everyone agreed that the added facilities were needed; however, student opinion was far from unanimous on the merits of the individual buildings. One student critic described hulking, monotonous Barrows Hall, which blocked the traditional Telegraph Avenue view of the Campanile, as something Sonny Liston designed with his gloves on.

Although space for faculty parking remained an issue, by the end of my four years many of the physical "growing pains" had been solved. But the growth of the University accompanied and created other changes, most notably in the mood of the student body.

We came to a University that was finally emerging from the grips of the Silent Generation. A *Daily Cal* cartoon characterized the undergraduate sentiment: a graduating senior is slapping the dean with his newly gained diploma, and the provoked dean snorts, "They get pretty independent *after* getting their diplomas." (Emphasis mine.) Of course, most students seemed involved with the same activities that occupied earlier generations of undergrads. Yet while mischievous Oski continued to reign as the campus symbol (although sharing his spotlight with a fountain-loving dog named Ludwig), the first breezes of change were already sweeping down Strawberry Canyon. Mass demonstrations and arrests in the spring of 1960 at the House Un-American Activities Committee hearings in San Francisco had drawn the University into the first student controversy of the decade. Critics branded Cal "the Little Red Schoolhouse," and charged that many students were either card-carrying Communists or hapless "Commie dupes." A HUAC witness testified that, "These youngsters don't know they're being used. At the University they are taught Darwin's Law and the name of God is never mentioned in the universities, and this makes them ready to join the Communist Party." There was hardly a night in the early sixties when *Operation Abolition,* the HUAC-sponsored film on the demonstrations, wasn't shown somewhere around the campus.

Increasingly students began focusing their attention on the problems of the University. Some went South, to Mississippi, to participate in the first sit-ins. Others protested discriminatory housing and employment practices in the Bay Area. Students initiated tutorial projects with ghetto children or counseled at Cal Camps. Dwinelle Plaza and later the steps of Sproul Hall were the rally sites for the days' issues: Cuba, disarmament, free speech, Vietnam, the Delano grape strike.

It was inevitable that students who were examining and questioning the institutions of society should turn their attention to the University, too. Many fought to abolish compulsory ROTC and discriminatory clauses in fraternity charters. "We are sick and tired of being cast as the silent generation!" cried one student editorial on the Communist speaker ban. "We demand not to be hampered by closed doors." The "Kerr Directives" were a constant target for student criticism.

While many campus controversies involved legitimate grievances and issues, frequently an underlying cause and theme was an uneasy feeling that the University was becoming increasingly impersonal and unresponsive. It seemed as though the University was run by a giant computer. When one student humorist wore a badge bitterly proclaiming, "I am a student; do not fold, bend, or mutilate," he expressed a popular sentiment.

While some faculty and administrators recognized the problem, the usual response was stout reliance on institutions which had served the University when it was much smaller and the student body was perhaps less cosmopolitan. Mario Savio's machine was born.

Six short months after we graduated, the combination of

increasing student involvement in non-academic concerns and the problems associated with the University's "growing pains" led to the Free Speech Movement. Using the tactics learned in the fight for civil rights, students made demands on a reluctant and unbelieving administration. The *Daily Cal* cartoon that amused us as freshmen was hopelessly out of date: students were no longer waiting until after their graduation to assert their independence.

Although the most striking development of our four years at Cal was the increasing student activism and involvement in broad university and social concerns, many of my most vivid memories are of the enduring University: stealing Stanford's goal posts, bonfire rallies, Friday beer at the Rathskeller, being roused on football Saturday mornings by the Straw Hat Band, buying ice cream from the Crunchy Munchy man on the way home from class. Not every campus controversy involved pickets and petitions; we struggled with the knotty dilemmas of a girl running for campus "Ugly Man," a dog—Wazu—on the ballot for ASUC president, and the propriety of a thirty-two-foot nude painted on a construction fence to publicize a campus art festival.

Despite the apparent anonymity of the burgeoning campus, most of us remember Cal for the close and enduring friendships we made there. And for all that we complained about those lines, Cal's size offered a staggering diversity of experience—in politics: from Maoists to Birchites; in entertainment: folk singers to Rudolf Serkin; in life styles: scrubbed blond sorority girls to raggedy TAFF beats and beyond (TAFF was the Berkeley police acronym for the Telegraph Avenue Freedom Fighters). There was an advocate somewhere on campus for every imaginable and some unimaginable causes. It was the strength of Cal that in the course of four years we were each exposed to a full, sometimes bewildering, range of ideas and opinions.

Four years away from Cal the view is a counterpoint of startling change alongside the fond and familiar. Disruptive growth fades from memory when compared to the personal friendships that have grown beyond Berkeley, and the intellectual skills that underpin adult careers.

There is no question in my mind that our generation has had a profound impact on the University. In our era, the University moved a step farther from the isolation of the ivory tower. As students we fought to play new roles; we were not content to be scholastic sponges, absorbing and regurgitating academic information; we responded to the need for greater participation in the affairs of the University and our society. We cleared the way for the turmoil and controversy from which new definitions of the relationship of student, university, and society are emerging in a world that is, if not brave, at least new in its problems of mass scale.

"I remember my stroll through the halls at Boalt and how intrigued I became with the atmosphere. Everything that I saw, from the Moot Court Room to the great Library, seemed to reflect a tradition of excellence and a focused commitment to achievement; yet the law school complemented the great diversity, individualism, and openness of the Berkeley environment."

LARRY W. SONSINI

Larry W. Sonsini

ARRIVED AT THE UNIVERSITY OF CALIFORNIA at Berkeley in August 1959, much earlier than other freshmen. I temporarily moved in with a high school friend, Bo McAdam, who was playing on the Cal varsity football team. Bo was eating dinners at the varsity training table, and I tagged along, not really knowing where else to go. It was then that I met Coach Pete Elliott, who came up to me and asked who I was. I told him that I had been invited to play freshman football, and he informed me that the freshman team didn't report for another thirty days. I had a month to acquaint myself with the campus. To this day I remember the special places that I wandered, Eucalyptus Grove, Strawberry Creek, Edwards Field, and Strawberry Canyon, my stroll near the Chancellor's house. I soon joined a fraternity with a wonderful location on Warring Street next to Memorial Stadium.

During my first two years at Berkeley, I was under the guidance of the Cal athletic department. My first year I played on the freshman football team under a young coach named Mike White (who later coached the Cal varsity to a couple of Bowl appearances) and some wonderful assistants, including an Old Blue, Truck Collom, and at times a former Cal quarterback, Joe Kapp. I remember the adrenaline rush of wearing the blue and gold in Memorial Stadium and on the floor of the Los Angeles Coliseum. We won the Pacific Eight Freshman Football championship that year. The next season I was invited to play rugby under the immortal Doc Hudson. I have fond memories of

Coach Hudson, for he epitomized the competitive spirit, the value of tradition and the rewards of relentless perseverance. Rugby was a "family affair" at Berkeley for coaches, players, students, and fans (Doc Hudson maintained a dental practice while he coached). We didn't play in front of crowds; those that came were just part of the whole team. Like football, playing rugby at Cal was a great confidence builder. Competition was intense as we met with world-class teams like the New Zealand All Blacks and traveled in Canada for the World Cup competition. You can imagine the excitement I enjoyed when my son Peter was part of Cal's 1988 national championship rugby squad.

For reasons I don't recall clearly, I left Cal athletics after my sophomore year. Reflecting back, I remember that there was so much the Berkeley campus offered in terms of academics and culture that seemed to overshadow my commitment to the athletic program. I knew I could play at a competitive level, but I also knew that the attraction of the Berkeley curriculum would dilute my concentration on the playing field. Although I second-guessed this decision for a number of years, the support of the athletic department was remarkable. I was asked to stay involved in the program, and as a result I found myself announcing freshman basketball games in Harmon Gymnasium, serving as the play-by-play spotter at the Cal football games, and occasionally acting as a recruiter for the football program. To top things off, I was able to make some money for watering, by hand, the end zones at Memorial Stadium (the field was grass then) every Sunday morning. Needless to say, the experience and confidence I gained doing the public announcing work later proved invaluable to me in the pursuit of my career as a lawyer.

Academically, I initially placed emphasis on pre-med courses, for I always thought that I would go to medical school. I remember boiling animal parts in my room at my fraternity house, spending time in the labs, and developing camaraderie with medical students. However, one day during my senior year as I was walking by the Boalt Hall School of Law, which I had walked by every day for four years, I decided fortuitously to visit the office of the Dean of Admissions to learn about the law program. I remember my stroll thorough the halls at Boalt and how intrigued I became with the atmosphere. Everything I saw, from the Moot Court Room to the great Library, seemed to reflect a tradition of excellence and a focused commitment to achievement; yet the law school complemented the great diversity, individualism, and openness of the Berkeley environment.

I entered Boalt Hall in September 1963 and there embarked, as with every other law student, upon a three-year excursion into the transformation of how to think in a creative and responsive way. I remember my first set of exams. I studied harder than at any other time in my life and memorized everything I could: every case, every fact situation in every case, every decision, the reason for every decision, and scored poorly. It was then and there that I recognized that memorization is but a minor tool in the educational process of the law. I began to appreciate the importance of pushing my imagination, creative thought, communication skills, and decision-making as hard and as consistently as I could. I fell in love with the judgment demands of applying the law to the day's practical problems.

It wasn't difficult to decide what I wanted to do as a lawyer. Somehow or another I became enamored of corporate law and particularly the regulation of stock markets and corporate finance. I signed up for the securities regulation classes, and that began my long association and deep respect for Professor Richard Jennings. I later became his research assistant and ultimately took over teaching his classes. Actually, I owe Dick for the direction I took in joining a law firm. I wanted to go to New York (where I was born) to practice with one of the Wall Street firms. I was intrigued with the cachet of Wall Street and the influence and creativity that security lawyers could apply to a myriad of transactions ranging from private financing to mergers and acquisitions and the like. Professor Jennings pointed out to me that there was a young firm located in Palo Alto, California, that was getting involved in representing businesses at early stages of growth. That led me to set up an interview with John Wilson, who was the second most influential person in launching my career.

It was a rainy day in April 1966 when I was driving an old Volkswagen "bug" across the Bay Bridge down the peninsula to Palo Alto; a place I had only visited when our football and rugby teams traveled to the Farm. It was a Saturday morning, and I found myself on a peaceful lane next to Stanford Hospital. I remember to this day walking into John Wilson's office. Here was this very distinguished gentleman sitting behind a desk wearing a blue suit and a bow tie as if he were preparing to address a group of elders. I had never felt more relaxed than while talking to John Wilson about my aspirations. He is just made that way. I immediately knew that I could work with this man. I joined the firm in September 1966, one month before the birth of my son, Matthew.

It was a very small law firm then, with a dream of representing growing companies in the technology industry. I was the first employee of a rather informal partnership that got formalized upon my employment. John Wilson came out of the East Coast, went to Yale Law School with the likes of Byron "Whizzer" White and Gerald Ford and had big law firm experience in Cleveland. Pete McCloskey, later a congressman, ran against Richard Nixon for president of the United States and was an ex-marine and former district attorney. Roger Mosher, a classmate of Pete's at Stanford Law School, previously worked in a large San Francisco law firm. These three men, each so different, were the driving force in the firm and were the influence in my early career. To this day I think of them among the most effective lawyers I ever knew.

So there I was, a Berkeley grad in Stanford territory working with an entrepreneurial group of lawyers embarking upon a dream. It was so fragile then, but luck was on my side: I happened to have been at the right place at the right time. However, notwithstanding the fact that I was in Palo Alto, my ties to Berkeley remained strong. The athletic department asked me to get involved, and my first assignment was to recruit a young man named Lynn Swan, who had distinguished himself on the football field at a Northern California high school. I entertained Lynn and his mother and father at dinner and attempted to impress upon him all that Berkeley had to offer. The next day I learned that he had dinner with O. J. Simpson, and decided to attend USC. He distinguished himself as an All American and later as an All Pro with the Pittsburgh Steelers. I wasn't asked to do any further recruiting of athletes for Cal.

In the late 1960s, the seeds that grew into the technology industry in Silicon Valley were just beginning to take root. The entrepreneurs were young, energetic, and committed to the application and development of high technology. It was irrelevant where you lived, what hobby you had, or where you were educated. What was important was your ability to commit, create, and apply your abilities and instincts. The capital necessary to feed the imagination of these entrepreneurs and build businesses came from a relatively new group of investors, known widely today as venture capitalists. Like the entrepreneurs, the early venture capitalists were every bit as entrepreneurial and risk adverse. And so a partnership began. A mixture of the venture firms and a few of us lawyers who were trying, together, to feel our way in building new companies and industries. Most of us knew each other, understood our roles, and were committed to technology. We each asked ourselves questions. The entrepreneurs, whether their small enterprises, some located in garages, could survive the start-up phase. The venture capitalists, whether they could manage the risks associated with untried ventures. And we lawyers asked whether we could continue to provide the diverse solutions demanded by these growing enterprises and yet compete with the larger law firms.

Consequently, I was fortunate to develop my career amongst a mixture of some of the most creative and influential personalities in the country, those who put together the most successful of the venture capital firms; and the great entrepreneurs. These men, Tommy Davis, Robert Noyce, Ken Oshman, became clients and friends as did many other Silicon Valley pioneers.

During the 1970s, the focus in Silicon Valley was primarily microelectronics. Most of the clients we represented were involved in making instruments and semiconductors of one kind or another. I spent my time working with these firms on almost every issue one must address in building a competitive global enterprise, as well as responding to the challenge of rapid technological change. Wall Street was just beginning to discover Silicon Valley in the 1970s. Fortunately, there were some locally-based investment bankers like George Quist, Tom Weisel, and others. As a result, investment banking firms started to arrive, and legal, accounting, and banking services took hold. The computer age arrived with a variety of complementary businesses.

It was clear by the late 1970s that the infrastructure and fabric of an entire industry was coming together in Silicon Valley. First, there was the presence of the great universities, at Berkeley and Stanford. Second, there was the breeding ground for such technologically advanced companies as Fairchild Semiconductor, IBM, Hewlett-Packard. Through all of this our young law firm was growing, and I was building upon my experience.

In the late 1970s we had approximately fifteen lawyers wrestling with the challenge to grow to service the needs of our growing clients, to continue to service the start-up company and to remain in partnership with developing businesses; to develop the disciplines and skill to represent emerging growth; to perform the task of the initial public offerings and provide diverse disciplines as the companies grew into major industrial powers. It was an aggressive business plan, but we were fully committed. We grew as a firm to serve our rapidly growing companies.

We entered the 1980s with economic confidence. The original formula hadn't changed; it just became more expansive. As the computer companies like Apple Computer, Sun Microsystems, and others took hold, other entrepreneurs formed to provide products and services essential to the computer age. Our law firm expanded from 25 lawyers in the early 1980s to over 250 as we entered the 1990s, one of the largest, if not the largest, law firms in the country without a branch office. With the retirement of John Wilson, I remain as the only one left from the group I joined in 1966.

It was in the 1980s that I began to teach law at Boalt Hall. What a great honor it was for me when the eighty-eight-year-old Dick Jennings called and asked if I would take over his courses while he continued to work on a book. And so in 1985, I began to teach the securities regulation courses at Boalt, which I continue to do to this day. Every Monday morning I take the same ride to Berkeley that I did that day in April 1966 when I came back from that visit to John Wilson. I pass many of the same structures, although the names of the companies have changed, as I approach the serenity and majesty of the Berkeley campus. I walk the same halls at Boalt that I did that day as an undergraduate with the same feeling of enthusiasm. As I teach my course, every once in a while I flash back to the days when I was there listening to Dick Jennings. I started teaching to give something back to Cal. But I still find myself taking more than I give. Teaching at the University not only energizes my spirit but continues to sharpen my skills.

As I reflect on all of this, I am aware that the momentum that began in the late 1960s has gathered even greater force in the 1990s. From semiconductors to computers, our industries have greatly diversified. Software companies, biotechnology companies, entertainment and telecommunications companies, reflect the legacy of some of the things that got started when I first landed in Palo Alto. We continue to face every increasing challenge to expand our industries and maintain the entrepreneurial spirit. In a way we are still just beginning, and I like it that way. I suppose the singularity of my career has caused me to miss a number of things along the way; but the way I look at it, it's what's ahead that counts. Consequently, my days at Berkeley do not seem long ago. The University experience is very reflective of my experiences over the past twenty-eight years. After all, "Let There Be Light" could very well be the theme of the technology revolution.

"As I never really came to the University,
so also I have never really left it. Most
of my life I have lived close to the
campus physically and intellectually.
The University is still, as it was when I
rode in my buggy to the campus, a
member of my family."

MARION SPROUL GOODIN

Marion Sproul Goodin

A S AN ENTERING FRESHMAN in the 1934 class, I did not
"come" to the University of California. I was born there
seventeen years earlier.

In 1917 my mother and father were living in a Berkeley
bungalow on Grant Street. My paternal grandparents lived in an
equally modest house just around the corner on Rose. My father
had a month previously been advanced from the lowly position
of cashier at the University to the potentially somewhat more
promising one of acting assistant comptroller, and a short time
later was to add the duties of acting secretary of the Regents. Both
of these positions opened up as a result of the hasty wartime
leaves of superiors, and from my father's exemption from military service as an asthmatic. However, they were not just something he fell into by chance. Rather, they were the initial steps in
the fulfillment of the dream with which he had graduated from
Berkeley in 1913.

This was a far cry from the dream with which he had
entered Berkeley, but both dreams came from his enthusiastic
response to a unique personality. I hasten to add that their effect
on my father was the only conceivable point of similarity
between the two men.

That my father had an entirely classical education at
Mission High School was no accident. My grandfather had been
a teacher in Scotland before he came to California. He had a certificate from a normal school in Glasgow, and he had been admitted to and completed one year at the University of Edinburgh

medical school. There is no doubt but that he was determined that his two sons should graduate from a university, and no question in his mind that a classical preparation was the ticket of admission. However, my father, who had worked at odd jobs from his early school years, found a job sometime after the San Francisco earthquake and fire with one Charles McEnerney, a man with a shadowy background, dubious professional credentials, but almost certainly valuable political connections, who had sold himself to the city as an engineer and been put in charge of resurveying San Francisco. His principal educational talent, however, was scientific. He hired my father and another Mission High student, supplied them with a level and transit and turned them loose. My father came from a family of some sophistication where education and books were valued but not one where worldliness was countenanced, let alone prized. Though my father was born in 1891, the Gay Nineties had passed the family by. Stern Presbyterianism was the order of the day. Whether or not Charles McEnerney thought that youth was wasted on the young, he certainly thought youth was wasted on Presbyterians, and he set about to correct this deprivation. He took his young assistants to Mayes Oyster House, where he introduced them to oysters and allowed them to sip his champagne; he took them to the theater; he devised such entrancing high jinx for the Saturday morning "staff meetings" that my father's five-years-younger brother, Allan, attended voluntarily.

The lure of this exposure to *la dolce vita* led my father, in spite of the fact that he rarely received his stipulated salary, to conclude that the life of a civil engineer was the life for him. He graduated from Mission High in the Christmas Class of 1908. Berkeley, at that time, accepted freshmen only in the fall. In the intervening six months, my father went to night school to make up the required mathematics, and the following fall he was admitted to the College of Engineering at Berkeley.

Somewhere in the next four years the dream of an engineering career came up against the harsh reality that he had no natural talent and no real interest in the field of engineering. He was an unusual engineering student from the start. Engineers were known to be clannish, whereas my father participated in all phases of student life—politics, sports, the YMCA—and took courses from famous professors in fields far removed from the engineering curriculum. He came quickly to believe that the University of California was the greatest institution in the world, and that Benjamin Ide Wheeler, its president, was the ideal model for a fulfilling and fruitful life. He resolved to stay there, and of course, he did. He worked one year after graduation as an "efficiency expert" for the Civil Service Board of Oakland, and then returned, at less salary, to the University. To the best of my knowledge, he never, even in the dark days, regretted it.

243

This is a long tale to justify the assertion that I was born in the University, but without it, it would be difficult to convey forcefully my feelings that the University was by way of being the sixth member of our family, and that Benjamin Ide Wheeler was our highly respected godfather. He is a legend at Berkeley.

And so, on July 15, 1917, I became the newest member of the R. G. Sproul family, the others being my mother and father and the University. I would be greatly surprised if my father would not have preferred, and my mother have conceived it her duty to produce, a boy. Such disappointment was, however, substantially alleviated by my good judgment in the choice of my birth date. I was born on Benjamin Ide Wheeler's birthday. Until the day he died, my father had an autographed photograph of Wheeler in his study. Under the picture was Wheeler's signature and the date July 15, 1854. At the lower edge of the picture, in pencil, my father had written Marion Elizabeth Sproul and my birth date.

If my father had experienced some disappointment at the arrival of a girl, and did not, in truth, have a consuming interest in babies of any sex, this was not true of my grandfather. He had and greatly loved two sons. A girl was a delightful novelty, and it was he who was responsible for my first physical exposure to the powerful presence of the University in our life. It was his custom on Saturday afternoons, when he had finished his week's work at the Southern Pacific Co. in San Francisco, to return to Rose Street, eat his lunch, go to the library to return and replenish his books, and then to walk all over Berkeley, the streets, the hills, the campus, with his friend John Flynn, a fellow Scot and a printer. After I arrived, the custom changed to pushing me in my buggy, usually on the grounds of the University. Mr. Flynn reported that my grandfather gave me careful explanations of the names and functions of the buildings, and in particular, called my attention to the very considerable beauties of the physical setting.

When I was four we moved from Grant Street to Elmwood Avenue, to a larger redwood house. I was now beyond a buggy. Accordingly, the Saturday afternoon buggy rides were replaced by walks with my father. We walked sometimes around Berkeley, then more nearly rural and thinly populated than now, especially in the north campus area; sometimes on campus where we explored buildings; and sometimes in the Berkeley hills where the Big C was our special charge, most critically at Big Game time when the hated Stanford tried to paint it red and white.

On Sunday afternoons my father often worked at his office and when he did, I went along. On these excursions I had the solemn responsibility of keeping track of his keys, housed in a thick and heavy leather key holder. I took great pride in selecting the right key and opening the big front door of California Hall. Once inside, I was allowed to use his secretary's typewriter to work on an unending detective story I was writing. This kept me very busy and reasonably quiet.

When I was ten we moved to Piedmont Avenue at the northeast corner of a property that later became the site of International House. This was not by chance. The University knew that it wanted to acquire this property for the Rockefellers, and they feared that the owners would escalate the price when they learned of the buyer. Accordingly, they enlisted several University families to buy the houses as they came on the market at a normal price. None of the houses had been built with children in mind, and all significantly lacked outdoor play space. It did not take our gang of kids long to come up with an ingenious solution.

We quickly learned how to get into the adjacent stadium, and, whenever it was not being used by the varsity, we took it over for our football games, track meets, and treasure hunts. These last took place on Saturday afternoons directly after the game. We went under the bleachers, starting at the top and crawling down to the field, picking up coins or other items of interest that had been dropped during the game. The rules provided that the money was pooled and shared, but exotic items belonged to the finder.

We lived very briefly on Piedmont Avenue and made one more move to Tanglewood Road, also briefly, before we reached the President's House on the campus, where my mother and father lived for twenty-eight years and we children lived until we were married. We always called it the PH and we all still think of it as our house. All the high holidays and great occasions of our young lives took place there: the formal dances of our sororities and fraternities (in what the houseplans called the ballroom but which was known to us as the basement); the christening parties of all eleven grandchildren and their Easter egg hunts; my wedding; the Sunday night potluck suppers that kept our family intact despite the increasing amount of time our parents were away from us. We loved that house, so much so, that when my children learned that no one was going to live there when Grandpa and Grandma moved out, they suggested to me that we buy it—it was such a neat house. And it was.

Living on the campus, we were, of course, even more tightly interwoven with University life. One of my brothers delivered the *Daily Cal* to University offices (and if he was sick my mother or father substituted). My older brother was the longest lasting batboy in the baseball team's history, faithfully in attendance at the field back of Edwards Stadium every afternoon after school. We had tickets to and attended virtually every athletic event staged by the University until we reached college age. I went to my first Cal basketball game much earlier when we still lived on Elmwood, and it was far from the routine occasion it became. I went with my father and Guy C. Earl, then a Regent. The game was at night in the old Harmon Gym, a charming octagonal brown shingle building in somewhat dilapidated condition. Inside, the perimeter was ringed with a narrow balcony perhaps four rows of seats deep, and that balcony tipped seriously down towards the floor and jiggled ominously when anyone jumped up in excitement. I forgot my fears, and any traces that remained were obliterated when I was taken at the end of the game to the Varsity, a now long vanished hangout of students at Bancroft and Telegraph, for a soda.

Athletics, however avidly followed, were not the only excitement of our life on campus; there was the constant parade of house guests: the Charter Day speakers and other prominent visitors to Berkeley; princes and princesses, presidents and prime ministers, sultans and shahs. We children were not included in the great state occasions. Nonetheless, we were living in the same house and did encounter each at more unbuttoned moments. We often ate breakfast together. The library at tea time in late afternoon was a common ground. And finally, added to what we could ourselves observe, there was the added fillip of the backstage gossip of the maids. Thus we learned that Willa Cather was exceedingly shy and very precise in her requirements. She requested breakfast in her room and did not appear at tea time in the library. Her tea was taken *very* late in the evening, in her room, and she gave the maid exact instructions as to the making up of her bed. On the other hand, the Sultan of Morocco was an easy and charming guest who made only one request. He asked that, as he wore only silk slippers and found our climate cold, a hot water bottle be put under his feet at meals. These contacts, however fleeting, opened up to us the world beyond Berkeley and gave us a sense of what sort of men and women moved on that larger stage.

This was brought home to me most kindly by a Charter Day speaker I missed, Jan Masaryk. He came to Berkeley in the spring of 1939. He was at that time the Czech ambassador to Great Britain, and he came in place of Dr. Edward Benes and read Dr. Benes' speech and then spoke in his own words of the deepening plight of his country.

In the fall of 1934, I registered at the University, finally an official member of the community. As near as I can remember, there were something over 3,000 other freshmen. In the whole University there were 13,336 students, 10,573 of them undergraduates. When I graduated four years later, the student body had grown to 16,324. In the program of my graduation, 2,500 names are listed. This seems today a high percentage of the entering class to graduate, but of course, I cannot be sure all who graduated that day had entered in 1934. So even in 1934 Berkeley was already big (two-thirds as big as it is now) and grew bigger before I left in 1938. As I had come from a high school of 100 students, I could hardly have been unaware of the change in scale, but I have no recollection of being overwhelmed by the size either in those first days or at any time in the four following years. It was home. My father, I believe, feared I might be daunted by the numbers. At any rate, he offered me the possibility of going to an Eastern college if I wished. I was flabbergasted at the time, and I can still not believe he was serious, or else he counted on my refusing, as I did. Berkeley was, in his eyes, always the best University in the world. If I had gone elsewhere I would have believed the matter was with me, not the school. Years later when my oldest son, his oldest grandchild, went to Harvard, he took it very hard, although he laughed when I observed that he might prefer to have Rob demonstrating on President Pusey's front lawn than on his own. (Rob entered college in 1964, so that idle comment made me something of a prophet.)

If Berkeley's size did not awe me, my eyes were opened by the diversity of opinion that flourished on campus, by the simple fact that I came to know people who said they were communists, some of whom I think actually were. Conventional wisdom seems to hold that radical thought arrived unheralded and full-blown at Berkeley in the 1960s. Perhaps it appears so in contrast to the 1950s, but there was certainly radical ferment in the 1930s. I think we were generally more civil, but no less intense. It was, after all, the time of the worst of the Great Depression. We had the Spanish Civil War and the Lincoln Brigade. We had Upton Sinclair's campaign for governor. Closer to home we had the vexatious questions as to whether there were communists on the faculty who were indoctrinating students, as many legislators believed, and whether political speech could be allowed on campus property. There was a lot to debate, and an abundant variety of debaters. I came from a conservative town—believe it or not, Berkeley was conservative in 1934—a moderately conservative family, and a very conservative school. I had a lot to learn, and not a few things to unlearn. The campus atmosphere forced me to think about questions it had never occurred to me to put to myself before.

Learning to think also took place in classrooms, not invariably, but often. It was Joel Hildebrand's proud claim that it was he who taught me to think, an accomplishment of which he was still reminding me when I was a grandmother. It may even be true. To fulfill my science requirement, I landed in his course, Chemistry 1AB, rather than in the easy, rather pleasant, nonstressful geology course that was the usual safe haven of nonscience majors. This was because my father considered Joel Hildebrand a great teacher. It was my father's settled belief, often urged upon all of us children, that it was better to take teachers than subjects, that you learned more from a great teacher no matter what his subject than you learned from a mediocre one no matter how close to your heart his material lay. Hildebrand knew that I was an English major and he felt that his course was very likely my last chance to learn to think. Whatever it was that took place in the study of English literature, it was not, in his view, thinking. It was probably recreation and as such he enjoyed and valued it, but it was not thinking. In order to make the most of the short time he felt he had to save me from a life of total incoherence, he put me in his own advanced lab section, which was otherwise filled with boy geniuses who had cut their teeth on home chemistry sets. In those innocent days, Hildebrand's chief campus wide fame came from his Big Game lecture in which red and white substances were turned to blue and gold in spectacular displays. That was fun, but it was more important that he taught me to be both systematic in the way I learned and imaginative in how I used what I knew. I never entirely signed on to the notion that the study of the non-sciences required no thinking, but I am grateful to him for an appreciation of how the sciences did their thinking. He was as pleased as I with the A I finally earned, and he certainly took as much credit.

My father recommended other teachers from time to time, but to a diminishing degree after my freshman year. One other recommendation was particularly memorable. The course was named "Progress of Civilization" and the teacher was Frederick Teggart. Professor Teggart had a many-hatted career, at the Bancroft Library and as a member of both the history and the political science departments, but his quarrelsome temperament had made difficulties wherever he was, despite his scholarly attainment. My father thought very highly of Teggart and did not want to lose his talents at Berkeley. He persuaded the Regents to create a department, Social Institutions, of which Teggart was the entire faculty. I accepted this recommendation grudgingly. I thought I had no interest in the social sciences and by then I had more courses in my field that did interest me than I could fit into the remaining time. One lecture was all it took to convince me of my error. Teggart was a superb lecturer with a highly original mind. He led his classes to rethink all manner of received truths, and he made the process of doing so exhilarating. If Hildebrand had ever taken Social Institutions 1AB, even he would have revised his dictum about the poor quality of thinking outside the hard sciences.

I have singled out these two courses because they were far afield from my major and so make good examples of my father's advice. I would, however, be remiss if I did not express my appreciation to all of the faculty of the English department in which I spent the major part of my time and, in particular, to James Clive. I first met Professor Clive, by pure good luck, in the freshman compulsory composition course. Thereafter, I took every course he gave. He shamed me into mastering (as opposed to muddling) Middle English well enough to understand more exactly, and hence to understand more fully, Chaucer, and he had the gift of making fresh and vital not just Chaucer, which was easy, but all the lovely archaisms of Elizabethan verse and prose.

As I never really came to the University, so also I have never really left it. Most of my life I have lived close to the campus physically and intellectually. The University is still, as it was when I rode in my buggy to the campus, a member of my family. When all my children were first in school from 8:30 A.M. to 3:00 P.M., I was re-admitted to the graduate division and actually took courses for credit for a year. I considered continuing to a Ph.D. but with a husband and three children, it seemed a foolish indulgence, an unusable credential. However, I still have in my desk drawer a souvenir of that year—the certificate of Honorary Dismissal, which permits me re-entry to the University. Who knows? Perhaps I will yet use it.

"No generation of students has had available as rich a heritage as the present one and in no place can this great heritage be more fully realized and enjoyed than on the Berkeley campus of the University. It is there for the student to sample and to adopt to his needs. It is to be found not only in the libraries and laboratories, but in the ideas and wisdom of the scientists and scholars who make up this rare community."

DONALD H. MCLAUGHLIN

Donald H. McLaughlin

THE VERY NAME UNIVERSITY implies a range of involvement that has no earthly limit. It extends from distant galaxies to subatomic particles and from organisms as simple as a single cell to a complete man, and includes even his supernatural speculations. It is concerned with all manner of organizations and their functions, from the social habits of primates to such modern monstrosities as the corporate conglomerate. Furthermore, each individual in his relation to the entity known as the university brings his own characteristics into play and responds in his own way to the stimulus the institution gives him.

In each of my three associations with the University—as a student on the Berkeley campus, as a member of the faculty, and as a Regent—my concept of the University acquired new dimensions, for each led me into activities, problems, and opportunities that arose from different roles and responsibilities. My progress from freshman in 1910 (the lowest of ranks on the Berkeley campus with the possible exception of dean) to the lofty and serene post of elected professor emeritus has exposed me to all extremes.

As a student, I completed a program of study in the old College of Mining that by contemporary standards would be regarded as shockingly narrow and almost vocational. Yet in its emphasis on mathematics, geology, and the physical sciences and on their application in elementary engineering problems, it provided a sequence of studies against which progress could confidently be measured. Good habits of work had to be acquired if success was to be won. The pattern was accepted as reasonable, and without protest, at least by the students I knew best, for each had a clear sense of purpose and an appreciation of the aid the University was giving him in attaining his objectives. It perhaps neglected "the training of the whole man," whatever that highly subjective idea may mean, but if it did, I doubt if many of the widely scattered graduates of the college have been seriously handicapped in their diverse careers. I must admit, however, that completion of the program was accompanied by a smug sense of accomplishment and by a feeling of superiority over less fortunate classmates in the softer fields. Eventually, however, the limitations of our knowledge became more apparent, which fortunately sharpened the desire for further training and for better preparation, not only in the specific subjects that were sampled as an undergraduate, but in new and still unexplored fields. All in all, the old curriculum, narrow as it was, stimulated further effort and really served us well.

My return to the campus as a professor and a dean occurred much later, after some seasoning in the Army and in geological exploration in the high Andes of Peru and other remote places, as well as after the mellowing effect of sixteen years on the faculty at Harvard. In my new assignment, my old respect for the faculty and students at Berkeley did not suffer by comparison with the best of my associates and colleagues in these wider activities, nor did it with the way other academic institutions with which I had gained some familiarity were meeting the responsibility of training able young people.

Berkeley had, of course, changed in the long interval and so had I. A far better appreciation on my part of the significance of the other fields of learning besides science and technology brought wider contacts with faculty and students, which I could enjoy in spite of the occasional necessity of concealing old and persistent prejudices. A certain degree of tolerant skepticism was helpful in restraining my enthusiasm for some of the academic concepts that waxed and waned in popularity in the dominant liberal tradition of the times.

At the end of the thirties, the old College of Mining appeared to have outlived its usefulness and was transformed into a department in the College of Engineering, in which the students could be prepared more broadly for careers in the sciences and technology related to discovery and benefaction of the mineral resources of our small planet. In the old days, the excitement and adventure in exploration and mining attracted a particularly lively type of student, with imagination and boldness as well as inherent ability, and from them came leaders whose names are still remembered with respect in distant parts of the world, as well as on this continent, not only in mining regions but in the high places where decisions are made.

Today, with more exacting preparation in the sciences as well as in subjects that should provide better understanding of human relations, more time intervenes before a student can attain the satisfactions of professional practice. The field still attracts the intellectually venturesome, but, unfortunately for us in engineering and mining, many of the best are diverted into pure science and others, less commendably, are lured into foreign activities before they have adequate preparation for effective service.

The sequence of sophisticated studies now required for a career with the resources of the earth puts a very different light on the slogan that an early evangelical organizer of the College of California expressed when he hailed the establishment of a chair in the humanities as a victory of "minds over mines." Perhaps I am overstating my case by claiming that mining—or mineral technology as it is now called—ranks in intellectual content with moral philosophy and other humanistic concerns, but on the basis of comparative contributions to the welfare of humanity we might make a reasonable case.

Still later, when I had slipped from grace and become a corporation executive, I had the privilege of serving as a Regent of the University of California, which allowed me to participate in the delicate procedures of a governing board that had, not without wisdom, delegated wide powers to the administration and the faculty, but that nevertheless was still held legally responsible for the welfare and conduct of the University. In times of stress and public criticism, it was not an easy position to fill, particularly when sharp differences existed among well-intentioned people who regarded themselves as friends of the University. I was appointed to the board in the midst of the oath controversy and my term ended fifteen years later as the current, even more troublesome turmoil was starting. The University, however, survived the dire predictions of disaster over the unfortunate oath episode and it hopefully will emerge intact from the difficulties of these turbulent times, probably with a better understanding of the scope of academic freedom and with a more steadfast devotion to it on the part of the Regents, as well as a clearer recognition of academic responsibility on the part of the faculty, both to their students and to a somewhat disturbed, but still, generous, electorate.

No generation of students has had available as rich a heritage as the present one and in no place can this great heritage be more fully realized and enjoyed than on the Berkeley campus of the University. It is there for the student to sample and to adopt to his needs. It is to be found not only in the libraries and laboratories, but in the ideas and wisdom of the scientists and scholars who make up this rare community.

The very magnitude of the heritage could be overwhelming to anyone who felt he must not neglect any part of it. Fortunately, the individual—especially an enthusiastic young student—is apt to have his interest concentrated on a particular field, on an appealing idea or on a hope that seems of dominant importance to him and that guides his efforts to master what is known and to him appears to be relevant. He is rarely dismayed by the magnitude of the task he sets for himself and pushes ahead with vigor to gain competence necessary to break into new ground. The able ones can reasonably expect to become true professionals—as philosophers or as historians, as teachers or as scholars, as well as in fields such as medicine, engineering, and law, where only the adequately trained can meet the demands of their calling. Beyond this worthy level of attainment, the gifted few in each field, using their learning and skills as a firm base, will go on with imagination and clear vision to explore the unknown and to make their contributions to the knowledge and the thinking of the future.

As one of the principal custodians of this vast intellectual heritage, members of the faculty cannot fail to recognize their personal duty to devise and employ the most effective means of transmitting to the successive generations of students the segment of contemporary knowledge that they command. They should know and use the best techniques of teaching—and realize that no one approach suits all subjects and all individuals.

An emphasis on excellence has long been a characteristic of the University. It has endeavored to, and succeeded in, attracting outstanding scientists and scholars to its faculty—and in holding them. There is nothing snobbish in insisting that the privilege of enrollment must be earned by careful and demonstrated preparation, and that excellence in all its manifestations is an ideal to be sought. The University, in meeting its responsibilities for the welfare of the country, must continue to set as its first priority the training of the most competent men and women it can select from any walk of life and preparing them to the best of its ability to participate constructively, honestly, and with high competence in meeting the demands of their many future callings. It has settled for no less in the past and can confidently be expected to maintain the even more exacting standards now required for future performance.

During the fifteen years I had the honor of serving as one of the Regents, three new campuses were acquired, architectural plans prepared, and faculty engaged. Each of the new campuses is now vigorously alive and each has the potential of becoming a major new university. Projections were also made for physical growth of the older units and some measure of architectural distinction was achieved in spite of the artistic handicaps of the times. Educational objectives to insure a common commitment to highest standards and excellence and yet to permit a desirable degree of diversity were defined and adopted by the appropriate agencies to provide sound guidance for each campus. It was a time of outstanding achievement in which all the widespread groups that participated in the efforts—Regents, administrative officers, faculty, alumni, and students—can take lasting pride. The record will continue to command respect and admiration long after the disruptive troubles of the times have been forgotten.

"At Cal I learned the importance of 'spirit,' enthusiasm, and competition. The rooting section in Memorial Stadium was segregated into men's and women's areas. Men wore white shirts as background for the regular massive color card stunts at half time. No 'red' was tolerated. When someone wore red, there were loud shouts of 'take it off.' During Big Game week, the Berkeley Fire Department trucks were officially painted blue and gold by the City to avoid the amateur painting of these colors by students."

WALTER E. HOADLEY

Walter E. Hoadley

L ITTLE DID I REALIZE when I first came to Cal how my life would be substantially shaped by my undergraduate and graduate learning experience on campus during 1934–42. I had very positive expectations, but events have far exceeded my fondest dreams.

My parents and grandparents were hard working and God fearing, each with less than a high school education. Their hope was for me to go to college. To this end I was continually urged and expected to do my best in school—mildly rewarded when I succeeded and scolded when I fell short.

I also had strong support from teachers, clergy, and others who took an interest in my future. During the Great Depression I attended Mission High School in San Francisco, where I received much guidance. On occasion, teachers would require my attendance at 6:00 A.M. classes to help prepare me for the qualifying examinations for college.

When I eventually received my A.B. degree in 1938, I truly believed that my parents and supporters had earned it with me.

My life-long career as an economist was started by a Mission High civics teacher who had become concerned over widespread joblessness. One morning she asked our senior civics class how many of our fathers were out of work. Twenty-seven hands went up out of thirty. She promptly changed the course to "economics," even though she knew little about the subject. This initial experience with change, later reinforced continually at

Berkeley, set a long-standing precedent for me to expect change and to try to be a part of it. For me, there was also a great awakening of interest in the future. Forecasting has received my highest priority as a professional economist.

After graduation from high school, I had college scholarship offers but none offered a lower cost to me (twenty-six dollars per semester) than Cal, with the advantage that I could also live at home in San Francisco. I commuted by streetcar, ferryboat, and electric train to Berkeley. The commute proved to be an excellent study hall. I had never been on the Berkeley or any other campus until my first day as a freshman. I was naive. So much so that I was surprised, even disappointed, when I attended my first class and the professor was not in cap and gown. Whenever I had seen a professor in the movies or in a news photo, academic garb had been worn.

As I pursued my first year studies, I came to realize that in some instances my freshman course was a repeat of high school, probably because several of my teachers had lived in Berkeley and knew their academic peers. All this combined to give me a helpful momentum for the years ahead.

My family's finances were limited, forcing me to work for six months to earn the tuition before entering Cal. A fraternity was out of the question. Then I learned that fraternities had to meet minimum academic standards to remain on campus. Some who needed academic help were ready to negotiate a discount membership, an early practical lesson in economics. A non-resident membership was offered by the Kappa Alpha house. For a token payment I could eat lunch with the brothers and have some social privileges so long as my grades were Honor Roll quality.

There was another requirement that I be "active" on campus. I chose the *Daily Cal* editorial staff, which was one of the best decisions I could have made. I was forced to meet campus leaders and to become well acquainted with the University's facilities. I became eligible for free press "passes" to campus and off-campus events, broadening my academic and social life at almost no expense, and in addition, I worked part-time, mostly at night, on the San Francisco waterfront handling rail and ship freight cargo. The pay was thirty-five cents per hour . . . if there was work to be done. No work, no pay, and a loss of my ten cent carfare. My dock work gave me valuable experience as a blue collar employee in an atmosphere of union-management tension. As I contemplated my future, I rapidly understood that more education was the only way to advance beyond the docks.

University academic rules at the time did not allow freshmen to take any economics courses, and my first year at Cal was marked by impatience to get on with my contemplated major field. In fact, this freshman edict proved invaluable. I found time to explore non-economics courses as well as complete other requirements toward graduation. Equally important, my extra-curricular activities broadened my perspective. The *Daily Cal* sharpened my writing skills and improved my general knowledge. I also found opportunities to learn more about public speaking, leading to a life-long experience on the platform.

UC Berkeley's Class of 1938 has been closely knit since we first gathered on campus in August 1934. In large part this was because the Berkeley YMCA was extremely helpful. Entering freshmen who had been high school leaders were invited to come to Berkeley a week before classes started to learn about the University, its traditions, customs, and activities. We learned class organization early. The dress code for men on campus was fairly strict: freshmen could only wear moleskins (plain drab slacks), lofty sophomores wore blue jeans, and upper classmen corduroys which seldom or never were laundered in the hope that they might stand alone; few ever did.

The Class of '38 was proud to win the Frosh-Soph Brawl as freshmen as well as sophomores. Stanford never got to paint the Big C on "Tightwad Hill" when '38 had the "vigilante" responsibility. Class events were routinely successful. By graduation, a '38 Club of '38 men provided the core group for future regular reunions. Much later, the women formed their own '38 Club. Eleven hundred out of 2,700 classmates became life members of the California Alumni Association at commencement, despite the $100 fee.

At Cal I learned the importance of "spirit," enthusiasm, and competition. The rooting section in Memorial Stadium was segregated into men's and women's areas. Men wore white shirts as background for the regular massive color card stunts at half time. No "red" was tolerated. When someone wore red, there were loud shouts of "take it off." During Big Game week, the Berkeley Fire Department trucks were officially painted blue and gold by the City to avoid the amateur painting of these colors by students.

I covered some of President Robert Sproul's speeches for the *Daily Cal,* always wary of a "correction" call from the President's office. Provost Monroe Deutsch was a cordial human being whose positive comments on almost any news development gave me constructive insights. Dean Robert Calkins of the College of Commerce launched me as an economist by giving me a temporary job as a research assistant on a pre–World War II project for the California State Planning Board. Several others became valued mentors: Ira B. Cross, banking and finance; Paul S. Taylor, labor; Joe S. Bain, industrial organization; Gerald Marsh and Douglas Chretien, public speaking; and Laurence Harper, constitutional law. Each opened the doors of my mind as well as opportunity.

When I became eligible as a sophomore to take an economics course, I was excited and anxious to learn. I was also delighted with advanced public speaking courses. My enthusiasm never diminished. I was later to graduate with a major in economics and a minor in public speaking.

One of my most impressive freshman courses was Professor Joel Hildebrand's Chemistry 1AB. I also met a laboratory partner, Virginia Alm, who became my wife in 1939. That initial chemistry has lasted through more than fifty years of marriage.

While financing my Cal education had been a never-ending challenge, something always turned up when the need became acute, thanks to someone at the University. I left the docks when I was invited to be a reader at thirty-five dollars per month in public speaking and eventually a teaching fellow and head teaching fellow at sixty-five dollars per month in economics.

Several honors came my way: in my field of economics, Phi Beta Kappa, *Daily Cal* editorial awards, and selection as class valedictorian. As graduation on May 21, 1938, approached, the class leaders carefully planned Senior Week, a time for relaxing and farewells between the end of finals and commencement in Memorial Stadium. The theme was "A Roamin' Holiday," appropriate because the class participants gathered each day in a different Bay Area recreation-entertainment place for fun and food. I shared the Senior Week responsibilities. However, my attention was diverted to the preparation of my valedictorian address. Without the public speaking classes and faculty support I never would have been chosen. I faced the commencement audience of thousands in awe, but the experience boosted my confidence for future speeches to other large audiences as well as radio and television. Our class of 2,700 graduates received diplomas from President Sproul individually in a meticulous procedure which assured that the right person got the right diploma. Virginia and I announced our engagement at graduation and were married a year later. Meeting on the Cal campus added a memorable milestone in our lives.

My progress in economics at Cal had reaffirmed a desire to attend graduate school on campus. Virginia was helped by the UC placement office to find a position as a secretary (using her English major training). I had hoped for a teaching fellowship in economics, but was told that traditional preference was given to non–UC Berkeley graduates. Luck did me a great favor. Enrollment in Economics 1A skyrocketed in the fall of 1938 because of a recession which aroused widespread student interest in the subject. No one else was available to fill the unexpected open teaching slot. At the end of the semester I won the "best teaching fellow" award and had a job for the next two years.

My teaching assistant pay was for nine months, August

through May. This meant I needed a summer income. Thanks to my labor professor mentor, Paul Taylor, and my interest in labor economics sparked by my father, a New Deal Democrat and railroad union president, and the differing economic views of my mother, a conservative Republican, I received a summer job offer to serve as a junior economist on the staff of the California Governor's Commission on Reemployment. Cal helped me please both my parents. Professor Taylor found another job for me in the summer of 1940 as a field investigator for the U.S. Bureau of Agricultural Economics. I interviewed 170 families from Oklahoma and Arkansas, "Dust Bowlers," and after submitting my report, was encouraged to write a master's thesis on the more precise subject, "A Study of 170 Self-Resettled Families: Monterey County, California, 1940." Professor Taylor chaired my committee, and I completed my M.A. degree in labor economics.

My next goal was the Ph.D. degree in economics with a minor in constitutional law. The course work was a mixture of the exciting and the technical. Getting ready for the formidable written and oral "Preliminary Examination" was a full-time challenge. Meanwhile, the clouds of World War II were gathering, and many of my '38 classmates were getting military commissions. I failed the required perfect eye standards.

Thanks to the grace of God, I successfully passed my "prelim" on Friday, December 5, 1941, two days before Pearl Harbor. I found my dream job as assistant to the president of the Dollar Steamship Line, and was scheduled to report for duty on December 8, 1941. A prompt call came from my prospective boss postponing my new job "until this incident is over."

Once again, the University came to my rescue. Because of earlier research for the State Planning Board on defense preparation, I was almost immediately hired to join an expanded University organization to train personnel for war rather than the defense industry. The emphasis was on practical rather than theoretical economics. I had a lot of retooling to do to become an effective teacher.

As soon as the shock of the war declaration subsided, the need for economics and financial intelligence increased sharply. I was called to Chicago by a former Berkeley visiting professor who headed up a special economic research-intelligence unit at the Federal Reserve Bank. He told me that he remembered my ability but not my name. However, he did remember my wife Virginia as a wonderful bridge player and thus tracked me down. Soon thereafter we moved to Chicago. My duties quickly involved the financial needs of machine tool and paper manufacturing companies in the Midwest and New England states. Subsequent assignments covered other industries and areas until victory in Europe seemed inevitable. When attention shifted to Asia, my war-time task was to serve as economic advisor to the Civil Affairs Training School at the University of Chicago where military finance officers were being readied to re-establish the banking systems in Japan and Germany.

World War II had interrupted the completion of my doctorate in economics. My thesis concerning the economics of the petroleum industry still remained to be written and a final oral examination. Progress on the thesis during the war years had been virtually impossible; now I could concentrate. I was awarded my Ph.D. in economics in 1946, and I joined Armstrong Cork Company, now Armstrong World Industries, in 1949 as corporate economist.

As my professional responsibilities broadened so did the number of my foreign contacts. My economic education which had its birth at Berkeley became more globalized.

In 1960 I was named a public director of the Federal Reserve Bank of Philadelphia to represent the general public in the Mid-Atlantic region and eventually became chairman of the Conference of Chairmen of the twelve Federal Reserve Banks. In 1966 I joined the Bank of America as senior vice president and chief economist. This move brought the Hoadleys back to the San Francisco Bay Area, an economic and family round-trip after nearly twenty-five years.

Many campus contacts were re-established. Some faculty mentors still active provided opportunities for reminiscing and speculation about the future of the University. I served the Class of 1938 as president. Many activities with the California Alumni Association afforded me opportunities to work closely with the administration, faculty, and students. Serving as an alumni Regent reinforced my knowledge of the speed and intensity of change in higher education generally and the University of California specifically.

To be named Alumnus of the Year in 1993 was a crowning honor. It is also a life-long reminder of what the University of California has done, and continues to do, to influence and enhance the lives of its students, its alumni, the people of the Bay Area, the state of California, our nation, and the world.

My University of California–rooted economics enhanced my supplemental skills first learned at Cal. They have enabled me to face innumerable challenges with considerable confidence, but also with a high sense of reality and pragmatism.

For Virginia and me to say "thanks Cal" seems so inadequate. We can never hope to repay fully what our campus experiences have meant to us in shaping much of our lives. But we will keep trying.

"Our grandchildren may have never known what it was like to cross the bay in a ferryboat, or to ride the Number 6 streetcar down College Avenue, or to get a pitcher of punch at the Claremont Hotel for five dollars which would last throughout the evening while they danced. What they do know is that they have attended one of the best universities in the world. . . ."

BOBBE PAULEY PAGEN

Bobbe Pauley Pagen

OESN'T GROWING UP IN A COLLEGE TOWN always cast a magic spell on the youth surrounded by the college and by all its influences? That is the way it seemed to my teenage friends and me during our school days in Berkeley. There wasn't a Cal football game, track meet, basketball game, or any sporting event that did not affect us in some way. We knew about Tightwad Hill and the painting of the Big C and the Big Game long before the entering lowly freshman. The University of California was as much a part of us as the lofty campanile which we saw and heard every day.

There was a horror story going around Willard Junior High School, where I went before entering Berkeley High, that if you happened to be one of the unlucky ones up in the campanile when it struck noon, the noise of the chimes striking twelve times might drive you to jump overboard or at least split your eardrums and deafen you forever. Although we took this with a grain of salt, we were never there at either noon or midnight.

Going to Berkeley High, as I did, seemed like a natural step to Cal and, although exhilarated by the sporting events, we all had the gnawing problem in back of our heads of making the right grades in the proper subjects in order to be accepted into that awesome magical place.

In passing the University of California track field every day on my way to Berkeley High from my home, little did I visualize that as vice president of the student body I would one day be giving medals to Jesse Owens and Glen Cunningham on that same field for setting new world records in the Berlin Olympics of 1936.

I was born in Modesto, California, at the Bald Eagle Ranch which my great-grandfather had built for his first home. Modesto has a large archway through which one enters the city. On the arch was a sign "Modesto—Water, Wealth, Contentment, Health." Each night the letters were lighted, which I well remember as a youngster. I take particular pride in that sign because of my great grandparents' participation in the development and growth of Modesto which now has a population of 180,000.

My great grandfather, Robert McHenry, came to the San Joaquin Valley around 1850. In 1885 he became the president of the First National Bank of Modesto, and his son, Oramil, succeeded him as president. Robert became a leader in the cause for irrigation in the Central Valley, and upon his death, Oramil continued the quest for water for the wheat fields which was the main crop for many farmers at that time. My grandfather, Oramil, became an alumnus of the University of California only a few years after its founding in 1869. He built the McHenry Library which now is the McHenry Museum. Robert McHenry began the construction of his home in town in 1882, which now, more than 100 years later, is being restored to its original state and is being preserved as one of California's historical landmarks.

Robert married Matilda Hewitt, who as a young girl traveled by wagon train across the plains with five other siblings from Ohio to California.

Perhaps it was more than moving to Berkeley as a teenager that held my interest in the University of California. Maybe it was the series of events that would follow that would tie me to Cal for the rest of my life. I spent four wonderful years at UC Berkeley, where I formed some beautiful friendships, not the least of whom were Betty and Bill Monahan. Bill had just retired as athletic director at UC Berkeley and was now going to work for a concern headed by Ed Pauley. Ed and I always called the Monahans our cupids, because they introduced us in Los

Angeles the year I graduated, and we were married one year later. Ed, also a UC Berkeley graduate, Class of 1923, was later appointed to the Board of Regents of the University, and I delightedly found myself back on my beloved campus saying a "tearful hello" to everyone to whom I had said a "tearful good-bye" earlier.

It was through Ed's efforts and our affection for the University of California system that UC Berkeley has the Edwin W. Pauley Nuclear Science Center, and the soon to be built Pauley Gallery, both in the Lawrence Hall of Science, and the Barbara McHenry Pauley Ballroom in the student union. (During the Great Depression I was one of the students lucky enough to have a job in the ticket office which was then in Stephens Student Union.) A Pauley track is at UC Santa Barbara, and UCLA has the Pauley Pavilion.

Among the lasting friends I had made was the Dean of Women Lucy Stebbins, who looked like a dean of women is supposed to, with the right amount of decorum to demand respect though she always had a twinkle in her eye. Among my priceless possessions is a book of poems which she gave me called *A Shropshire Lad* by A. E. Housman. In it is written, "For Bobbe Jean's library of poetry—with memories of a happy year and affectionate good wishes for the years to come, From Lucy Ward Stebbins." Her assistant, Dean Bobbie Davidson, was very much a dean, but was full of fun. They both became fast friends.

Another woman friend was Ida Sproul, wife of the president of the University. She was always giving of herself whether it be serving tea to the students or reading a piece of literature to them.

At the time that I was in school during the depression years, the country was seeing a red Communist in every window and under every bed. As a result, Upton Sinclair, a socialist labor leader, and Harry Bridges, head of the Longshoremen's Union, had been refused permission to speak on campus. However, they could speak outside of Sather Gate. Imagine what a howl of protest there would be today! As vice president of the student

273

body, it fell to me to make the speech (after all, I had majored in public speaking) before that unpredictable group, announcing it was leaving certain important gifts to the University from the Class of '36, I had the effrontery to say, "one of our big football stars has just given us a great scare; he has caught the *red* measles." Encouraged by the cheers and applause, I added, "The Class of '36 leaves bigger and better soapboxes from which our distinguished speakers could speak outside of Sather Gate." Maybe it was just as well that President Bob Sproul was out of town and absent from the podium that day. However he soon heard about it, and later called me into his office to see him. He politely and calmly explained that the University could not support the views of these two gentlemen and what they stood for. I, on the other hand, stated that I felt it was the right of the students to hear from prominent leaders of any group, and I thought that it was part of our college education. I apologized for any embarrassment in which I may have put him and the University. In spite of our unsettled differences we formed a friendship which lasted many years.

After the Second World War, Ed was appointed U.S. Ambassador of Reparations by President Truman. On one of Ed's committees, he chose Bob Sproul as a member, for a mission to Moscow. General Eisenhower was the hero of the day in Moscow and all over the world. Ed and I were invited to stay at Spaso House where the U.S. ambassador makes his home. Ambassador Averill Harriman and his daughter, Kathy, were in residence at that time. It was around lunch time when we heard a great commotion at the entrance to Spaso House. Ike had brought a Russian general in with him to lunch! This was unprecedented. To the Harrimans' knowledge there had never been a Russian, let alone a Russian general, inside of Spaso House except officially. They entered laughing, arms around each other. Our relations with Russia at that point were very high indeed! I had first met Eisenhower at an official dinner in a bombed-out house in Berlin. Among the guests were Admiral and Mrs. Radford. She and I were among the first American women visitors into Berlin after the war, and found out in our initial conversation that she not only knew of my hometown Modesto, but had been engaged to my uncle! Here we were, the only two American women in Berlin, and we were practically "kissing cousins." When Eisenhower spoke at a luncheon at UCLA years later, we recalled that incident and decided that "it's a small world after all."

The University of California continued to play a role in my life with my second marriage to Bill Pagen, four years after Ed's death. We were married by a classmate of mine and good friend, Federal Judge Tom MacBride, at his and Martha's home in Lake Tahoe, California. Tom is a retired United States District Judge for the Eastern District of California. He and Martha have generously created a Charitable Remainder Unitrust that will fund a faculty library at Boalt Hall.

Bill could not have been more involved with the University, although this time at UCLA. In fact, in 1992, he received the UCLA Alumnus of the Year Award, the oldest and highest award UCLA gives for dedicated service of an outstanding alumnus. It was a well-deserved award. Bill died a year later from pulmonary complications which became too much for even for the fighter he was! We, his family and friends, are all warmed by the fact that he lived long enough to be recognized for his brilliance and love for the University.

Another event which stands out in my mind was when John F. Kennedy spoke in the Memorial Stadium on Charter Day in 1962. He was introduced by Ed, then chairman of the Board of Regents. We had the same kind of rocking chair at our home that Kennedy used for his bad back, and the same embroidered pads made by the girl who had made his cushions at the White House. We flew this equipment from Los Angeles to the President's house in Berkeley, where President Kennedy was staying and where he used the chair. That rocker is now proudly displayed in our home with words "Kennedy's Chair" embroidered on the chair cushion. It is one of my most cherished possessions.

The advice given to all contributors to this book was to

275

write about ourselves at Berkeley, and how Berkeley influenced our lives. I looked in our yearbook and it listed the following after my name—ASUC vice president, and a member of Alpha Chi Omega, Prytanean (a women's honor society of which I am still a member), and ASUC Executive Committee where it reads, "Bobbe Jean McHenry has exhibited leadership in advancing new ideas. She represented the ASUC at the Student Institute of Pacific Relations Conference. In connection with this she held weekly meetings with students of different races to help them become more a part of the general campus. In regard to a woman's dormitory, she had a campus vote to register public opinion and contacted alumnae groups." The resume continued, "Women's Executive Committee, Finance Committee, Forum Governing Board, a member of Treble Clef (we sang the opera *Boris Godunov* with the University of California Symphony), the *Occident*—the campus literary magazine." The Women's Judicial Committee was formerly the Women's Student Affairs Committee which was "coordinated with the Men's Judicial Committee as the disciplinary force in the student government on the campus. It also focused on the regulation of student conduct in examinations."

As for my interests, I majored in public speaking, but anthropology, paleontology, and music were my favorite courses. I especially admired Marjorie Petray, my music professor, for being very accomplished and an able teacher. I particularly remember with fondness Professor Barrows, the poli-sci professor with the sonorous voice. You could hear his "harrumph" from one end of Wheeler Auditorium to the other. Two of my public speaking class professors I also remember: Professor Perstein, who ably challenged our thinking processes, and Professor Flaherty, whose poems we memorized.

As a member of the Deputations Committee, which also encompassed the Forum Board for student debates, it was my lot to speak at high schools about the statewide University of California and my beloved Berkeley. Every big and little town was anxious to hear about our famous University. We were asked all kinds of questions. I like to think that maybe we played a little part in persuading an aspiring student to go to our Cal.

Most of my life I've been married and had the role of homemaker, mother of three wonderful children, and grandmother of eight. Among those who are following in our footsteps attending Cal are a daughter, one son who graduated from UC Santa Barbara, and two Cal grandchildren. One granddaughter will graduate this May. One grandson received the same American Legion Award in grammar school that I had received in Modesto.

I'm afraid that I never became a celebrity as are the other contributors to this book.

Our grandchildren may have never known what it was like to cross the bay in a ferryboat, or to ride the Number 6 streetcar down College Avenue, or to get a pitcher of punch at the Claremont Hotel for five dollars which would last throughout the evening while they danced. What they do know is that they have attended one of the best universities in the world and have been taught by the finest faculty, and that the University of California at Berkeley has produced the highest number of Nobel Prize winners of any other university and is a distinguished public university in medical research. There are far too many honors accredited to this University for me to list.

Having been the president of my freshman class, I am proud to continue on as permanent president of the Class of '36, and thus, the University of California in all its greatness and glory continues to be a part of my life.

"By the end of my sophomore year, I was totally and irretrievably in love with Cal, with all it offered and stood for. The stature of its faculty, the ability and diversity of its student body, the breadth of its offerings—both intellectual and extra-curricular—made me realize how fortunate I was to have been admitted to this institution."

ADRIAN A. KRAGEN

Adrian A. Kragen

I ENTERED CAL IN THE FALL OF 1927 not knowing what to expect and certainly not anticipating that it would be the opening for me of tremendous opportunities and a wonderfully fulfilling life. In fact, I probably came to the University as a sort of relief station after working for a few years. I was a very mediocre high school student with little or no interest in education. I had quit high school without graduating and tried my hand at working in businesses requiring little or no skill. I decided to try the college scene when a fellow worker suggested that our jobs were dead-end, with which I agreed, and said we could get into college by studying for two or three years at a preparatory school. I decided to try that route. My friend stayed and took my job. Bates Preparatory attracted mainly rich kids who had been unsuccessful in public school or who were lazy. I was paying the tuition with my own money and worked very hard. As a result, the administration recommended me for admission to Cal after eleven months of study at Bates.

The University was an entirely new world to me. None of my family had ever even thought of going to college. I am sure my parents were very surprised when I told them of my decision and because of my prior high school record were sure I shouldn't last very long in this new venture. My fellow students, the faculty, and even what I considered to be the mammoth size of the physical plant and the whole concept of higher education had never been within the scope of my imagination. However, I quickly became acclimated to this new world. My first semester I enrolled in

History 4A with Professor Franklin Palm and enjoyed the course so much that I decided that history was to be my major. David Prescott Barrows, with his broad ranging lectures, introduced me to the area of government and of course made a tremendous impression on all of us when, on the first Friday of the semester, he strode into Wheeler in the full uniform of a brigadier general. I enrolled in Economics 1A with Ira Cross and was introduced through his excellent lectures not only to basic economics but to what I regarded as outrageous eccentricity when in the sixth or seventh class he said, "Will the couple necking in the seventh row please leave" and waited until they did. I began to meet people—both students and faculty—who brought me to understand the value of a good education, and I quickly decided I was going to work diligently to become part of what I regarded then and still consider to be an elite group.

Of course, it was difficult as a twenty-year-old freshman who had been in the "real world" to accept the hazing of eighteen- and nineteen-year-old sophomores. Luckily I was not told to roll a peanut with my nose down Bancroft Way, but it was demeaning to be required to wear a freshman beanie.

In high school, I had placed an undue emphasis on participation in athletic activities. At Cal I soon found that I was not up to University standards as a participant, but that I could have real enjoyment participating in intercollegiate athletics as a spectator. I entered into that phase of activity enthusiastically, and it has been an important and pleasant part of my life and that of my family ever since.

Every aspect of my university life at Berkeley was enjoyable though I had to endure during the first semester the long commute from my parents' home in San Francisco. Even that had its compensation with the fun of riding the ferryboats in both good and bad weather and forming friendships with other commuter students. As the days wore on, I began to wander about the campus, enjoying its beauty, to lounge at Sather Gate, and to become a part of the campus scene. To supplement my financial resources, I took a job washing glassware at the zoology lab, which, although it was a somewhat smelly occupation, gave me a view of another part of university life.

I cannot say that I enjoyed my first experience with midterm examinations, although I did enjoy the rather decent grades the readers gave me, and examinations soon became a normal aspect of university life. I worried about the results every time I finished my blue book, but I did well enough to become a member of Phi Beta Kappa.

My sophomore year included two milestone events that affected my life thereafter. First I met a young lady, Billie Bercovich, as a blind date at a sorority dance, and very quickly hoped she would be in my future. The second event occurred because I had decided to take a rather heavy course overload and wanted one course that would not be too demanding. I consulted friends who were juniors. They suggested that Jurisprudence 10AB, an introduction to the common law via Blackstone, would be fun, that I could easily get an "A" from the lecturer, an Oakland lawyer. Therefore, I enrolled in the course and on the first day found that the Oakland lawyer was no longer giving the course. Rather, it was a young professor in his first year of teaching at Boalt Hall, Roger John Traynor, and he was very demanding. However, I found the course to be great and Professor Traynor to be inspiring. He changed my life. I decided to go to law school and Professor Traynor became my father confessor and mentor, responsible for many of the wonderful events that have happened to me in my chosen profession. He embodies what has been often said, "A great teacher can give you inspiration and change your life." In my seven undergraduate and law school years at the University of California at Berkeley, I discovered some great teachers but none has had the influence on me that Roger Traynor had: as he later influenced all of the state and the country when he became a justice, then Chief Justice of the Supreme Court of California, unquestionably the finest state court justice in the nation.

By the end of my sophomore year, I was totally and irretrievably in love with Cal, with all it offered and stood for. The

283

stature of its faculty, the ability and diversity of its student body, the breadth of its offerings—both intellectual and extra-curricular—made me realize how fortunate I was to have been admitted to this institution.

During my junior year I lived in a lodging house on Union Street, about where the entrance to Zellerbach Hall is now situated. There was a little cottage on the rear of the lot. Four law students lived there; one of them was Bernard Witkin, today the guru of California's law writers. From Bernie and his housemates I obtained a view of the breadth of interest which I believe has always characterized Cal students. Day or night in this cottage, discussions went on about as diverse a catalogue of subjects as was possible and, of course, intriguing disagreements. I began to appreciate then how much other students contribute to one's learning process.

My junior and senior years enabled me to broaden both my knowledge and perspective. I had the tremendous experience of delving into anthropology under the tutelage of those legendary giants of the subject, Professors Kroeber and Lowie. I was brought to realize how important and how fascinating was the study of the roots of our civilization. Professor Charles Gulick made his class in economics appreciate the values and defects of the labor movement, and how important it was to understand its place in our society. I explored United States history with Professor Laurence Harper, himself a Boalt Hall graduate, and Professor Bolton, who was a world renowned expert on Western history. In my senior year I joined the honors course with Professor Guttridge, which, because of the breadth of the material we covered, expanded my outlook and my understanding of our historical background.

Starting with my sophomore year, I joined the University debate team, and in my senior year served that unit as debate manager. Unfortunately, the year I took office, the dean of students decided to eliminate the twenty-five dollars a month stipend previously paid the holder of that office. Maybe it was the depression that caused the change, but I could surely have used

the twenty-five dollars. Despite that deficiency, I enjoyed pro-
moting and doing the essential acts necessary to stage debates
with students from Oxford, Harvard, and many universities
from California and other states. In those days, major events
such as the Oxford and Joffre Medal debates filled old Harmon
Gymnasium. Today I wonder if even the most prestigious
debate group would fill 800-seat Wheeler Auditorium. In
those days before television, 50,000 or more people went to
Memorial Stadium to watch our football team play St. Mary's,
Santa Clara...

In my senior year, I remember the thrill of moving into
the just-opened International House where, in contrast to my
Spartan and mediocre room at the lodging house, I enjoyed a single room with maid service for twenty dollars a month. I also
had the opportunity to meet students from many foreign countries, a valuable experience for one who had never been east of
Sacramento. I obtained some understanding of diametrically different styles of life from my own, of the students, from such countries as Japan, India, Germany, England, Singapore. This
exposure was invaluable after I graduated from law school and
started to deal with people whose lifestyles and backgrounds
were significantly different from ours. International House was a
very important part of the educational process at Cal.

Also in my senior year I became assistant ticket manager
for football, which meant additional income, but also that I
could see only the second and third quarters of each game. It was
an interesting experience for one who normally never left any
game till the last gun had sounded. It also gave me an idea of how
the business end of an athletic program operated. Harry Davis,
the ticket manager, was a good manager but Bill Mead, the other
assistant, and I were irritated with him when he insisted we
recount thousands of dollars to find a fifty-cent discrepancy.
I now think that training too has served me well in my professional life.

In my senior year I became (with Robert Bridges) the
reader for Professor Palm's History 145/146, a course on the his-

tory of modern Europe very popular with sorority and fraternity members and athletes. In addition to its being the highest paid reader's position on the campus ($550 each semester), it provided me experience in preparing and reading examination papers which I used when I returned to Cal as a professor. It also gave me an indication of how to react to some of the most heartrending stories you will ever hear about the reason for a student's poor performance in an exam! Bridges and I were regaled with more reasons for class absence and other misfeasances or nonfeasances than we ever thought existed.

I graduated in 1931 with highest honors in history. The question now was whether I should go to Boalt Law School or Hastings in San Francisco for my law education. Money was very tight in the midst of the depression. I chose Hastings because I had a job with a small law firm serving papers and doing odd jobs, and I could live at home. I was second in my class at the end of my first year. However, I missed Berkeley too much to continue at Hastings. When I met with Dean McMurray, himself a Hastings graduate, to request admission to Boalt, he told me that Boalt did not accept Hastings transfers. Heartbroken, I called on Professor Traynor, and with the assistance of Professor Barbara Armstrong, my admission to Boalt was obtained. I did not and think few, if any, of my classmates realized at that time that Boalt Hall, a comparatively small and somewhat provincial school, had one of the finest law school faculties in the country. We understood that we were receiving a fine legal education, and our professors were excellent, but we had no concept of how high their colleagues at Harvard, Yale, Columbia, and other prestigious eastern schools rated them. I found out about the reputation of that faculty after I started attending American Law School Association meetings in the 1950s. Boalt was especially unique in having the only female law professor in the country, a wonderful teacher and scholar. While Harvard, Yale, Chicago, and other law schools would not admit women at all, they were in my class at Boalt and accounted for about 10 percent of the class. Boalt Hall was a nice compact building that meant the faculty could not evade the students, as they frequently could and did at Harvard and Yale.

The world renowned legal scholar Max Radin had an office as big as a small coat closet, as was Professor Armstrong's. However, in his minute office, with its desk stacked high with books and articles, Professor Radin was always willing to reach into that pile of materials for an article or book which would be helpful to our problem. Professor Kidd, who often called the class "only fit to be ribbon clerks," was also always ready to help with any student crisis, even to bailing out a student who had a brush with the law. Professor Traynor shared his office with the *Law Review* for which he was faculty adviser. When I was freed for the second and third quarter of a football home game and came up to sit with my now wife Billie, there were always a half-dozen of the law professors watching the game.

Leaving the somewhat sheltered life of a Cal student in 1934 was not ideal. It was then the height of the depression and only a few of the top ten students got jobs. I did get a job full of opportunities for experience but lacking in compensation. However, Cal was never far from my being: I spent time with Professor Traynor discussing tax law and attended all Cal football and basketball events. I even tried to go back to Boalt to get a S.J.D. but was turned down by Dean Dickerson who told me Boalt was a poor place for such an endeavor. I never forgave him for this slight to my school.

When in 1940 Roger Traynor persuaded then Attorney General Warren to give me a position as deputy attorney general, my debt to Professor Traynor and to Cal was heavily increased. In addition to being a great man, Earl Warren was one whose devotion to Cal exceeded my own. Later as Governor, he was able to implement this devotion to the benefit of the entire University system. I had contact with him while he was the Chief Justice of the Supreme Court of the United States. At his request, I interviewed students from California law schools and recommended one each year as his law clerk.

In 1944 I joined the Los Angeles law firm of Loeb and

Loeb, and I saw more evidence of the value of my Berkeley education. I became associated with Herman Selvin, a Cal undergraduate and Boalt Hall alumnus, the finest lawyer I have ever known and as loyal to Cal as anyone who ever attended the university.

In 1951 I was offered a tenured professorship at Boalt Hall including an endowed chair. There was very little hesitation by myself or Billie when I discussed the offer with her. I said "yes" even though it meant a 75 percent reduction in income. In fact, when at dinner in Perino's restaurant in Los Angeles, Dean Prosser was making the offer of the professorship, Billie weakened my negotiating power by saying "wonderful" or "great" or some similar statement at every mention of Cal, Boalt, or Berkeley. It was our belief that being a member of the Cal faculty was the ultimate achievement.

Returning to Boalt after eighteen years was a revelation. Not only had the school left the old building and started the process of increasing its student body, but Dean Prosser had brought enormous visibility to the school and nationwide recognition of the quality of its faculty and student body. Dean Prosser had told me that the faculty was "sort of indecently fond of each other," and it was, in fact, probably the most congenial faculty of any major law school in the country.

I hope that I have inculcated in my students my own feeling of the greatness of the school generally and my own loyalty.

My four-year stint as vice chancellor under Chancellors Glenn Seaborg and Edward Strong gave me a wider view of the campus family and the all-campus dedication to maintaining the prestige of the institution. Because I was assigned the task of transferring the administration of the intercollegiate athletic program from the ASUC to the Berkeley administration, I became very close to that program as well, and I have witnessed the evolution which has made Cal one of the foremost universities in the country ensuring that athletes are truly student-athletes, with a major emphasis on academic progress while building quality teams.

The draconian effort to meet the increasing budget diffi-

288

culties which have resulted from the past year's turn-down of the California economy with early retirement offers, salary cuts, and other expedients would be anticipated in the normal course to drastically reduce the quality of the academic offerings at Berkeley. But we appear to be able still to attract new young faculty of the highest caliber as well as world-renowned professors. This is due to the University's fine reputation in the academic world and to the loyalty of its alumni, who are giving loving support, in both financial and personal involvement. As the members of my class are planning our sixtieth anniversary reunion, we find that we have contributed, not only to the legal profession but to the prestige and welfare of Cal. Many of us have been in the judiciary; some have held high office in the State Bar. Many have lent luster in their representation of clients in pro bono activities.

This great Cal spirit makes me somewhat inordinately proud that I graduated from this wonderful institution.

289

"The beauty of the campus and
the Berkeley hills left a deep
impression, but deeper still was
the intense intellectual life of a
graduate department."

JOHN W. GARDNER

John W. Gardner

I SPENT MY EARLY BOYHOOD in the midst of lima bean fields crisscrossed by neatly paved streets with streetlights. The company that developed Beverly Hills as a real estate venture had laid out the streets; and all the land that had not yet been sold for houses (most of it at that time) was leased out to the farmer who raised the beans.

Beverly Hills was a very small village, separated from Los Angeles by eleven miles of open country dotted with oil derricks. There were three or four stores. Everyone knew the one policeman. In fact, everyone knew everyone else.

I spent two of my school years at Punahou School in Honolulu. We lived at Waikiki, which was in those days a wonderfully peaceful residential area. After the third year of high school I spent a year traveling around the world with my brother and grandparents.

For my brother and myself, the University of California and Stanford University—Cal and Stanford—were household words from early boyhood and in this we differed not at all from other boys the length and breadth of the state. But of course the words stood for football teams. Our awareness of the institutions to which the teams were attached was dim at best.

In 1929 I entered Stanford, spent three years as an English major, and then took a year and a half off pursuing the odd notion that I could write the Great American Novel. Failing that, I returned to college in 1934 and received my A.B. in psychology in 1935, my M.A. in 1936.

I was married in my senior year to a girl of extraordinary grace and beauty, Aida Marroquin. When we first met, two years earlier, she spoke no English and I could not converse in Spanish, but it was a negligible barrier.

The next two years were spent earning a Ph.D. degree and serving as a teaching assistant in psychology at the University of California. It was a new world of concentrated effort and single-minded commitment to one field.

To me the University of California was the faculty and graduate students of the Department of Psychology. Together they formed a small and intensely preoccupied society within the University, intimately in touch with other psychologists throughout the nation and the world, but not always in touch with the rest of the University.

The faculty made a particularly deep impression on me. There was Warner Brown, my principal advisor, a man of cool, keen intellect whose personal warmth and kindness were hidden by a rather austere manner. There was Edward Tolman, the favorite of every graduate student, one of the great psychologists of his generation, a tall, gracious, humorous man, full of ideas, questions, impulses, and warmth toward others. There was Jean MacFarlane, a superb teacher and a wise, perceptive, understanding human being. There was Robert Tryon, a big, genial man with an original mind and a remarkable gift for friendship.

They still represent the University in my memory—and it's a good way for the University to be remembered. They had an unselfconscious devotion to their field, an intellectual commitment that communicated itself to every newcomer. At many points in my career it has been essential that I understand research and research people, and the ideas and ideals of the academic world. My comprehension of those values was deepened and strengthened in my period at Berkeley.

The one additional item that must be mentioned is the Bancroft Library. It contained (still contains), among other things, one of the great collections on Spanish colonial days in the West, presided over by Herbert Bolton. Bolton's older brother

Thaddeus was one of the distinguished figures in the early days of American psychology. Capitalizing on that thin connection, I paid a call on Bolton one day to obtain some guidance in the study of California history, a field I had no business paying attention to when I was intensely busy working toward a degree in psychology. He worked out a reading list for me, and I began a leisurely exploration of California history that has continued to this day.

It was, perhaps, an odd diversion for a psychologist, but it was just another theme in the omnivorous reading that began when I was five and continued for some forty years. In my mid-forties I began to limit my reading to fields in which I was directly active at the moment—a necessary step if I were to accomplish all the homework necessary in those busy years. The years have not grown less busy, and my reading has never regained the undisciplined breadth of earlier decades. Now, when starkly clear priorities and the viselike pressure of time constrict my interests, I thank God for that early aimlessness.

In summary, my experience at Berkeley was typically that of a graduate student, more intellectual than social. The beauty of the campus and the Berkeley hills left a deep impression, but deeper still was the intense intellectual life of a graduate department.

When I left Berkeley, my objectives were simple—to be a good academic psychologist, to do great research, to rise in the academic ranks, to write articles and books.

It was a short career. I pursued those objectives on college faculties for four years. Then, following the attack on Pearl Harbor, I went to Washington to work with the Federal Communications Commission for a year before joining the Marine Corps. I was eventually assigned to OSS and served overseas in Italy and Austria.

When I first arrived in Washington, I was asked to head the Latin American section of the Foreign Broadcast Intelligence Service. Since I had a good knowledge of the Spanish language and of Latin America I had no doubt of my intellectual capacity to handle the job. But I was astounded when I began to receive good marks on my administrative ability. It was wholly contrary to my image of myself, wholly at odds with my plans for the future. I had never run anything. I had no ambition to run anything. From my earliest years, I had thought of myself as a student, an observer, pleasantly detached from the mainstream of the world's action. From that point on, my life was to be governed by constant conflict between the life of action and the life of reflection.

When I left the Marine Corps after the war, I joined Carnegie Corporation and spent nineteen rewarding years, in which my two lives were pleasantly combined. Though I spent the last ten of those years as president of the Carnegie Corporation and the Carnegie Foundation for the Advancement of Teaching, I found ample time for reading and writing. My first book, *Excellence*, was published in 1961.

A more important product of the Carnegie years was an intensive education in the plans of men, the nature of innovation, what it takes to nourish creativity, and all the ways in which good ideas flourish or fail. My second book, *Self-Renewal* (1964), a study of the life and death of institutions and societies, was drawn wholly and directly from that experience.

The years with Carnegie were family years. When we moved to Scarsdale in 1946 our two daughters, Stephanie and Francesca, were just beginning school; when we left they had completed college, (Radcliffe and Stanford, respectively) and were both married.

Fairly early in the Carnegie years, I began to travel to Washington to fulfill consulting assignments, first in the Department of Defense and then more widely—the Office of Education, the Department of State, the White House. By the time I joined President Johnson's Cabinet in 1965 I was thoroughly familiar with the bureaucracy.

I did not accept the cabinet post eagerly. Though my position at Carnegie Corporation was highly visible, I was not a public man and still am not. It was no pleasure for me to plunge into the world of press conferences, ever present photographers, and endless public interaction with my fellow human beings.

Nevertheless, my commitment to public service was real and deep, and has remained so. When I resigned from the Cabinet in early 1968, I found, after weighing an extraordinary variety of invitations, that what I wanted most of all was to continue—in a private capacity—to concern myself with the same range of problems that had engaged my attention as Secretary of Health, Education and Welfare. I accepted the chairmanship of the Urban Coalition, a private organization concerned with the problems of the cities.

My life has been one of continuous change. It would suit the tradition of complacency in autobiography to say that the change was all good and growth-producing. But who knows what other, better paths I might have taken.

"College is becoming more and more
a place to expose the student to the
techniques of acquiring new
knowledge rather than one for the
absorption of past wisdom."

DANIEL E. KOSHLAND JR.

Daniel E. Koshland Jr.

"Hey, Freshman, where's your dink?" The words came anonymously from an overlooking window as I walked up the winding stairs to Bowles Hall. I pretended I hadn't heard but I wondered what a "dink" was and whether the mystic voice was registering friendly hostility or hostile hostility. Only that spring I had been a lordly high-school senior, comfortable in small, familiar surroundings. On that September 1937 day I was entering the renowned University of California with 3,000 other freshmen and everything seemed insecure.

Before arriving on the Berkeley campus I had obtained a copy of the catalog of the University, which even in those days was the size of a small telephone book. I had read the fantastic smorgasbord of courses in that catalog—differential equations, Sanskrit, physics of the nucleus, physical chemistry, oriental art, international law, history of religion. Whole departments were devoted to subjects that I hadn't known existed. Subjects with which I was familiar were not learned in a single course but involved in an unbelievable proliferation into esoteric specialties. I couldn't even understand the descriptions of the advanced courses. Like a child on a merry-go-round, I was exhilarated by the adventure but just a little scared at the speed with which I was moving.

How quickly moods change. A month later I was wearing my dink properly and happily explaining to my younger sisters, parents, and friends how Cal worked. By my sophomore year I knew everything. Now, twenty-seven years later, I return as a professor at the same University and wonder whether the idyllic world I remember ever really existed. Are reminiscences ever valid or do nostalgia, egotism, and forgetfulness conspire to distort our memories of past events? I do know that the University had a tremendous impact on my life intellectually, socially, emotionally, politically, and morally. Some of its influences were not felt until many years later; others are perhaps still unrecognized. Some of the effects were in the form of direct technical training which was immediately utilized; others involved intangible attitudes which appeared in many forms over many years.

Perhaps the most lasting impact was the result of the stimulation of great teachers, strong personalities with that indefinable charisma which builds legends. I remember my first freshman class from Professor Joel Hildebrand. As he began his lecture in the sloping amphitheater of the lecture hall, the buzz of whispered comments, rustling papers, and clattering books gradually subsided. When his words became audible to me midway in the room, he was explaining the kinetic theory of gases and I settled down to take notes, impressed by the lucidity of the presentation. The lecture proceeded swiftly and clearly and I left the hall knowing what a fine lecturer could do with a complex subject. When I came to the second class, on Wednesday, Professor Hildebrand was handing out blue books, the blank books which signaled an examination, and I and my bewildered neighbors were wondering what was occurring. Professor Hildebrand returned to the rostrum and with a slight twinkle in his eye said, "Some students have asked me what the blue books are for. Apparently they missed the announcement at the beginning of my lecture last time that we would have a short quiz on the contents of my first lecture at the beginning of my second lecture. By the way, it is my practice to announce quizzes at the opening of my lectures." Needless to say my fellow freshmen and I did miserably on that first quiz, but Professor Hildebrand never again had to ask for quiet when he entered the classroom. The speed of light could be measured by the time between Professor

Hildebrand's entrance and the moment of attentive silence in the class. If this had been only one flashy gimmick in an otherwise prosaic course, it would not be worth remembering, but it was typical of the imaginative understanding of human nature and the ironic amusement of the master teacher which pervaded his approach to all aspects of that course.

Other great teachers reveled in the excitement of the classroom and played on the audience of students in the way a great conductor draws the best from an orchestra. Ira B. Cross in economics and Robert Kerner in history seemed to gain sustenance from a large classroom filled with eager students. There was an electric atmosphere in each of these classes and I would no more have thought of missing a Monday, Wednesday, or Friday lecture by Kerner or Cross than I would have missed the Cal-Stanford game. In the midst of the 1938 Czechoslovakian crisis, Kerner would frequently be late for class. It was a rule at the University that the class would leave if a professor was more than ten minutes late. On some occasions, about nine minutes after the starting time of class, Kerner's secretary would arrive and say, "Professor Kerner is on the phone talking to Premier Benes and won't be finished for a few minutes. Those of you who would like to leave can do so." Not a student moved. Sometimes Kerner would return from these phone calls and proceed to lecture exactly where he had left off the previous time. On other occasions he would plunge immediately into the then current Czechoslovakian crises. We felt we were living history, perhaps helping to make it, and certainly understanding how it was made.

Kerner made one prediction after another about the future of Europe in those troubled times and almost invariably he was right. Some of us sitting around the dormitory rooms would compare his "batting average" with those of well-known columnists of the time. Invariably Kerner's predictions were more accurate. One day one of us asked in the question period, "Professor Kerner, how is it that you are so much more accurate in making predictions than the columnists in the daily press?" Kerner was not a modest man and we knew he would like the question. His reply was, "Columnists read the daily newspapers and each other. I read history and geography. The history of Russia is the urge to control ice-free ports. The history of Middle Europe is the desire to control outlets to the sea. Ideologies come and go; the facts of geography remain. If the columnists would read more history and geography instead of each other, they might be better predictors." Kerner's course, with its probing analysis of the underlying factors of history, remained with me for many years as the difference between a penetrating understanding and mere knowledge of superficial data.

Kerner vehemently denounced Hitler and was steadfast in his predictions that Hitler would plunge the world into war. At this period in 1937 many newspapers were stating that the fears were exaggerated and that one could "do business with Hitler." One day a student asked Kerner if his statements weren't rather extreme in view of many contradictory reports. "Perhaps," suggested the student, "the truth lies somewhere in between the statements of Kerner and those of the daily press."

Kerner replied icily, "If I say two and two is four and the paper says two and two is five, that doesn't make two and two four and a half." I remember Kerner's four and a half whenever proponents of compromise suggest there is not truth but only a muddy middle between opposing views.

Not all professors made their impressions on their students in a large classroom. I had Professor William C. Bray in an advanced course in chemistry laboratory. In most laboratory courses a slavish following of textbook recipe allows one to complete a laboratory experiment and only later during the write-ups does one comprehend the purpose of the three-hour laboratory. I had begun in the usual manner in the first period of Professor Bray's course when he entered the laboratory and stopped by my desk.

"Koshland," he said, "what are you doing there?"

"I'm on page six," I replied, "weighing out manganese dioxide."

"Yes, yes," he said impatiently. "I can see that is where

you are. But why are you doing it?"

"Because the lab book says so."

"But why does the lab book ask you to do that?" said he, and so the conversation went. I was desperately delaying for time, knowing that I did not understand what I was doing, and Bray in a loud voice was pursuing the questioning to my infinite embarrassment. In about thirty seconds it was clear to him that I did not have one single sophisticated thought on this experiment and for four and a half subsequent minutes Professor Bray persisted in questioning me on what I thought might be the purpose of the experiment, how the manganese dioxide might react, and so forth. When he had finished with me, he moved on to the next student in the laboratory and went through the same procedure. The students at the farther end of the lab benches had a little time to organize their thoughts but the difficulty of the questions increased proportionately, and as he left the laboratory every student in the class had been subjected to a painful interrogation. In the second laboratory session twenty-five chemistry students all arrived completely prepared, having read at least two articles in addition to the textbook. Bray didn't disappoint us. He continued the questioning procedure then and throughout the course, and pretended never to notice the dramatic improvement in the competence of our replies.

Since my profession has been in academic life, many of the techniques of these professors have been invaluable to me. I have used a variant of Professor Bray's approach, for example, in large lecture classes. If I ask a rhetorical question such as, "Why do you believe the genetic code is so universal," I find the class usually sits passively awaiting my expected answer to my own question. So now, after a moment's hesitation, I say, "Mr. Smith, what do you think?" Mr. Smith struggles with the answer, sometimes successfully and sometimes not. If Mr. Smith fails, I may try a few other students or answer the question myself. But whether the question is answered correctly or not is immaterial. Every future question finds each student struggling for an answer in case he should be the victim to be called on. As a result, when the answer is forthcoming, it is more meaningful and more fixed in the memory of the student. I am not sure I would have the courage to use this technique or to bear some of the frightful silences that result if I could not look back with gratitude and respect on the teaching of Professor Bray.

Far more important than these individual techniques, these professors imparted a zest for learning, an enthusiasm for penetrating thinking, and a love of their subject which was contagious. I didn't want to be a historian but I was determined to enjoy something as thoroughly as Professor Kerner enjoyed history. I always enjoyed learning and I can't say the University really introduced me to that. In high school I soaked up science, English, and history and wanted to learn as much about as many things as possible. The difference at the University was that I was for the first time exposed to probing deeply beneath the surface. I learned that there were men who felt they were just beginning a subject long after most men thought they had mastered it, men who would never rest until their research revealed basic understanding. William Whyte, in his admirable book *The Organization Man,* makes the point that the successful businessman, the successful scientist, the successful comedian, in fact the successful anything, is the man who is driven by internal fires. Fame can act as a spur and money can act as a spur but the men who lead to new frontiers push themselves on even after they have more fame than they can absorb or more money than they care to spend. The University of California, with its fantastic catalog of courses, offered the chance for a student to explore until he found an area of enthusiasm and then to learn from the great explorers of the mind how to follow that enthusiasm to new horizons.

Today I read frequently how big the universities are and how the poor student becomes a cog in the automated machine. Cal is today twice as big as when I was an undergraduate but the change from 15,000 to 27,000 probably would never be noticed by an undergraduate student. Maybe because nobody told us it was big and heartless, it never occurred to us to worry about it. I didn't want to, and would have been uncomfortable if forced to sit for long hours alone with a professor. I wanted professors to be available for brief, spirited sessions during office hours and they were. (I remember one spirited battle with Professor Cross when I thought I had discovered a fatal flaw in the professor's argument. I dashed into his office hour expecting to slay the dragon. With a benign smile and Socratic questioning he led me step by step until I realized with horror that I was about to contradict my opening postulate.) I expected and enjoyed the fact that my professors were inventive scholars of international renown and it was assumed that they would never have achieved these reputations if they spent all their afternoons chatting with undergraduates. With very few exceptions, I found the professors of the University accessible and willing to talk to me in any legitimate discussion (and I find that to be true of the University today). I always had the feeling, however, that as soon as the question or argument or advice which I was requesting was taken care of, the professor had something else to do. That did not make the professor less attractive; the fact that his time was of value to him made it clear he was sharing something of value with me. Occasionally we were puzzled by professors who seemed overeager to talk to us. Didn't they have anything better to do with their time?

Contact between professor and student is achieved in many ways and having taught at a small, highly select graduate university (The Rockefeller University) and the big, bustling University of California, I believe one of the great assets of American education is that there is such an enormous variety of institutions. The small liberal arts college and the vast complex university each are performing vital and different functions. The small liberal arts college cannot offer the variety of the big university. The big university cannot offer the warmth of the small school. Each, however, can do an excellent job in its own sphere. No one suggests that New York City can have all the culture, financial power, amusement centers, etc. of a big metropolis and at the same time the personal recognition and sleepy serenity of a small town. I wonder why the press expects a big university to have both.

In this regard I remember a comment by Professor Paxson of history after a dinner at Bowles Hall. It was a custom to invite a well-known professor to dinner at Bowles Hall for an evening of social conversation with ten or fifteen students. A student asked Professor Paxson what he felt the role of a professor in a big university was. Did he feel that a lot of the warmth and friendliness was lost in such a large institution? Professor Paxson answered, "I don't know about the role of the university but I can tell you about the role of a professor. I view myself as a busy farmer. Some say I should spend all my time looking for the bad seedlings and coddle them and nourish them and worry over them. I feel that my job is to spread the manure. If it is good manure, the good seedlings will grow."

The "Hey, Freshman, where's your dink" phenomenon was extended to many other aspects of living, intellectual as well as physical. In every university there is usually a course or two in which the students spend hours in the laboratory, work weekends and nights, lose sleep, and overwork at the expense of other courses. It is traditional to curse the incompetence of the designers of the course and the immorality of the exploitation. Yet it is these courses which stand out years later. I remember most distinctly what I learned in the class and the character of the other individuals who shared the ordeal with me. Some in their moments of adversity helped their colleagues generously in time and effort. Others, bent on solving their own problems, monopolized source books and left equipment in disarray. The importance of friendships formed in dire peril has, of course, been observed many times, but I believe the significance of the shared ordeal in a university education is frequently overlooked. Just as the education and formal training of the college prepare a student for subsequent life, so the social challenges and moral challenges become preparation for later obstacles. The terrors of the "dink" or the "impossible course" are surmounted, only to be replaced by new challenges, with the same uneasy feeling in the pit of the stomach. The new job, the move to a new town, the step to propose a new theory, each produces its own worries, but now the

308

worries only serve to remind us of past fears that proved to be groundless. Happiness has been defined as the construction of hurdles just high enough for one to jump. The University helped us raise the level of the hurdles and helped give us the confidence that we would be able to jump them.

The various aspects of student government gave the fledgling politician a chance to experiment. The student body of 15,000 was sufficiently large to require campaigning and organization, but sufficiently protected so that the costs in time and money were within the reach of busy and not so wealthy students. I remember forging a coalition of liberals to battle the reactionary entrenched forces in my sophomore year. Clearly we were the good guys and the entrenched forces were the bad guys. But by the time the senior year had been reached I was somewhat dismayed to find that some of my regular colleagues had deserted to the foe and some of the apparently irredeemable villains had seen the light and joined our side. Years later, when I was first elected to a school board, a veteran board member turned to me and said, "I'll give you one piece of advice that I had to learn the hard way. Everyone's motives are noble." At first I didn't know what he meant. Gradually, as I listened to groups present arguments before the school board representing the ACLU, the American Legion, the Republican Club, the Taxpayers Association, the Little League, etc. I learned that every group sincerely believed it was acting for the general good. The advocates of low taxes (who just didn't happen to have children in school) were there to protect the economy from disastrous overburdening and the advocates of high taxes (who just happened to have five kids in the public school system) were there to protect the most precious heritage of our country—free public education. So I reinforced what I had learned at Berkeley earlier—it wasn't always easy to separate good guys and bad guys on the basis of motivation. Minds can be changed by exposing procedural flaws, pointing out misjudgments of ultimate results, criticizing unproved assumptions, but no minds will be changed by denouncing your opponent's morality.

I learned another invaluable lesson during political action at Cal. In one office I held I appointed only those whom I considered best qualified, but intellectually and socially these people came from a very small group. As a result, my effectiveness in converting the majority to support the ultimate recommendations was severely limited. So I found that the "best man" in terms of political effectiveness cannot always be decided on the narrowest professional grounds.

For a while Berkeley dropped out of my life except for an occasional sentimental visit or a reminder of a lesson learned long ago. When the war ended, I went back to graduate school, getting a Ph.D. at the University of Chicago and proceeding toward my original goal—a career in biochemistry. My professional career between 1946 and 1965 was entirely in eastern academic institutions. Then, in 1965, I received a phone call from Professor Horace Barker, chairman of the Department of Biochemistry at Berkeley, asking me if I would be interested in coming to join the faculty. We were at the time living in Bellport, Long Island, under fairly idyllic conditions. I had a joint appointment at Brookhaven National Laboratory and the Rockefeller University, allowing me to combine the facilities of an excellent research institute with those of a small, stimulating university. My wife had a job at Brookhaven. Our home was three blocks from the children's school and one block from Great South Bay. The cultural attractions of New York City could be enjoyed while living in the country. I had just the month before declined an offer from an eastern university after soul-searching discussions in which my wife and I concluded that we could not live in a better place. But the morning after my call from Dr. Barker, I decided I should at least look over the Berkeley campus, and after a week on the campus I had succumbed once again to the pulse of Berkeley. I thought I made the decision on cold logic—the fine academic standing of the faculty, the facilities to do good research, the high ability of the students—but my wife claims that sentiment played a major role, that she knew after that first phone call we were ultimately fated to move. I can't argue too strongly because the campus today looks as attractive to this middle-aged professor as it did to that callow freshman.

To understand why Berkeley is appealing to a scientist it is necessary to understand the many roles of a professor in a modern university. There is, first of all, the role of lecturer. Part of the enjoyment of lecturing is in the act itself, the challenge of generating enthusiasm and imparting knowledge. Part, however, depends on the caliber of the audience. An eager and sophisticated group of students provide more challenge but also more rewarding responses. There is, secondly, the role of scholar in stimulating his colleagues, which not only makes daily life more pleasant but provides invaluable sources of material in both the preparation of lectures and research. Finally, there is the role of research, perhaps the least understood face of university life as far as the lay public is concerned.

My field of research in biochemistry involves the study of enzymes. Enzymes are the tiny catalysts that control the dynamic processes of all living systems. Nerve conduction, muscular contraction, vision, the digestion of food, and the synthesis of building materials, to name a few, are all controlled by enzymes. When the enzymes operate correctly we are well. When they are deficient or malfunctioning, we are ill. Each mammalian cell, which is about the size of one billionth of a drop of water, contains about 10,000 different enzymes, each with its own specific function. A yeast cell is simpler than a mammalian cell and has only about 3,000 different enzymes, but many are very similar to the mammalian ones. It is sometimes humbling to realize how similar the lowly yeast cell is to the higher animals. It is also fortunate, since we can perform many experiments on yeast cells which would be impossible on man.

In my laboratory at Berkeley students at various levels of development—undergraduate, predoctoral, and postdoctoral—are doing research on enzymes. Each has his own problem, which he will pursue with help and guidance from me but whose success or failure will depend primarily on his own dedication and initiative. One student, for example, is studying sozyme, an enzyme which catalyzes the degradation of bacterial cell walls. From that study we hope to understand why enzymes are so incredibly efficient, far more so than any man-made catalyst. Another student is studying an enzyme from *Salmonella typhimurium* in order to understand genetic defects in the enzyme architecture, defects which we know are the causes of genetic diseases. A third student is studying an enzyme which synthesizes a building block for DNA and which we hope will serve as a model for studies on the role of enzymes in metabolic control. Each of these students is receiving educational credits and serving an apprenticeship and yet each is at the same time pressing back the frontiers of knowledge and adding to the health of our country and the world. There is thus no clear line between research and teaching, education and public service. As in every good symbiotic relationship, everyone benefits. The government gets the services of dedicated and talented youngsters at a nominal price. The students are given the opportunity of participating in real research while acquiring an education.

To illustrate how research in biochemistry is pursued, I might describe a specific problem in our research on biological control mechanisms. To understand the significance of these mechanisms, consider what happens when you cut your finger. At first blood rushes forth. Gradually the bleeding subsides and a clot is formed. Later new skin is formed and finally the production of new skin stops. Control mechanisms are vitally involved in each step. An enzyme, thrombin, must be activated in the clotting mechanisms. If it is not, we would bleed to death, as happens in hemophilia. If it is activated too soon or in the wrong place, thromboses can be formed, as occurs in some types of heart attacks. The enzymes producing skin must be dormant until activated and must be inhibited or "turned off" when they have finished the job. If not, we would continue to produce scar tissue, a situation analogous to cancer, in which uncontrolled growth occurs.

One pervasive feature of control enzymes is the "cooperativity phenomenon." This had originally been observed in hemoglobin by the Danish scientist C. Bohr many years ago, but had never been explained. We and others had puzzled over this phenomenon for a number of years when suddenly it occurred to us that a combination of features—the flexibility of the enzyme molecule, the presence of numerous subunits in an enzyme, the manner in which activators and inhibitors bind—could be combined to make a reasonable qualitative theory. To test the theory, however, we would need quantitative predictions and one young man, George Nemethy, set out to derive the appropriate mathematics. Another young man, David Filmer, programmed these equations for the computer so we could compare our theory with experimental results. To our pleasure we found that we could explain the experimental phenomena quantitatively as well as qualitatively by the theory.

One puzzling feature, however, was the finding that the computer produced not only curves which duplicated the observed phenomena but also some curves of a type which had never been observed in nature. All the previous observations in hemoglobin and control enzymes showed "positive co-operativity," in which the first bound molecule helped the second molecule to bind and the second molecule helped the third and so forth. The anomalous curves predicted an opposite behavior, "negative co-operativity," in which the first molecule made it more difficult for the second molecule to bind. No such phenomenon had been observed, so we published the predictions derived from the computer and tried to find some systems which fit these new types of curves. After a year of looking and finding nothing, we went on to other things.

Some years later, a graduate student, Abby Conway, was studying an enzyme in carbohydrate metabolism and found some peculiar behavior. At first we did not know how to interpret the data and then we remembered those computer curves. Indeed this enzyme was behaving just as the computer had predicted. More recently we have found several other enzymes which show this "negative co-operativity" and scientists in other laboratories around the world have also verified that these anomalous computer curves do appear in nature. We are now pursuing other aspects of this problem, e.g., is it possible these types of co-operativity are important in the functioning of nerves, and are also exploring what new insight into regulation can be deduced from the theories.

This example illustrates many of the features of scientific research. There is a combination of deliberate logic and unexpected luck, theoretical hypothesis and detailed experimental technique, grand design and day-to-day opportunism. The student who will succeed will need dedication, general knowledge, and technical skill. He will also need qualities that frequently surprise an outsider. He will need emotional courage to survive the long periods of "bad results," which can be incredibly disheartening. He will need ingenuity and a willingness to question authority, because creativity in science is more a matter of inventive imagination than disciplined logic. Logic and rigor are needed to establish a hypothesis but its conception usually involves thinking the unthinkable, combining ideas in ways which are considered preposterous. "Light rays bend," "man is descended from apes," "a stone and a feather fall at the same rate in a vacuum"—all preposterous but true. Berkeley abounds in the type of student who enjoys such challenges and it is a professor's delight to watch their minds develop and to have their help in solving the riddles of nature.

It is inevitable to compare the Berkeley of then with the Berkeley of now. The Berkeley of nostalgia has apparently little relation to the Berkeley of the present television image. But neither of these pictures is a true picture of the campus. Then, as now, there were some boring lectures and badly run laboratories. Then, as now, there were rebels and the state legislature considered Berkeley a "hotbed of Communism." Then, as now, people wondered whether the University was too big. Then, the students were considered frivolous, spoiled, and unserious. Now they are considered unwashed, unshaven, and uncivil. But then, as now, the individuals who behaved badly, the poor lectures, and the students who wanted out were a tiny fraction of the total.

There are some real differences, however, in the Berkeley
of the not too distant past and that of the present. In general the
students are now better trained and more professionally motivated than in my days as an undergraduate. This motivation and
seriousness explain to a large part their lack of interest in student
government whose control is then left to a minority. The high
motivation of most students requires higher standards at the University, which in turn puts greater pressure on the students. This
added pressure is accepted understandingly by those who have
chosen their careers, because the benefits of more rigorous training are obvious. It is more difficult to justify to the student who is
still seeking his niche, and the heavy burden of study then leads
him to question whether his required courses are relevant to his
present and future needs. As the high schools get better, students
want new experiences at the college level, and so increased
opportunities are created in research and extracurricular projects. College is becoming more and more a place to expose the
student to the techniques of acquiring new knowledge rather
than one for the absorption of past wisdom. The sciences have
had the easiest accommodation to this need because it is in their
tradition to integrate teaching and research. The humanities are
also progressing in this regard and Berkeley is pioneering in procedures for educational development and student-initiated
courses. The highly publicized political rebellions of today are
also more extreme than those of the past, partly because of the
more intense mood of students, partly because the legacy of the
civil rights movement has changed protests from verbal jousting
to physical obstructions. The latter must, and will, be resolved,
since it threatens the delicate balance of any community dedicated to reason and scholarship. The composition of the student
population has changed. The colleges are no longer recruiting
from a small fraction of the population, but rather, from essentially the entire population. Finally, the complexity of the world
and the proliferation of knowledge has signaled the growth of the
graduate school, and its integration into the campus as a vital
part, not a mere appendage, of the University community.

In the last analysis, however, the University today isn't so different from the University of twenty-five years ago. Its catalog is bigger, its faculty more distinguished, its physical plant larger, its students of higher quality, but Berkeley isn't just the sum of its parts. It is an incredibly exciting complex which always seems about to burst asunder. The visiting lecturers are so numerous that the official University calendar can only record a fraction of them. The political crises are more intense and the soul-searching analyses of the role of the student, the professor, the administrator, and society, more prolonged. The critics of the University always seem like the blind man with the elephant—they can grab one part of its enormously complex structure and believe that is the whole. Yet Berkeley is emotional controversy and careful scholarship, football and beards, barefoot coeds and solemn Charter Day ceremonies, lecturing to three hundred students for one hour and guiding one student though senior research for one year, the tranquility of Faculty Glade and the cacophony of the Sproul steps, mass education and quality education rolled into one. You can say anything good or bad and it will be true, in some part, of the University. Except it's never dull. The pavement of Sather Gate throbs to the beat of the campus, and few who enter through those portals escape the fascination of Berkeley.

"Berkeley gave me the confidence
to strive in all disciplines and
recognize the tremendous
opportunities available to me."

MATT BIONDI

Matt Biondi

S HORTLY AFTER BEING ASKED TO CONTRIBUTE a reflection of my Berkeley experience, of which I feel very honored, I was reading a magazine on a flight home from Australia. One article in particular caught my attention because it dealt with popular athletes as role models. The author found society's "worship" of athletes to be a sad reflection on our cultural past and present; arguing that sports athletes are violent and shallow and aspire to win fame and fortune regardless of cost. I was quite surprised to read a brief mention of my name as someone who, by contrast, appeared to have a healthy approach to athletic competition. Although I credit my parents for giving me perspective beyond winning and losing, I believe Berkeley gave me the tools to respond to global interests and admiration in a way that has enriched the lives of those who have followed my swimming career.

When I arrived on the Berkeley campus in the fall of 1983, I was a shy, self-conscious kid eager to learn in the classroom and compete at the world-class level in freestyle sprinting. My first impression of Cal overwhelmed me with the sensation of witnessing a collection of every discipline, philosophy, and dress code known to this world. I was also impressed by the infinite possibilities which now surrounded me. Almost instantly, I felt liberated to pursue personal goals free from judgment and bias and began to challenge the perimeters of my personal development.

It was then that this underweight talented swimmer

from Moraga became a serious Olympic contender. No longer would I dedicate myself to superficial growth, as was the case in high school, or be intimidated by individuality. I had become fascinated with exploring the internal capabilities and self-imposed limitations of my mind and spirit. From this I learned the best path in life is an individual one to be determined solely from one's personal choice. Our greatest power in life is the power to choose.

I am extremely proud to have responded to the tutelage of Cal's aquatic coaches, Pete Cutino, Steve Heaston, and Nort Thornton, to the tune of eleven Olympic medals, just as I am proud of my education and the depth at which I was able to express myself to questions about who I am and how I was able to do the unique things I did. I have witnessed many athletes, intimidated by knowledge and growth beyond the physical, retreat to familiar territory within their sports discipline. Berkeley gave me the confidence to strive in all disciplines and recognize the tremendous opportunities available to me. With my success in the pool came the responsibility to entertain a public image. This was extremely difficult for me. It is therefore especially gratifying to be held as an example for others.

For being included in your list of outstanding Berkeley graduates, I say thank you for acknowledging my efforts. And to every individual who has contributed to the University of California, I say thank you for helping this still skinny swimmer to engage and celebrate all aspects of life and learning.

"Lecturing was the teaching art that Berkeley, above any other university in the country, brought to its full measure of distinction. . . . Berkeley taught me that a good lecture is as much a work of art as a good novel or essay or short story. I daresay none of the teachers who excited my mind in the 1930s ever actually thought of their lectures as works of art. But they were that."

ROBERT A. NISBET

Robert A. Nisbet

BERKELEY TRADITION, all but forgotten in my mind, was brought back to consciousness recently. I had just finished the final lecture of a course in social theory, one that had gone well during the term. The students had appeared to like it almost as much as I had myself. One of them, a transfer from Berkeley, came up after the final lecture and said, "You know, if this course had been at Berkeley, the students would have applauded you."

The praise, believe me, will not spoil me. I have learned, after three decades of teaching in a university, that the next time around I stand as good a chance of putting them to sleep. Try as you will, you can't win them all. The point of this, in any event, is not my teaching but a certain charming and, as I believe, wholly functional tradition at Berkeley: that of applauding the instructor at the end of a course and even occasionally after a particularly good lecture during the course.

I suppose my first reaction to the student's friendly words was one of mingled astonishment and pleasure that the tradition has, during all these years, survived. After the sometimes tidal disaffections at Berkeley in recent times, one finds himself wondering if any of the great traditions have survived. And I thought, as I walked back to my office, if this one has, no doubt a few other equally valuable ones have.

Not, heaven knows, that applause by itself is valuable. Applause has become very cheap in many quarters of our society. Courting applause is the slow drip that may damage a culture, even one that has remained as durable, generally speaking, as ours has before the buffets of depression and affluence. No, it wasn't the applause as such that mattered during my years at Berkeley, and I doubt that it does today. It's the context that is important. What was critical was the belief on the part of generation after generation of students that teaching was important: that good teaching should be acknowledged by rich applause and bad teaching by either a lowering of the volume of the applause or else sitting on one's hands. There were other ways, of course, that students in the 1930s showed their awareness of good teaching, their appreciation of it; but we can safely take the applause at the end of courses as the proper symbol of these.

The literary essayist and classicist William Arrowsmith has dourly remarked that one is as likely to come upon good teaching today in the American university as he is to come upon a clutch of Druids in the Mojave Desert. And, Arrowsmith goes on, you do not get Druids by offering prizes for Druid of the Year. If you want Druids, you plant forests.

Well, Berkeley had a full stand of forest on the campus in the 1930s, not yet bulldozed partly away by institutes and centers, and Berkeley also had its due share of Druids: remarkable teachers in all areas of the university; teachers whose characteristic and often brilliant way of expressing themselves was through the lecture. Lecturing was the teaching art that Berkeley, above any other university in the country, brought to its full measure of distinction.

I've never been able to understand the conviction in the minds of so many people, academic persons included, that good teaching cannot, virtually by definition, exist when it consists of lectures before large classes. Good heavens, Abelard transformed the mind of Europe in the first half of the twelfth century through lectures: often delivered, we are told, before thousands of students, who had come from all parts of Europe to hear him. But, it is commonly said, that was before there were textbooks for students to read; the lecture was indispensable. What nonsense! In the first place, there *were* textbooks, read, bought, and sold even as they are today; and in the second place, the lecture, the good lecture, the lecture given by a first-rate mind, is as indispensable to the thought process today as it was then. To assume that the value of something is the same when heard directly and personally from a distinguished mind as when one is reading it in a textbook is as absurd as to think that Shakespeare read is the same as Shakespeare enacted by a distinguished company of players.

Berkeley taught me that a good lecture is as much a work of art as a good novel or essay or short story. I daresay none of the teachers who excited my mind in the 1930s ever actually thought of their lectures as works of art. But they were that. True, works of art can be bad. But the mere sense, however dimly and subliminally held, that in preparing a lecture, that in delivering a lecture before a class, one is engaged in work not very different from what goes into the writing of an essay or short story, cannot help but give a lift to what goes on in the classroom.

There were some really distinguished lecturers at the Berkeley I knew in the 1930s as student and fledgling instructor. I will come to them shortly. For the moment I want to stay with the idea of the audience and audience response. I would argue that in the same way that there cannot be good novels, good plays, and good paintings except where there are good audiences, so there can't be good teaching except where there are good students. Berkeley had, and still has, them in abundance. By good students, I mean more here than minds of high native quality, more than literate minds. I mean students eager for, receptive to, and appreciative of what the classroom offers; students capable of and willing to distinguish between good teaching and bad.

When and in which department or school at Berkeley the custom began of applauding the instructor at the end of a term or after an especially good lecture I do not know. Alumni much older than I tell me they remember it. Henry Morse Stephens, Charles Mills Gayley, among others, knew the taste of applause for their memorable lectures. No doubt some of their predeces-

325

sors did also. Teaching, as is well known, has something in common with the theater. The lecturer in a classroom is both playwright and actor. To be sure, he would be despised if he ever forgot that in the long run it is content, not form or manner, that determines his success. The lore of Boalt Hall is, I am sure, still rich in tales of the style and eccentricities of the great Professor Alexander M. ("Captain") Kidd. But, for all his undoubted histrionic abilities, this remarkable teacher would not have survived very long had he not been also an immensely learned and very serious teacher of criminal law.

The kind of teaching that will earn a professor large and eager classes year after year is rarely if ever founded on histrionic technique or his reputation for being a great guy. He may be a decidedly effective person, magnetic in persuasive power, an eccentric, a showman, to some extent, but students are, at least in a place like the Berkeley I knew in the 1930s, quick to catch on to whether there is intellectual substance or not. If there isn't, all the platform technique in the world will not save the lecturer. If there is solid substance, there is no doubt, of course, that the allied possession of a strong or colorful personality, of personal mannerisms allowed to display themselves, can go on to establish the kind of reputation a Henry Morse Stephens had or, through so many years, a Joel Hildebrand had. But content and thrust of scholarly mind are vital.

Good students, the kind Berkeley has had in abundance all these hundred years—are almost impossible to deceive. The word gets around, the size and persisting identity of classes year after year tell a great deal, and over a period of time very few are in any doubt of who the really distinguished teachers on a campus are. That is, on a campus such as Berkeley where a tradition exists that manifests itself in discriminating appreciation of teaching.

In general I find formal teacher-evaluation schemes worthless. Quite often they become monstrosities of the educationists' analytical fancy, broken down into so many detailed items affecting so many aspects of the teacher and the classroom that they are regarded shortly as a bore by the students. And the average scores they elicit are valueless so far as genuine appreciation of teaching is concerned. I have seen many of these, including one—a product of some bureaucrat in the Office of Education in Washington, D.C.—in which several dozen items and questions were assembled and which included queries as to professorial dress, neatness, courtesy, good manners, etc. I had the feeling as I read it that none of the great teachers I had sat before at Berkeley would have come out very high on this aberration.

I don't think much either of annual teacher awards on a university or college campus. There were none in the Berkeley I knew, and none were necessary. What Michael Polanyi calls "tacit knowledge" should never be underestimated. It is one of the vital elements of the social bond. It is the knowledge we all have of a given condition or aspect of reality but don't try to put into words for the simple reason that by trying to put it into words we lose it. Everybody comes to know on a campus, even a large one, who the really great teachers are. But experience shows pretty clearly, I think, that the effort to single them out by special awards is self-defeating. A committee is called for. Candidates must be assembled for committee consideration. Proofs must be contrived to show why A receives an award but B does not. The result is almost inevitable: instead of great teaching being rewarded by solemn committee action, great teaching *gimmicks* are.

No, I think Berkeley, many years ago, hit upon the best means of stimulating and maintaining good teaching: through the applause that no teacher can ever be wholly immune to. I concede readily that there were, are, and will always be teachers at Berkeley, class applause notwithstanding, irremediably dull. Bear in mind, however, that they might be even duller were they not living in an atmosphere in which the Gayley, the Joel Hildebrand, the F. J. Teggart, the James P. McBaine, the Raymond J. Sontag—fine minds and scholars all—is widely known and duly appreciated as a great teacher. In any event, great teaching cannot be limited entirely to what goes on in the undergraduate classroom, vital though this is to the health of the university. There are teachers—I think of the remarkable Gilbert Lewis in chemistry—whose greatness lies in the seminar, in the research laboratory or in the study, where numbers are small and colloquy rather than lecturing is the form. This, too, is teaching.

Nor should the mistake be made—a common one these days—that there is somehow an impossible barrier between the scholarly mind and the distinguished teacher. I would, I am sure, fall easily for this alluring but largely false view of the matter were it not for my fifteen years on the Berkeley campus as undergraduate, graduate student, and faculty member. There I learned, or was to learn later, that those who had genuinely fired up my mind in the classroom or lecture hall were scholars: some, minor scholars, yes, others major scholars, but all scholars. I am sure there must be an exception to this, as there is to every generalization about human beings and human affairs. It's just that I don't know of any. I am not saying that the greatest teachers year in year out were the greatest scholars and scientists on the campus. No one would say that. I am only saying that one is exceedingly unlikely to find a faculty member in a university, regarded over a long period of time as a stimulating teacher, who is not also a scholar—minor or major, as the case may be—engaged continuously in the kind of research that is designed for publication before peers. I might have discovered this in my time on my own, but my Berkeley experience brought it home to me early and emphatically.

I recall vividly that even as undergraduates we took much pride in what was known, or believed, to be the scholarly stature of one of our teachers. Often in student conversations about the faculty I could hear myself and others referring to someone as "the outstanding authority" in a given field. No doubt our characterizations were frequently in error, or at least in exaggeration. That doesn't affect the essential point, which is that even as undergraduates we found our sense of exciting teaching all of a piece with what we stoutly believed to be a teacher's scholarly eminence.

It was Frederick J. Teggart who excited me more than any other teacher, and the excitement began in his introductory course, Social Institutions 1AB, where he lectured before two hundred students year after year. The number would surely have increased, but Teggart had a fondness for 312 Wheeler and the room wouldn't hold any more. And, as was usually the case with Teggart, he refused to yield.

No doubt there was some degree of instant fascination with the materials he dealt with: the history of the ideas of progress, development, and social evolution; the comparative histories of institutions and cultures, all given focus by one of the most extraordinary minds of this century in the social sciences. On the other hand, I was almost equally fascinated by a few other subjects, considered simply as subjects, and I am inclined to think it was the teaching, the lecture presence of Teggart himself that made the difference.

This presence was formidable to both students and, as I later learned, faculty colleagues alike. Of Teggart it was said that whenever he changed his mind, the earth rumbled. Irish in descent, of fierce pride and profound stubbornness, he did not suffer fools gladly or endure with any visible patience inanities or even, it used to seem to me, amenities. He controlled more temper in a day than most of us do in a year. Jove-like in appearance, invariably distant and aloof when it came to students, he did nothing to seem the good guy and little by way of encouraging students even to come up and chat about anything. This in some ways was unfortunate, for in later years I discovered how gracious he could be with the students who, despite his manner, did go up to his office at 432 Wheeler to talk to him about their intellectual interests. And he could be as touched as anyone else by a student compliment, uttered to his face. It was just that he refused by any addition of bogus warmth to his manner, or by any pretense of being Old Chips, to seem to be courting either our visits or our compliments. And nothing horrified him more than faculty members he would occasionally hear about who seemed to believe that the role of teacher had the roles of father and mother and big brother built into it. He must turn over frequently in his grave these days at what goes on in the way of faculty invasions of student privacy, all under the guise of being "interested in them as human beings." From Teggart—but also a large number of other members of the Berkeley faculty in the 1930s—I acquired the conviction that has never for an instant left my mind: that in faculty members students want faculty members; nothing else!

Despite his often forbidding manner, Teggart would quite often be applauded during the term for a given lecture; and at the end of the semester he usually got an ovation. No one can tell me, knowing Teggart as I later came to, that such applause did not strike deep in his Irish soul. High though his standards were, his lectures could not have been as provocative, as filled with sheer intellectual life, had it not been for a student body in which the custom of applause existed and was discriminatingly followed.

And the applause, I will emphasize again, was in response to content that came, and could only have come, from a life of unremitting research in areas that seemed to him of vast importance. This suggests something else to my mind about great teaching. It has to seem important, even at times almost evangelically important, to the man teaching. Only then, I am inclined to think, will students think it important. There is an old saying in law that it is important to *be* just and also to *seem* just. Of university teaching, great teaching, that is, I will say: its content must *be* important and also *seem* important.

Teggart made it seem profoundly, almost world-saving in importance. And this began with the freshman course that he taught for so many years. On his best days, from the moment he strode into the room, he appeared quite literally to displace atmosphere. Whether a given theme seemed, on its own terms, either remote and abstract or, depending upon student omniscience, easy and obvious, Teggart's manner could make the theme seem, at one and the same time, assimilable and worthy. Some of us used to think there was a certain missionary quality in him, and this, provided it is united with bona fide intellectual content, is all right too.

The Oxford University Press has recently published a book of mine. Its title is *Social Change and History: Aspects of the Western Idea of Development*. It is, as it should be, dedicated to Teggart. Whether the title itself, the structure and theme of the book, or a large part of its content, it is hard for me to imagine much of it having come into existence on my typewriter apart from the lectures Teggart gave us thirty-five years ago in Social Institutions 1AB. It's not the first book I've written that owes a good deal to Teggart's ideas, nor will it be the last. But this one seems hardly more than a new rendering of what was in fact a freshman course at Berkeley in the 1930s. For all the fascination of the ideas in that course, lasting fascination as events have proved, I don't think they would have impressed themselves on my mind as they did had it not been for a quality of greatness in the way the ideas were given to us in lectures. As I say, it is terribly important to *look* as if what you are saying is important. Teggart always did.

But so did a good many others on the Berkeley campus in the 1930s. The lecturers I heard during those years included some who, at any given time in a semester, impressed me as much as Teggart did. There was Hildebrand in chemistry, Neuhaus in art history, Thompson in medieval history, Palm in modern European history, Cross in economics, Barrows in political science, Kofoid in zoology, Adams, Loewenberg, Dennes, and Strong in philosophy, Potter, Bronson, and Cline in English. There were many others I heard about on the campus from students and whose lectures I would occasionally drop in on (another highly auspicious custom then prevailing at Berkeley). But these I have mentioned are the ones I heard the most often, along with Teggart. Actually, as I think of it, I wasn't even enrolled in all the courses represented by the names I have just listed. I certainly knew no chemistry and never enrolled in a single course. But such was the fame of Hildebrand as a teacher that I found it pleasant occasionally to join someone and wander up to the old Chem Aud. The same was true of several others. From all of them I got, I think, the same basic and lasting lesson I learned most profoundly from Teggart: teaching must begin with something worth saying but it will acquire due luster only in an atmosphere that is made favorable to good teaching by students who, by tradition and custom, show discriminating appreciation of it.

ๆ.   ๆ.

Something else I learned at Berkeley that has remained intact in my mind is the importance of diversified teaching. I mean, teaching by one and the same man of lower division, upper division, and graduate courses. In many places today this is supposed to be an impossible combination. The experience of Berkeley in the 1930s showed that it isn't. Most of the men I admired as teachers taught at all three levels and, on the clear evidence, with much success. I studied under George Adams in philosophy and Frederick Teggart in social institutions at each of the three levels, and I found both men stimulating and rewarding intellectually at the graduate or upper division level as I had found them in the introductory course.

The last suggests another striking feature of the Berkeley scene: the fondness of the great on the faculty for the introductory, *freshman* course. I do not know whether this tradition has survived; I hope it has, for it is hard to think of anything better calculated to sink deep the roots of learning than to be confronted, as a freshman, with the light and leading of a university. It was considered a mark of prestige in the 1930s to be allowed by one's department to teach the introductory course. From one end of the campus to the other you could find men of National Academy stature teaching freshman physics, chemistry, history, philosophy, zoology, and so on.

True, not all of them did it really well, measured simply in terms of eloquence and of arresting personality. Herbert E. Bolton taught the introductory course in Spanish-American history for decades. He took great pride in it, as I well recall. He was not, however, at his best in this course: too frequently anecdotal, often dry and pedestrian. What did it matter? Thousands upon thousands of students through the years took the course, applauded him vigorously at the end and knew the experience of having been taught by a man, famous in the world of historical scholarship, who had literally traveled by foot, horseback, and raft each and every route taken by the early Spanish explorers in the Southwest. Is there any wonder in the fact that for so many years an unending stream of Spanish-American historians went forth from Berkeley to populate other university campuses in the country?

There was David Prescott Barrows; not one of the University's major scholarly figures, to be sure (though I believe his *Berber and Black* remains to this day a classic), but a man of immense devotion to scholarship nevertheless and a very humane and cultivated mind. He was emphatically one of the University's great men, and his life as teacher, scholar, political figure, military leader, university president, as well as his deep and genuine love of political philosophy, were to be appreciated by many thousands of students who took his Political Science 1AB in Wheeler Auditorium.

Such was the prestige of the introductory course in Berkeley in the 1930s that when, upon Teggart's retirement, I was permitted to take over his freshman course I felt a sense of accomplishment not to be exceeded in later years on the occasion of my first article published, my first book, or my accession to the full professorship or to high administrative office. And when that day came, as it had to, given the agony and sweat that went into the preparation of my lectures, on which I first received applause from students for a lecture, my destiny as a teacher was forever fixed. I repeat, nothing can save a man from giving a bad lecture or course occasionally; or at least I have not been saved. But, given the background of Berkeley as I knew it in the 1930s it is impossible to give a bad lecture or course and not be made depressed by the knowledge.

It was the tradition of great lecturing—a tradition, as I have emphasized, that was as deep in the student body as in the faculty—that alone made it possible for a university as large as

Berkeley to stimulate as many minds as it did and to send them forth in the worlds of scholarship, creative arts, professions, statecraft, and business, fully the equals of those who had chanced to go to one or other of the great private universities where numbers were smaller. Certainly there were other elements in the elixir that made Berkeley the first state university campus to reach parity with the greatest of the private universities. World-renowned research, especially, in those days, in the physical sciences; outstanding leadership from presidents such as Wheeler and Sproul; vigorous faculty government through which the University's Academic Senate became a veritable model of the academic republic in action. I take away from none of these. But it was the tradition of teaching and, within this, the tradition of great lecturing that made it possible for the University's other resources to become transmitted to generation after generation of students.

The genius of the system was that undergraduates, including newly enrolled freshmen, were exposed to great intellectual presences. Barrows *looked* like a great man; Bolton *looked* like a historian-explorer, Teggart *looked* Jove-like in wisdom, Hildebrand *looked* like a scientist. If, as is by now so widely known as to be scarcely worth the repeating, motivation is an indispensable part of genuine learning, much is owing those teachers at Berkeley who, simply by appearing day after day before young undergraduates, including freshmen, and lecturing to them from the loftiness of sometimes world-renowned scholarship, awakened in at least a few students—the forever vital few—a desire to be like them.

Carlyle didn't exaggerate the role of heroes in history or the importance of hero-worship. To a large degree, that is what *university* education is all about: hero-worship in academic context. Call it, if we will, emulation. Few are the creative figures in history whose powers were not first elicited by a youthful desire to be like some admired exemplar or teacher. This, in any mind of innate strength, doesn't make for imitation. There is a universe of difference between emulation and imitation. The Greeks emulated one another, generation to generation in the Golden Age of Athens. They most assuredly did not imitate one another. In *emulating* Plato, Aristotle tried to become as unlike Plato in mere content of thought as possible. He remained, however, a Greek.

In a very real sense, we had our heroes on the campus in the 1930s. There were the heroes one managed to take courses from directly, and there were the heroes one might not ever perhaps have heard lecture or even seen, but who were heroes nonetheless. I never had a course from, never saw until later years when I was an instructor, Kroeber in anthropology, Sauer in geography, Tolman in psychology, Radin in law, or Linforth in classics. They were heroes all the same to many of us. We knew about them. They were movers and shakers. They made the campus, as we dimly realized, a profoundly exciting intellectual scene.

I thought the Berkeley air was the freest I had ever breathed when I got there in the fall of 1932. It was free in the sense that what one did thenceforth academically was a matter of free choice. Curricular requirements were few, the elective system was happily flourishing, and one had the feeling that he was making his own intellectual destiny instead of obeying the curricular lares and penates of grade school. The manifest success of Berkeley's free, highly elective system taught me something that has never left my mind, either as teacher or during the decade I served in deanship and vice-chancellorship, as administrator. This is the essential irrelevance of curriculum—with its inbuilt pressure to both ritualize and bureaucratize learning—as compared with *the simple presence of good courses and good teachers* from which one can choose freely.

At Berkeley, with its free elective system, we made our own way. This was exciting in itself and it was also, as I look back on it, a wonderful way in which to learn to walk, intellectually. The idea that there should be some carefully conceived design in what one takes in college, that each course should be architecturally related to each other course, is, I will always believe, one of the most pernicious ideas in academia. Only the individual human mind is capable of the fusion, the synthesis, that is, without any question, necessary to intellectual cultivation. Such fusion, such synthesis, cannot be had free, as the gift of curriculum design committees. Bear in mind that I am talking about general, or liberal, education. Obviously within a given discipline, mathematics, chemistry, law, there has to be something of a design, something of before-and-after relationships among courses. These, however, flow from the subject; not from committees earnestly trying to impose.

It was possible to take wild conglomerates of courses in the Berkeley of the 1930s: a course in Shakespeare side by side with one in corporation finance (I speak from experience, very pleasant experience), with a third, drawn from zoology, added in last-minute caprice. Somehow they fused, or at least I thought they did, which is as good. One does not get indigestion from mixture of foods if they are all good; only from bad food or from mindless overindulgence. I had industrial organization from Robert Calkins, going the very next hour to an equally fine course by James Allen on the Greek tragedies, in translation. Perhaps I was deluded, but I thought the two went together extremely well—a consequence, I am convinced, of the fact that both courses were taught by eminently humane and alert minds, each concerned with exploring a major area of human experience: social organization and man's fate.

To this day in my own advising of undergraduate students I refuse—sometimes to their tender dismay—to advise them, except with respect to the minimum essentials which the faculty in its wisdom has laid down for each and every student mind on the campus. I have to go that far; I can't break the law. But I don't have to go any further, and I don't. "What shall I take?" Take what you feel like taking; shop around; try courses out; find out what *students* think are good courses; take what interests *you*. But please don't bother me with requests for telling you what you ought to take. Such is my system of advising; or, I should say, such was the system of advising I found at Berkeley in the 1930s, fell in love with, and have remained faithful to ever since. And, to give a happy ending to this, I can report that around nineteen out of twenty students later tell me they are glad I advised them as I did.

This is one final element of the Berkeley scene that stays with me, has had immense influence in my own life and that fits perfectly my conception of what is required in any scene of first-rank university teaching. I'm referring to a deeply rooted faculty tradition of individual scholarship; scholarship done by individuals rather than by bureaucratic institutes and centers in which responsibility for meeting a payroll and keeping the organization together drives out individuality of work.

The Berkeley campus was alive in the 1930s with individuals who were dedicated to scholarship the very individuality of which made it easy to combine with teaching. And what astonishing numbers of hours each day they gave to this scholarship. There was never a morning in the week when Teggart was not at his desk in 432 Wheeler by seven o'clock. And when he left at the end of the day it was carrying a full briefcase. What student in the history of that period will ever forget Bolton and the hours he spent in Bancroft Library? There was a dilapidated couch in Bolton's study, and until a University regulation made it necessary for the Library to be cleared utterly of people by 2 A.M. Bolton would often work through the night, occasionally cat-napping on the couch, and could frequently be seen early the next day heading down Telegraph for a shave and breakfast. There was the remarkable Professor William Popper in Semitic languages (for decades he *was* the Department of Semitic Languages), who, he told me, had trouble sleeping after about four o'clock in the morning, so went to the campus, and when he left to go home for dinner it was often to return an hour later to get in some more work before bedtime. And up in physics, as all the world now knows, the cyclotron was being perfected in the early 1930s by a man named Ernest Lawrence who also counted as a misfortune each night not spent largely in the old radiation laboratory with young colleagues and graduate students.

I don't want to exaggerate reality. Of course there were

337

drones on the faculty. There are anywhere, at all times. I only mean that for many of us the *style,* the enduring *image,* of Berkeley was created by the spectacle of these men and many others like them. They saw in scholarship a calling. And the Lord knows, in that day—which was before there were around-the-calendar institute salaries to fatten regular income or publishers fighting to give substantial advances of royalties on books— scholarship *had* to be a calling. And it is well to bear in mind that the men I am referring to, the Teggarts, Boltons, Poppers, received no reward in the form of any reduction of teaching load. Three full courses a semester was standard in the humanities and social sciences, and this included a graduate seminar. I recall no complaints. As Stephen Pepper in philosophy—another distinguished lecturer (his Esthetics was one of the most famous of the courses on the campus) and also scholar used to say: "We come to teach." Teach they did!

And in the teaching and in their mere *presence* they created, in the minds of the tyros, a respect for, a rooted desire to be engaged in scholarship of one's own. You didn't have to be told, much less threatened with loss of promotion, that research and scholarly writing were expected of you. It was in the air. It was simply what one did, just as meeting a minimum of three courses a term was what one did. Who needed to be told?

Yes, I know there were those who did little if any research, though they were not many, and there were more whose research was at best of minor significance. I'm not trying here to summon up remembrance of a never-never land. I am saying only that the essential character of Berkeley in the 1930s was set for us by those who taught, who took immense pride in their teaching and who also put before us, by example, not preaching, the incontestable verity of continuing scholarship. I said above that exposure to the scene at Berkeley makes it impossible for any of us who drew from that scene to give a bad lecture and course and not feel guilty about it. I can say much the same about scholarship. Limited many of us may be in our own scholarly contributions, but I daresay none of us could forsake scholarship in one form or other and not feel very guilty about it.

At its best Berkeley was much more for us than simply a place where we took courses, got grades, and received a degree. It was an intellectual scene, a place where ideas flourished and where, through the presence of a Tolman, a Sauer, a Lawrence, or a Teggart, these ideas took root in one way or other and produced still other ideas. Talk all we will about curricula, teaching, and felicitous relationships between students and faculty, the simple test of a distinguished university has to do with none of these but solely with whether or not it is an exciting scene of ideas. This is what, over a period of nearly a century, Berkeley, Harvard, Chicago, Columbia, Michigan, and possibly one or two other places have, or have had in common. You could, in an almost literal manner, feel the Berkeley campus pulsate as you walked onto it in the 1930s, and I venture to guess you still can. So, I found in later years, was this the case with each of the other universities I have mentioned. And it is the dire lack of this vital quality that can make certain otherwise renowned universities in the country dull and infertile. They ransack academia for name scholars, they pay staggering salaries to a few stars, they pride themselves on the masterful way in which students are housed, meet one another, meet with faculty, see members of the administration, and so on. But they remain, year after year, decade after decade, dull. There is no feeling of pulsation as one walks on their campuses.

What it takes for a university to become an intellectual scene, a setting for ideas, a field of pulsation, I do not know for sure, any more than I know what is required to produce a fifth century B.C. Athens, an Elizabethan England, or a Renaissance Florence. Great minds and spirits, yes, but this is only to restate the question. Why do they come to a place and why do they stay—oftentimes when those of fainter heart flee—and why are their numbers reproduced generation after generation, even though not every generation of a Berkeley or Harvard, any more than every generation of a Renaissance Florence, is as great as the one before, or after? Who knows? We can guess, speculate, and imagine. And that, despite twenty-five hundred years of intellec-

339

tual awareness of the problem involved, is about all we can do.

The best I can come up with—and it's not a full answer even if correct—is that good audiences somehow come into existence, which in turn make it worth the while of good creative minds to come and then to remain, and, in the process, to improve the audience, and thus attract still more creative minds, ad infinitum. So I come back to where I began this essay: the indispensable value of a good audience and its applause, its *discriminating* applause. Berkeley somehow acquired this many years ago; it still has it, at least in degree, and as long as it has it, the occasional slipping away of a few faculty minds will not make much difference. Neither will a demonstration or even a riot, now and then. It's the applause that matters.

"An education is like an index, which is very useful for the topics you want to look up, but 99 percent unused. What is important in an education is the 1 percent that you manage in some mysterious way to build into your permanent self."

GEORGE R. STEWART

George R. Stewart

MANY PEOPLE ARE FASCINATED by what are called "Little-known Facts of History." One of these—in my personal history—is that I am a degree-holding alumnus of the University of California. Once, after I had been a professor at Berkeley for about thirty years, I got a notice from the Alumni Association that I was in the "lost" list.

To be sure, I am an alumnus by nothing more than two terms of residence and a Master of Arts, that is, by only the narrowest of margins. Accordingly, when anyone does me the honor of thinking about my career at all, he associates me with Princeton (four years, A.B.) or Columbia (two years, Ph.D).

Granted that the M.A. is the shadowiest of degrees, still I am proud to confess that in the course of earning it I spent my one year as a graduate student in the Department of English at Berkeley, and I am ready to write something about that experience, because it produced important results in my life.

On what was, if I remember correctly, a fine August morning, I came upon the campus by one of the west entrances, looking for the place to register—a tallish young man, wearing glasses, on the slim side. I had recently been seriously ill, and I doubt if I gave much impression of energy and durability. You might not have predicted that, forty-nine years later, I would still be able, as now, to write about that morning.

Since what I got out of the University necessarily depends upon what I took into it, I must record that I was, in that month, a little past my twenty-fourth birthday. I had entered

Princeton in 1913. That was the college which people in these days are likely to call "F. Scott Fitzgerald's Princeton." Naturally, like most Princetonians of the time, I resent that label. Fitzgerald was in my class, and I knew him. But there was a lot more to Old Nassau than what you get from *This Side of Paradise*. For instance, I came to graduation with a very solid education, as a major in English literature.

Still, as I shall point out later, I do not altogether defend that education. Come to think of it, however, I do not know that I wholly defend any kind of formal training. An education is like an index, which is very useful for the topics you want to look up, but 99 percent unused. What is important in an education is the 1 percent that you manage in some mysterious way to build into your permanent self.

After graduating, I went into the Army, and was left with a permanent disability. This, too, must be rated as a little-known fact, and my work record fails to indicate, I suppose, that the disability has slowed me down greatly.

Of course, as it would be only conventional to put it, I learned a lot in the Army. But I mean this in more than a conventional sense. Like other educational systems, that of the U.S. Army is about 99 percent waste, but the other 1 percent, I think, did build itself into that complicated entity which, always changing, has been my personality, or character, or simply my *me,* throughout the years.

One thing that the Army does not do is to provide an intellectual or artistic atmosphere. I remember getting some good reading done, while stretched on an army cot, and I even studied a little Anglo-Saxon on my own. Still—and this is most important—when I came to Berkeley, my intellectual life had been in abeyance for two years, and was ready, so to speak, to break loose.

As I walked across the campus, that August morning, I had a cylindrical mailing case under my arm. I found the registration desk, rather charmingly placed, out of doors, near the present bridge across the creek, not far from the northeast corner of the present Life Sciences Building. I approached the two girls there, pulled something from the mailing case, and handed it across. As it happened, my credentials from Princeton had not arrived, and I had brought my diploma along. If proof was needed that I was a college graduate, here it was!

The girl looked at it, and found it all in Latin, of which she did not read a word. But she could see the orange-and-black ribbon. She said, "That's a pretty one!" And so I was admitted, without the aid of a computer.

I went on then to Wheeler Hall, and began, as one might put it, to enter into my kingdom.

Since I was already as old as I was, my social adjustments, such as they are, had been pretty well shaped, and I cannot attribute much in that connection (for better or for worse) to my months at Berkeley. Few sentimental memories of college days arise in my recollections of the time. I believe that there were some athletic teams operating, and I even saw a few football games, but not in much spirit of old Alma Mater. I had some social life. I roomed for most of the year with Paul Fussell ('16), thus further cementing a friendship that was begun in high school and still lasts. Two friends whom I came to know that year are Will Dennes of our Philosophy Department, and Homer Davis, who was for many years president of Athens College in Greece.

My real experience of that year, however, was intellectual, and that is, after all, as it should be with a graduate student.

And now, let me admit it, my judgment of the University in that year—and of the Department of English in particular—is definitely ambivalent. So, since a happy ending is preferable, let me in the beginning get rid of the adverse comments.

Graduate study in English seemed to me, even with my then meager experience, to be inadequate. In fact, if it had been better, I might have stayed on for my Ph.D. To be sure, such study was not well organized in general through the country at that time, as I was to discover at Columbia too. But at Berkeley it was definitely unsatisfactory.

There was little tradition of graduate work. Not more

than three or four Ph.D. degrees in English had ever been given. Out of nineteen professors and instructors listed in the Announcement of Courses, only five had the Ph.D., and most of the others had no degree above A.B.

One trouble was—and this has tended to be true of the department ever since—that some of the best-qualified men had been drafted into the general service of the University. Charles M. Gayley was one of the three "war deans," and Walter Hart was deeply involved with Summer Session. In addition, I was interested in American literature, and "Billy" Armes, who had been giving those courses, had just died.

Putting all these causes together, one has no difficulty in seeing why the offering in courses was thin and somewhat marginal.

Moreover, the graduate students themselves were mostly candidates for a teaching credential, and were merely working off a course requirement. At the risk of being deemed an intellectual snob, I must record that most of them failed to bring me much stimulus. Of all the students whom I came to know during that year, only one, to my knowledge, went ahead to the Ph.D.

Gayley was giving no graduate work, and I had a so-called pro-seminar (mostly seniors) with him. He was so busy over in California Hall that he taught his course, I am afraid, in a somewhat left-handed manner. I am glad to have had some experience with his personality, but I got little from the course. From much that I have heard about Gayley, I am sure that he was, at his best, a superb teacher, and I am sorry not to have experienced him thus.

I took a course each term with Wells. The first one, in the theory of fiction, was so overrun with the kind of student that I have just mentioned that the classes were slow and dull. The second course was in essay writing, against a background of American literature. And here we can move over to the positive side.

Many alumni must still remember Chauncey Wells, though he died more than thirty years ago. He had only the A.B.

degree, published almost nothing and was regarded by some of his colleagues as not counting for much. I got a great deal out of his course, and my other contacts with him at this time, not to mention what I got from friendship with him during my later years in the department.

In the first place, he did much to inspire and to shape my style of writing, and nothing, after all, has been more important in my life. At first I floundered around in the course, not doing very well. Then I sensed the virtues of what he was trying to teach, and I began to learn how to approach his ideals. I treasure from that time what I still consider one of the highest compliments ever paid me. Toward the end of the term, he read one of my short essays to the class, and then ended by saying simply, "I wish I had written that."

During that year I was not yet committed to English, and I took some work in Russian with George Noyes and Alexander Kaun. I abandoned that study, and soon forgot nearly all of my Russian, but in one curious detail that work left traces. From Noyes' discussion of the aspects of the Russian verb I learned, or thought I learned, some ways of handling English tenses, and I have made some use of that knowledge.

With Herbert Bolton I took a course in the history of the American West, and I find it not too much to repeat the cliché "It opened up a new world for me." Out of that course has sprung about half of all that I have ever written.

Having thus discussed the courses, we can pause for generalizing speculation. Particularly, because of this course with Bolton, I sometimes wonder what my life would have been if I had come to Berkeley with Paul Fussell in 1913, as I might well have done, instead of going East. At Princeton I experienced only a restricted curriculum just breaking out of the bounds of the old time Greek/Latin/mathematics alliance. There were, for instance, no departments of anthropology or geography, and in later years the geographers have sometimes hailed me for their own. At Princeton, as far as I know, there was no course in Western history. Moreover, the requirements were so strict as to discourage much experimenting with courses, though I managed to do some. If I had been an undergraduate at Berkeley, I might well have been fascinated by some kind of work that did not even exist at Princeton. Joel Hildebrand keeps telling me that he would have caught me and made a great chemist out of me, but in that case, I would not have written the books that Joel has very much enjoyed reading.

To return to 1919—as would be expected by the general tenets of graduate work, I spent my time and energy much less on my classes than on more direct preparation for the master's degree. The formal requirements were usually complicated and elaborate, and I think that their existence (as compared, for instance, with the much simpler ones of today) is an evidence of the immaturity and uncertainty of the department at that time. Probably one can postulate it as a general rule, no more in educational processes than in other human activities, that people protect themselves by spelling out and setting up rules and regulations when they lack basic confidence in themselves.

Besides passing a specified number of hours of courses, I was required, along with the other candidates for the M.A., to write a thesis and to take five separate examinations. In fact, since one examination was duplex, there were really six examinations—four written and two oral. They were 1) English literature, 2) English language, 3) the field of the thesis, 4) the history of criticism, 5) the duplex examination in composition, that is, written and oral expression. The degree, in fact, was a difficult one, perhaps harder to attain then than it is now, though such comparisons across the gap of the years are hard to make.

I cannot help wondering now how anyone could commit himself to take so many examinations, and I suppose that few candidates took them all in one year. But the courage of youth, or even its rashness, is a marvelous thing, and I went ahead, perhaps being somewhat encouraged by the not very stiff competition.

The examination in literature I passed on the basis of a good honors course at Princeton, plus some reading that I had done in the Army and since then. I did the one on language with the help of one undergraduate course at Princeton, a little study of Anglo-Saxon on my own while in the Army, and some cramming, at which Homer Davis and I sometimes worked together.

The history of criticism was something about which I knew very little, but for this examination there was a prescribed minimum list of writers, such as Aristotle, Longinus, and Lessing. Though I had to approach this reading as a chore in cramming, it opened up a new field to me, and I have been grateful. Though I passed the examination without distinction, I may add the cryptic remark that, without Lessing, *Storm* would not have been the same.

The examination in the field of the thesis (oral, one hour, three professors) took care of itself, and there was nothing much that you could do in immediate preparation for written and oral expression.

In spite of the help that I had from Chauncey Wells, I was still an awkward and uncertain writer, but I managed to pass the written part.

As for the examination in oral expression, I am even yet not quite sure what that one was supposed to prove or test. Perhaps the examination was designed to keep you from getting your degree if you displayed too much of a Siskiyou County accent, or to weed out those who did not possess the presence and voice to conduct a class. As the examination was conducted, you were handed half a dozen mimeographed sheets, each with a paragraph from some standard author. You took your pick, and had a short time to inspect what you were going to present. Then you went to the front of the room, and read the passage aloud to the assembled company.

I chose something from Carlyle, and barely passed. I believe that I mispronounced *gibbet,* a word about which (along with half a dozen others) I remain uncertain to this day. The question of hard or soft *g* fails to bother me with *gibbon, gin, ginger, gypsy,* and their kin, but I have never mastered that other one. I think, however, that it would really have been a pity if my young career had been gibbeted.

Of all of my experiences during the year the preparation of my master's thesis was, I think, the most important. Though Wells, my adviser, gave me some good help, I worked chiefly on my own, as I did later on my doctoral thesis and as I have done throughout my life. My subject was *Robert Louis Stevenson in California,* and it became, as I realize now, a good start toward a Ph.D. thesis. By what should be rated as cruel and unusual punishment, each successful candidate had to deposit a copy of his thesis in the University Library. There mine has been for almost half a century, and every now and then someone gets it out and reads it! I have no protection against this invasion of my youthful privacy, and I tremble at the thought of the callousness that must be revealed. All such authors should at least have the refuge of a statute of limitations, providing that after a certain number of years (the fewer the better) all master's theses shall be burned, on the correct theory that by that time everything useful in them will have been put into print. I myself have never reread the thing, and possibly it is not so bad as I imagine. Still, at least two of my colleagues have read it, and in their presence I feel always a certain affectionate but pitying attitude, as who should say, "He's not a bad sort, really! But did you ever read his master's thesis?"

At least, I reply defiantly that I learned a great deal out of the process of preparing and writing it. From this work sprang a long number of "firsts" in my life. It was my first venture in western materials, and I began it even before I had felt Bolton's influence. I first learned the fascination of old newspapers, and I have been using them ever since. I made my first "discovery," which was Stevenson's *San Carlos Day* essay; I found it in the Monterey newspaper of 1879, and then was able to establish the authorship on internal evidence. By publishing this essay in *Scribner's Magazine* I did my first bit of scholarly-popular publication, thus essaying a difficult genre from which I have never escaped and at which I have never been wholly successful. By scouting around Monterey and Calistoga for people who had known Stevenson, I did not turn up any very important material, but I first learned of the pleasures and possible rewards of field work as opposed to library work, and I have done much work of that kind in preparing for my books. Also, for the first time, I tied up geography—and, one could say, archaeology—with a project, establishing the relationship between Mount Saint Helena and the Spyglass Hill of *Treasure Island,* and discovering by the aid of actual legwork that the vegetation of that island was remarkably like that of the Monterey Peninsula.

The English Department abolished the master's thesis a few years later. There are cogent reasons for such action. But I take this opportunity to record that the training offered me by that requirement has been of basic importance in my life.

Still another important experience of that year was the teaching of my first course. Then, as always, the staffing of the huge course in freshman composition was straining the capacities of the department. I was recruited to teach one section of it, at the same time continuing with my graduate work. Again I marvel at the courage of youth, as well as at the confidence to the point of rashness which the department thus displayed in me.

I had, as I remember, some twenty or twenty-five students, and such is the impression made by one's first class that I still remember some of their names and faces. One of them, in fact, lives near me in Berkeley. I sometimes see her and she remembers me, but I have never dared ask her what she thought of the class—though, if she remembered anything at all at this time distance, I could take that as a compliment.

Possibly, however, it was the best class that I ever taught. Certainly I buckled to the work with enthusiasm, with energy, and with something of what seemed to me of originality. I enjoyed a maximum of academic freedom, for nobody gave me any supervision at all. And, I must say, I would have been better off if someone had told me a few things, and I would have welcomed such counsel. But, after all, the people in the department were, themselves, too busy to bother much about what I did.

So I gained my first teaching experience in one of those small classrooms near the northwest corner of Wheeler Hall, though I have forgotten which floor. There is, however, nothing in this connection which is especially Berkeleyan. In those years following the World War all departments were pressed, and were only too eager to draft inexperienced people.

Now, when I add everything up, I see this period as a most remarkable year—from my point of view, deserving the title *Annus Mirabilis*. It may be termed, if you are looking for a superlative, the most important year of my professional life. In personal events other years may have been more decisive, but as the result of my Berkeley experiences of these nine months I entered into the main current of my career. Or, perhaps I should say, during that time I took my own little boat out into that current—vigorously, if not very skillfully, handling the oars, and with the University providing a helpful shove out of the slack water. Still, that is as much as you can expect education or an educational institution to do.

The greater part of the results of this year I must attribute to my own situation at that time. As I have recorded already, I was at a good age, and my creative and intellectual energies had been pent up by two years of inaction. I was due for a great outburst. On the other hand, I should be both ungrateful and less than honest if I did not attribute a portion of the results of this year to the University.

Appendix

ALBRIGHT, HORACE MARDEN. B.L., 1912, University of California,
Berkeley; LL.B., 1914, Georgetown University; LL.D., 1956,
University of Montana; 1961, UC Berkeley; 1962, University of
New Mexico. Staff member, Department of Interior, 1913–33;
including director, National Park Service, 1929–33. Executive vice
president, 1933–46, president, 1946–56, U.S. Potash Company. UC
Alumnus of the Year, 1952. Author of numerous articles and
recipient of many awards for work in conservation. Mr. Albright
passed away in 1987.

BAIRD, ZOË ELIOT. B.A., 1974, J.D., 1977, University of California,
Berkeley. Attorney-adviser, U.S. Justice Department; member, White
House legal staff, President Carter's administration. Partner,
O'Melveny & Myers. Senior vice president and general counsel,
Ætna Life and Casualty Company. Member, President's Foreign
Intelligence Advisory Board, 1993– ; President's Commission on the
Roles and Capabilities of the United States Intelligence Community,
1995– . Founder and chairman, Lawyers for Children, 1995– .
Member, Boalt Hall Board of Trustees, 1992– ; National Advisory
Council, Institute of Governmental Studies, 1989– . President
Clinton's initial nominee for attorney general of the United States.
Senior visiting scholar and senior research associate, Yale Law
School, 1996–1997. President, 1998–, Markle Foundation.

BIONDI, MATTHEW. B.A., 1988, University of California, Berkeley.
Member, national-champion UC Berkeley water polo team, 1984,
1985, 1987. Olympic medalist in freestyle and butterfly swimming,
1984, 1988, 1992. Co-founder, Delphys Foundation for marine
study. Inducted into Cal Athletic Hall of Fame, 1997.

BRICO, ANTONIA. A.B., 1923, University of California, Berkeley; D.M.,
1938, Mills College. Concert pianist, 1919 on; guest conductor of
major orchestras in Europe and the United States; conductor of the
Brico Symphony, Denver, Colorado; teacher of conducting, opera,
and piano. Ms. Brico passed away in 1989.

EDWARDS, RALPH LIVINGSTONE. A.B., 1935, University of California, Berkeley. Owner and producer of many radio and TV shows; creator, *Truth or Consequences* and *This Is Your Life;* winner of various TV Emmys. Eisenhower Award, #1 World War II bond sales; National Crusade chairman, American Cancer Society, 1962. Board of Trustees, Los Angeles Symphony, 1960. UC Alumnus of the Year, 1964; founding chairman, Robert Gordon Sproul Associates, UC Berkeley.

DIDION, JOAN. B.A., 1956, University of California, Berkeley. Staff member, *Daily Californian; Occident* literary magazine. Honorary member, *Keeping the Promise Campaign Committee;* co-chair, "Nobel Tradition" event, 1987. UC Alumna of the Year, 1981. Author of numerous books, including *After Henry, Miami, Slouching Towards Bethlehem, Salvador, Play It As It Lays, Run River,* and *The Last Thing He Wanted.* Recipient of 1999 Columbia Journalism Award. Her work often bears a distinct California context.

GALBRAITH, JOHN KENNETH. B.S., 1931, University of Toronto; M.S., 1933, PH.D., 1934, University of California, Berkeley. Lecturer, Harvard University, 1934–39; assistant professor of economics, Princeton University, 1939–41; deputy administrator, Office of Price Administration, 1941–43; board of editors, *Fortune* magazine, 1943–48; professor of economics, Harvard University, 1949– ; ambassador to India, 1961–63. Fellow, past president, American Academy of Arts and Sciences; American Academy of Arts and Letters. Author of numerous books, including *The Affluent Society* and *The New Industrial State.*

GARDNER, JOHN W. A.B., 1935, Stanford University; M.A., 1936, PH.D., 1938, University of California, Berkeley. Instructor in psychology, Connecticut College, 1938–40; assistant professor of psychology, Mt. Holyoke College, 1940–42; Marine Corps, 1943–46; staff member, 1946–55, president, 1955–65, Carnegie Corporation; U.S. Secretary of Health, Education and Welfare, 1965–68; chairman, National Urban Coalition, 1968–70. Founder, Common Cause, 1970; co-founding chairman, Independent Sector, 1980; chairman, National Civic League, 1994– . Recipient of numerous awards, including the Presidential Medal of Freedom, 1964. National leader in educational reform and author of books on education and leadership, including *Excellence* (revised 1984), *Self-Renewal* (revised 1981), and *On Leadership.*

GOLDBERG, REUBEN "RUBE" LUCIUS. B.S., 1904, University of California, Berkeley. Cartoonist, *San Francisco Chronicle,* 1904–5; *San Francisco Bulletin,* 1905–7; *New York Evening Mail,* 1907–21; nationally syndicated, 1921–64. Sculptor, 1964 on. Winner of Pulitzer Prize, 1948. The creator of *Boob McNutt, Ike and Mike,* and *Lucifer Butts* inventions. Author of *Rube Goldberg vs. the Machine Age.* Mr. Goldberg passed away in 1970.

356

GOLDMAN, RHODA HAAS. B.A., 1946, University of California, Berkeley. Member, Advisory Board, Walter A. Haas School of Business, 1991–93. Former trustee, UC Berkeley Foundation. She shared a commitment with her family to philanthropy and community involvement, as well as the arts and the environment. Mrs. Goldman passed away in 1996.

GOODIN, MARION SPROUL. B.A., 1938, M.A., 1940, University of California, Berkeley. A lifelong member of the UC Berkeley community, she and her siblings grew up on the campus and attended school here. Her father, Robert Gordon Sproul, was president of the University of California for 28 years. Her ties to the campus are many, including the Bancroft Library Council of Friends, Boalt Hall School of Law, International House, the University YWCA, and the California Alumni Council.

HAAS, ROBERT DOUGLAS. A.B., 1964, University of California, Berkeley; M.B.A., 1968, Harvard University. Peace Corps, Ivory Coast, 1964–66; White House fellow, U.S. Department of Housing and Urban Development, 1968–69. Chief executive officer, 1984–99; and Chairman of the board, 1989– , of Levi Strauss & Company. Fourth-generation Berkeley graduate and valedictorian.

HAAS, WALTER A., JR. B.A., 1937, University of California, Berkeley. Staff member, *Daily Californian;* Rally Committee; men's tennis team; Big C Society. Chief executive officer, Levi Strauss & Company, 1958–76; honorary chairman of the board. Member, Chancellor's Campaign Cabinet, Tri-Lateral Commission, National Commission on Public Service. Trustee, Ford Foundation. Owner, Oakland Athletics baseball team. UC Alumnus of the Year, 1984; recipient, Berkeley Medal, 1991. Cornerstone support from the Haas family helped build the new Walter A. Haas School of Business at UC Berkeley. Mr. Haas passed away in 1995.

HOADLEY, WALTER E. B.A., 1938, M.A., 1940, PH.D., 1946, University of California, Berkeley. Valedictorian and president, Class of 1938. Associate editor, *Daily Californian.* Retired executive vice president, Bank of America. Senior research fellow, Hoover Institute, Stanford University. UC Alumnus of the Year, 1993. Recipient, UC Berkeley Foundation Chancellor's Award, 1998.

KAPP, JOSEPH "JOE" R. A.B., 1960, University of California, Berkeley. Quarterback, UC Berkeley football team, 1955–58, All-American, 1958. Canadian professional teams, 1959–66, All-Canada, 1963, 1964; Minnesota Vikings, 1967–69, including National Football League championship finals, 1968, and Super Bowl IV, 1969. Recipient, Pop Warner and Voit awards, 1958; NFL Player of the Year, 1969; Vince Lombardi Award, 1969. Inducted into Canadian Football League Hall of Fame, 1984; UC Berkeley Sports Hall of Fame, 1992. Head football coach, California Bears, 1982–86; PAC-10 Coach of the Year, 1982.

KERR, CLARK. A.B., 1932, Swarthmore College; M.A., 1933, Stanford University; PH.D., 1939, University of California, Berkeley. Professor emeritus of economics and industrial relations; Chancellor, 1952–58, UC Berkeley; President, University of California, 1958–67. Chairman, Carnegie Commission on Higher Education and Carnegie Council on Policy Studies in Higher Education. Recipient of the Harold W. McGraw Jr. Prize for his contributions to education, 1990. He is credited with designing post-World War II higher education in California and has served six U.S. presidential administrations. The University of California expanded to nine campuses and doubled its 1958 enrollment during his tenure.

KINGSTON, MAXINE HONG. B.A., 1962, Teaching Credential, 1965, University of California, Berkeley. Senior lecturer, Department of English, UC Berkeley, 1991– . She is recognized as one of the nation's leading writers. Winner, National Book Critics' Circle Award, 1976, for *The Woman Warrior;* American Book Award for nonfiction, 1981, for *China Men;* PEN USA WEST Award for fiction, 1980, for *Tripmaster Monkey, His Fake Book;* Governor's Award for arts, 1989; and runner-up for the Pulitzer Prize in 1981. Her work has been adapted for the stage play *The Woman Warrior.* National Humanities Medal, 1997. UC Alumna of the Year, 2000.

KOSHLAND, DANIEL E., JR. B.S., 1941, University of California, Berkeley; PH.D., 1949, University of Chicago. Manhattan Project, 1942–46, including group leader, 1944–46; National Research Council Fellow, Harvard University, 1949–51; staff member, Brookhaven National Laboratory, 1951–65; including senior biochemist, 1961–65; affiliated professor, Rockefeller University, 1958–65; professor of biochemistry, UC Berkeley, 1965– ; including chairman of the biochemistry department, 1973–78. Editor, *Science* magazine. Recipient, Berkeley Citation, 1970; Clark Kerr Medal, 1994. Member, National Academy of Sciences. Recipient, National Medal of Science.

KRAGEN, ADRIAN A. B.A., 1931, J.D., 1934, University of California, Berkeley. Faculty member, 1952–73, professor, 1980–92, Boalt Hall School of Law; emeritus professor of law, 1992– ; faculty, Hastings Law School, 1973–80. Deputy attorney general under then–attorney general Earl Warren; vice chancellor, UC Berkeley, 1960–64; trustee, 1960–80, honorary trustee of the board and of the foundation, 1980– , Alta Bates Hospital; president, Guardian Health Foundation— Berkeley, 1976–80. Member, Bear Backers Council; Hall of Fame selection committee; chair, Emeriti Relations committee, Academic Senate. University endowed chair established in his name at Boalt Hall.

TJIAN, ROBERT T. B.S., 1971, University of California, Berkeley; PH.D.,1976, Harvard University. Professor of molecular and cell biology, UC Berkeley, 1979– . Investigator, Howard Hughes Medical Institute, 1987– . National Academy of Sciences Award in molecular biology, 1991; California Scientist of the Year, 1994. Member, National Academy of Sciences, 1991. His work has included major discoveries on the interactions at the chemical and molecular levels that determine how genes regulate the forms and functions of all living things. Recipient of the 1999 Research Prize from the General Motors Cancer Reseach Foundation.